Bloom's Classic Critical Views

HERMAN MELVILLE

Bloom's Classic Critical Views

Jane Austen

Geoffrey Chaucer

Charles Dickens

Ralph Waldo Emerson

Nathaniel Hawthorne

Herman Melville

Edgar Allan Poe

Walt Whitman

Bloom's Classic Critical Views

HERMAN MELVILLE

Edited and with an introduction by
Harold Bloom
Sterling Professor of the Humanities
Yale University

Bloom's Classic Critical Views: Herman Melville

Copyright © 2008 Infobase Publishing

Introduction © 2008 by Harold Bloom

All rights reserved. No part of this publication may be reproduced or utilized in any form or by any means, electronic or mechanical, including photocopying, recording, or by any information storage or retrieval systems, without permission in writing from the publisher. For more information contact:

Bloom's Literary Criticism
An imprint of Infobase Publishing
132 West 31st Street
New York NY 10001

Library of Congress Cataloging-in-Publication Data
Herman Melville / [edited by] Harold Bloom.
   p. cm. — (Bloom's classic critical views)
A selection of important older literary criticism on Herman Melville.
Includes bibliographical references (p.   ) and index.
ISBN-13: 978-0-7910-9557-7
ISBN-10: 0-7910-9557-6
1. Melville, Herman, 1819–1891—Criticism and interpretation. I. Bloom, Harold.

PS2387.H4 2007
813'.3—dc22

2007020561

Bloom's Literary Criticism books are available at special discounts when purchased in bulk quantities for businesses, associations, institutions, or sales promotions. Please call our Special Sales Department in New York at (212) 967-8800 or (800) 322-8755.

You can find Bloom's Literary Criticism on the World Wide Web at
http://www.chelseahouse.com

Series design by Erika K. Arroyo
Cover design by Takeshi Takahashi
Printed in the United States of America
Bang EJB 10 9 8 7 6 5 4 3 2 1

This book is printed on acid-free paper.

All links and Web addresses were checked and verified to be correct at the time of publication. Because of the dynamic nature of the Web, some addresses and links may have changed since publication and may no longer be valid.

Contents

Series Introduction	ix
Introduction by Harold Bloom	xi
Biography	xiii
Personal	3
William Ellery Channing "The Island Nukuheva" (1847)	5
Nathaniel Hawthorne (1850)	5
Sophia Hawthorne (1850)	6
Nathaniel Hawthorne (1851)	7
Nathaniel Hawthorne (1856)	8
General	11
Fitz-James O'Brien "On Young Authors—Melville" (1853)	13
"Sir Nathaniel" "American Authorship: IV. Herman Melville" (1853)	14
W. Clark Russell "Sea-Stories" (1884)	25
Robert Buchanan "Socrates in Camden, with a Look Round" (1885)	28
Edwin P. Whipple "American Literature" (1886)	29
Charles F. Richardson (1887)	29
Robert Louis Stevenson (1888)	29
Anonymous (1891)	30
Richard Henry Stoddard (1891)	32
Henry S. Salt "Marquesan Melville" (1892)	33
John St. Loe Strachey "Herman Melville" (1893)	43
William P. Trent (1903)	45
Carl Van Doren (1917)	46

Works   49

Typee   51
Nathaniel Hawthorne (1846)   51
Margaret Fuller (1846)   52
Henry Wadsworth Longfellow (1846)   52
James Russell Lowell (1848)   53
Thomas Low Nichols (1864)   53
Katharine Lee Bates (1897)   53
Jack London "Typee" (1910)   53

Omoo   54
Walt Whitman (1847)   54
Charles Gordon Greene (1847)   54
Horace Greeley (1847)   55

Mardi   57
Henry Cood Watson (1849)   57

Redburn   59
George Ripley (1849)   59

White-Jacket   61
George Ripley (1850)   61
Frederick Swartwout Cozzens (1850)   62

Moby-Dick   63
Herman Melville (1851)   63
Herman Melville (1851)   67
Herman Melville (1851)   69
Anonymous (1851)   72
Henry Chorley (1851)   74
Anonymous (1851)   76
Evert A. Duyckinck "Melville's *Moby Dick; or, The Whale*"
  (1851)   77
Horace Greeley (1851)   83
William T. Porter "Moby Dick, or The Whale" (1851)   85
William A. Butler (1851)   87
George Ripley "Literary Notices" (1852)   91
Archibald MacMechan "The Best Sea Story Ever Written"
  (1899)   93
Joseph Conrad (1907)   100

Contents vii

Frank Jewett Mather Jr. "Herman Melville" (1919)   101
Raymond Weaver "Herman Melville" (1921)   103
Lincoln Colcord "Notes on *Moby Dick*" (1922)   106
D.H. Lawrence "Herman Melville's *Moby Dick*" (1923)   117
Carl Van Doren "Mr. Melville's Moby Dick" (1924)   134
Charles Olson (1947)   138

Pierre   142
Anonymous "Pierre; or, The Ambiguities" (1852)   142
Anonymous "Review of New Books" (1852)   147
Anonymous "Pierre, or The Ambiguities" (1852)   147
Anonymous "New Novels" (1852)   160
Julian Hawthorne "The American Element in Fiction" (1886)   162

The Piazza Tales   162
Anonymous (1856)   163
Anonymous (1856)   163
Anonymous (1856)   164

The Confidence Man   164
Anonymous (1857)   164
Ann Sophia Stephens (1857)   165
Anonymous (1857)   166

Poetry   167
Anonymous (1866)   168
Richard Henry Stoddard (1866)   169
Edmund Clarence Stedman (1876)   170

Billy Budd   173
E.L. Grant Watson "Melville's Testament of Acceptance" (1933)   173
Karl E. Zink "Herman Melville and the Forms—Irony and Social Criticism in *Billy Budd*" (1952)   178
Wendell Glick "Expediency and Absolute Morality in *Billy Budd*" (1953)   187

Chronology   196

Index   198

Series Introduction

Bloom's Classic Critical Views is a new series presenting a selection of the most important older literary criticism on the greatest authors commonly read in high school and college classes today. Unlike the Bloom's Modern Critical Views series, which for more than twenty years has provided the best contemporary criticism on great authors, Bloom's Classic Critical Views attempts to present the authors in the context of their time and to provide criticism that has proved over the years to be the most valuable to readers and writers. Selections range from contemporary reviews in popular magazines, which demonstrate how a work was received in its own era, to profound essays by some of the strongest critics in the British and American tradition, including Henry James, G.K. Chesterton, Matthew Arnold, and many more.

Some of the critical essays and extracts presented here have appeared previously in other titles edited by Harold Bloom, such as the New Moulton's Library of Literary Criticism. Other selections appear here for the first time in any book by this publisher. All were selected under Harold Bloom's guidance.

In addition, each volume in this series contains a series of essays by a contemporary expert, who comments on the most important critical selections, putting them in context and suggesting how they might be used by a student writer to influence his or her own writing. This series is intended above all for students, to help them think more deeply and write more powerfully about great writers and their works.

Introduction by Harold Bloom

Moby-Dick—the epic of the White Whale, Captain Ahab, Ishmael the wanderer and his beloved, Queequeg the harpooner—shares with Hawthorne's fiction and much of Emily Dickinson's poetry the dark distinction of an ambivalent relation to the prime American literary prophet, Emerson. Transcendentalism, in its Emersonian versions, is as dialectical a mode as Nietzschean perspectivism, which has a debt to Emerson, whom Nietzsche rather ruefully admired.

The positive aspects of Emerson's dual vision inform Thoreau's *Walden*, Whitman's *Leaves of Grass*, and the writings of Margaret Fuller, but the subtle Emerson insinuates himself into those who reject him, including Herman Melville. Ahab stems from the Gnostic Emerson, even as Ishmael emerges from the Neoplatonic Emerson. Melville's struggle with Emerson, cosmological in scope, resembles Jacob's contest with a nameless one among the Elohim, in that it gives Melville the new name of Ishmael, just as Jacob is called Israel after his wrestling match, hardly with Yahweh but with the Angel of Death. Writing a letter to Hawthorne, Melville cataloged Emerson's transcendental terms that made up "the God within us" and judged them as suicidal: "As soon as you say *Me*, a *God*, a *Nature*, so soon you jump off from your stool and hang from the beam. *Yes*, that word is the hangman." Nevertheless only Ishmael-Melville survives the wreck of Ahab's whaler, and perhaps Melville owed part of his own endurance to Emerson's confrontations with fate, power, and illusion.

Unable to accept Emersonianism, or to reject it totally, Melville cultivated antithetical revenges upon the Sage of Concord, who is satirized first as Plotinus Plinlimmon in the novelist's *Pierre*, and then as "the mystical stranger," Mark Winsome, in *The Confidence Man: His Masquerade*. Though

Melville scribbled fierce marginalia in his copies of Emerson's *Essays, First and Second Series*, he nevertheless seems to have attended all of the mystical stranger's public lectures in New York City. At least from *Moby-Dick* on to the posthumously published *Billy Budd*, Melville remained unhappily haunted by the "deadly" Transcendentalist of Concord, Hawthorne's walking-companion.

How shall we judge Melville's total achievement, at its best? There is *Moby-Dick*, only (though defeated) rival to *Leaves of Grass* as our national epic, as our Homeric myth of origins. Plato fought bitterly against Homer, in the agon to be the educator of the Greeks, and Homer lost. Emerson happily greeted *Leaves of Grass*, though he later expressed some reservations. The great essayist never read *Moby-Dick*, but then he had little appreciation for prose fiction, including Hawthorne's. Henry James, unlike his brother William, condescended when he wrote of Emerson, who was unlikely to have gotten through *The Golden Bowl*, had he lived long enough.

Moby-Dick is flawed by undigested Shakespeare, yet even Homer nods, and what writer ever shall escape whipping? The *Confidence Man* has its enthusiasts, but I am not among them, and rather egregiously I find *Billy Budd* to be contrived, sentimental, and over-rated. Melville's poetry is marvelous to me, but metrically it is as distractingly hardy as the verse of Thomas Hardy. They are both major poets, but do not necessarily please the common reader. I have a particular fondness for nineteenth-century long poems, but my attempts to communicate my passion for Melville's *Clarel* and William Morris's *Sigurd the Volsung* to others have invariably failed.

The common reader (now a vanishing species) embraces *Moby-Dick* and two of the shorter tales: *Bartleby the Scrivner* and *Benito Cereno*. I would add the *The Encantadas*, *The Bell-Tower,* and a handful of meditative poems, particularly *After the Pleasure-Party*, but we scarcely would remember Melville now except for *Moby-Dick*, a central scripture together with *Song of Myself* and *The Adventures of Huckleberry Finn*. As I advance on seventy-seven, I want *people* when I read, which is why Shakespeare and Cervantes perpetually are supreme. Ahab and Ishmael (and the White Whale) join with Huck Finn and "Walt Whitman" in our national pantheon. That is achievement enough for any American writer.

BIOGRAPHY

Herman Melville
(1819–1891)

Herman Melville was born in New York City on August 1, 1819. He attended the New-York Male High School from 1825 to 1829. He then enrolled in Albany Academy but withdrew after his father's death in 1832. Melville worked at various jobs between 1832 and 1838, and in 1839 joined the crew of a packet sailing to Liverpool. After his return to New York he taught briefly and then in 1841 traveled on a whaler to the South Seas. In 1842 he jumped ship at the Marquesas Islands and then, after several months among supposedly cannibalistic native peoples, escaped by joining the crew of an Australian whaler. After a brief confinement at Tahiti as an accused mutineer, Melville spent several months in Maui and Honolulu, then enlisted in the U.S. Navy and sailed for home. After serving briefly in Boston, he was discharged in the fall of 1844.

After returning to Lansingburgh, New York, where his family had moved in 1838, Melville began writing a fictionalized travel account based on his travels, *Typee; or, A Peep at Polynesian Life* (1846). This book, Melville's most popular during his lifetime, was followed by a sequel, *Omoo: A Narrative of Adventures in the South Seas* (1847), which was also well received. His next book, *Mardi and a Voyage Thither* (1849), was not a success. From then on Melville's writing was increasingly ignored, and it was not until the 1920s that critics began to praise his later works, many of which were belatedly hailed as masterpieces.

Having married Elizabeth Shaw, the daughter of the chief justice of Massachusetts, in 1847, and with, eventually, four children to support, Melville continued to write prolifically, despite the poor reception of much of his work. His realistic sea stories, *Redburn: His First Voyage* and *White-Jacket; or, The World in a Man-of-War*, appeared in 1849 and 1850, respectively, and were followed by *Moby-Dick; or, The Whale* (1851), a heavily symbolic work partly inspired by his recent friendship with Nathaniel Hawthorne. Melville published *Pierre; or, The Ambiguities* in 1852 and between 1852 and 1856 wrote anonymous magazine stories for *Putnam's Monthly Magazine* and

Harper's New Monthly Magazine; these stories, among them "Bartleby, the Scrivener" and "Benito Cereno," were later collected and published as *The Piazza Tales* (1856). Melville's historical novel *Israel Potter: His Fifty Years of Exile* appeared in 1855.

In order to recover from a physical breakdown, Melville traveled in Europe and Palestine in 1856–57. His last novel, the satirical *The Confidence Man* (1857), was published shortly before his return to New York. After a series of unsuccessful lecture tours from 1857 to 1860, Melville became a district inspector of customs for New York Harbor in 1866, a position he retained until his resignation in 1885. His collection of bitter, disillusioned Civil War poems, *Battle-Pieces and Aspects of the War,* appeared in 1866 and was followed in 1876 by his narrative poem *Clarel,* which reflected his experiences in the Holy Land. *John Marr and Other Sailors* (1888), a collection of miscellaneous pieces, and the verse collection *Timoleon* (1891) were the two last works published during Melville's lifetime, both privately printed and issued in limited editions. Melville died on September 28, 1891, leaving his novel *Billy Budd, Foretopman* in manuscript. It was not published until 1924.

PERSONAL

William Ellery Channing
"The Island Nukuheva" (1847)

This is an excerpt from an 1847 poem by William Ellery Channing. It captures this transcendentalist poet's playful, early admiration of Melville's literary investment in the Pacific. It comes at the time of Melville's greatest fame during his life. Channing, a friend to Emerson and Thoreau, would have read Melville's *Typee* as welcome evidence of the essential and ideal goodness in man. To Channing, Melville's "Islanders" lived in "Paradise," basked in "perpetual" repose, enjoyed an endless summer, and assumed a perfect communal life. Students might find the poem useful in how it reflects the optimistic, transcendentalist preference for looking past the evil in man. *Typee*, however, does not do this. Notable is Channing's use of words like "perpetual" at a time when life in the Marquesas was under direct and mounting threat from Western germs, guns, and steel. Students exploring Melville's engagement with American preconceptions of the Pacific will find Channing's poem useful.

It is upon the far-off deep South Seas,
The island Nukuheva, its degrees
In vain,—I may not reckon, but the bold
Adventurous Melville there by chance was rolled,
And for four months in its delights did dwell,
And of this Island writ what I may tell.
So far away, it is a Paradise
To my unfolded, stationary eyes,
Around it white the heavy billows beat,
Within its vales profoundest cataracts meet,
Drawn from the breasts of the high purple mountains,
And to those Islanders perpetual fountains.

—William Ellery Channing, "The Island Nukuheva," 1847

Nathaniel Hawthorne (1850)

This simple 1850 notice by Nathaniel Hawthorne that he had "liked" Melville will point students to what is often counted as the most important encounter in American literary history—the picnic outing that took place on August 5, 1850, near Stockbridge, Massachusetts. Melville had just posed as "a Virginian spending July in Vermont" to glowingly review his mentor's prose in "Hawthorne and His Mosses." He would go on to dedicate *Moby-Dick* to Hawthorne's "genius." The intense friendship would wane in 1852.

I met Melville the other day, and liked him so much that I have asked him to spend a few days with me before leaving these parts.

—Nathaniel Hawthorne, Letter to Horatio Bridge (August 7, 1850), cited in Horatio Bridge, *Personal Recollections of Nathaniel Hawthorne*, 1893, p. 123

SOPHIA HAWTHORNE (1850)

In this excerpt, Nathaniel Hawthorne's wife, Sophia, captures for her mother the tension between Melville's "small eyes" and his "strange, lazy glance." Perhaps referencing her era's fascination with phrenology (the dubious study of how personality might be discerned in the features and measurements of the head or skull), Mrs. Hawthorne gives us a penetrating portrait of the earnest young Melville, seventeen years younger than Hawthorne. In noting the play between Melville's forceful internal calm and his external exuberance, she seems to be speaking about both the prose and the man.

We find [Melville] a man with a true warm heart & a soul & an intellect—with life to his finger-tips—earnest, sincere & reverent, very tender & *modest*—And I am not sure that he is not a very great man—but I have not quite decided upon my opinion—I should say, I am not quite sure that I *do not think him* a very great man—for my opinion is of course as far as possible from settling the matter. He has very keen perceptive power, but what astonishes me is, that his eyes are not large & deep—He seems to see every thing very accurately, & how he can do so with his small eyes, I cannot tell. They are not keen eyes, either, but quite undistinguished in any way. His nose is straight & rather handsome, his mouth expressive of sensibility & emotion—He is tall & erect with an air free, brave, & manly. When conversing, he is full of gesture & force, & loses himself in his subject—There is no grace nor polish—once in a while, his animation gives place to a singularly quiet expression out of those eyes, to which I have objected—an indrawn, dim look, but which at the same time makes you feel that he is at that instant taking deepest note of what is before him. It is a strange, lazy glance, but with a power in it quite unique. It does not seem to penetrate through you, but to take you into itself. I saw him look at Una so yesterday several times.

—Sophia Hawthorne, Letter to her mother
(September 4, 1850)

NATHANIEL HAWTHORNE (1851)

The final two entries in this section come from Nathaniel Hawthorne's journals. In the first, from August 1851, Hawthorne relates in his sober, yet affectionate style how the two stay up late into the night discussing "all possible and impossible matters." Hawthorne still exults in the heat of one of the most celebrated and swiftly burning literary friendships. The second entry comes from Hawthorne's time as American consul at Liverpool, a sinecure he secured from his old Bowdoin College friend, then president Franklin Pierce. These entries, recorded more than five years after the intellectually passionate Berkshire summers, convey Hawthorne's continued affection for Melville and bear no clear indication of how or why the friendship had cooled in intervening years. Hawthorne's words are important because they take note of Melville's physical and financial sufferings and careful measure of his altered character. But if "the spirit of adventure [had] gone out of him," if Melville had sunk into increasing gloom, Hawthorne also logs that Melville prefers not to "rest," but to wander "to-and-fro" over ultimacies, able "neither [to] believe, nor [to] be comfortable in his unbelief." In a second famous expression of Melville's persistent ambivalence over theological matters, Hawthorne reports him as having "pretty much made up his mind to be annihilated." Students interested in this famous friendship, or in how any of Melville's works take up practical or abstract theological issues may find Hawthorne's words of great interest. From his reproach of Pacific missionary endeavors in *Typee* and *Omoo* to his protracted meditation on the nature of evil, suffering, and authority in *Billy Budd*, Melville's work grapples with "Providence and futurity, and of everything that lies beyond human ken." Also, students exploring connections between Melville's life and his turn away from prose expression may find these representative personal extracts of some use.

Returning to the Post office, I got Mr Tappan's mail and my own and proceeded homeward, but clambered over the fence and sat down in Love Grove to read the papers. While thus engaged, a cavalier on horseback came along the road, and saluted me in Spanish; to which I replied by touching my hat, and went on with the newspaper. But the cavalier renewing his salutation, I regarded him more attentively, and saw that it was Herman Melville! So, hereupon, Julian and I hastened to the road, where ensued a greeting, and we all went homeward together, talking as we went. Soon, Mr Melville alighted, and put Julian into the saddle; and the little man was highly pleased, and sat on the horse with the freedom and fearlessness of an old equestrian, and had a ride of at least a mile homeward.

I asked Mrs Peters to make some tea for Herman Melville; and so she did, and he drank a cup, but was afraid to drink much, because it would keep him awake. After supper, I put Julian to bed; and Melville and I had a talk about time and eternity, things of this world and of the next, and books, and publishers, and all possible and impossible matters, that lasted pretty deep into the night, and if the truth must be told, we smoked cigars even within the sacred precincts of the sitting room. At last, he arose, and saddled his horse (whom we had put into the barn) and rode off for his own domicile; and I hastened to make the most of what little sleeping-time remained for me.

—Nathaniel Hawthorne, *Journal* (August 1, 1851)

NATHANIEL HAWTHORNE (1856)

November 20th, Thursday. A week ago last Monday, Herman Melville came to see me at the Consulate, looking much as he used to do (a little paler, and perhaps a little sadder), in a rough outside coat, and with his characteristic gravity and reserve of manner. He had crossed from New York to Glasgow in a screw steamer, about a fortnight before, and had since been seeing Edinburgh and other interesting places. I felt rather aukward [sic] at first; because this is the first time I have met him since my ineffectual attempt to get him a consular appointment from General Pierce. However, I failed only from real lack of power to serve him; so there was no reason to be ashamed, and we soon found ourselves on pretty much our former terms of sociability and confidence. Melville has not been well, of late; he has been affected with neuralgic complaints in his head and limbs, and no doubt has suffered from too constant literary occupation, pursued without much success, latterly; and his writings, for a long while past, have indicated a morbid state of mind. So he left his place at Pittsfield, and has established his wife and family, I believe, with his father-in-law in Boston, and is thus far on his way to Constantinople. I do not wonder that he found it necessary to take an airing through the world, after so many years of toilsome pen-labor and domestic life, following upon so wild and adventurous a youth as he was. I invited him to come and stay with us at Southport, as long as he might remain in this vicinity; and, accordingly, he did come, the next day, taking with him, by way of baggage, the least little bit of a bundle, which, he told me, contained a night-shirt and a tooth-brush. He is a person of very gentlemanly instincts in every respect, save that he is a little heterodox in the matter of clean linen.

He stayed with us from Tuesday till Thursday; and, on the intervening day, we took a pretty long walk together, and sat down in a hollow among the sand hills (sheltering ourselves from the high, cool wind) and smoked a cigar. Melville, as he always does, began to reason of Providence and futurity, and of everything that lies beyond human ken, and informed me that he had 'pretty much made up his mind to be annihilated'; but still he does not seem to rest in that anticipation; and, I think, will never rest until he gets hold of a definite belief. It is strange how he persists—and has persisted ever since I knew him, and probably long before—in wandering to-and-fro over these deserts, as dismal and monotonous as the sand hills amid which we were sitting. He can neither believe, nor be comfortable in his unbelief; and he is too honest and courageous not to try to do one or the other. If he were a religious man, he would be one of the most truly religious and reverential; he has a very high and noble nature, and better worth immortality than most of us.

—Nathaniel Hawthorne, *The English Notebooks*
(November 20, 1856)

GENERAL

The following extracts capture a wide variety of perspectives on Herman Melville and his work. They are arranged chronologically, all written before the "Melville Revival" that began in approximately 1917. What students should know first, perhaps, is that *Typee*, the author's first book, was his most commercially successful work. From then until the revival, Melville's work fared increasingly less well at selling significant numbers of copies or at earning the author accolades. The selections here reflect the idiosyncratic views of writers attempting to sort out the significance of a writer whose popularity waned. For this reason, the extracts are a fascinating window into both the works discussed and the time in which the criticism was written. The following entries track what many critics have deemed the tragic slide of Melville into bitterness and silence—a sketch of the author's literary and life trajectory that oversimplifies the matter.

Fitz-James O'Brien
"On Young Authors—Melville" (1853)

Mr. Melville does not improve with time. His later books are a decided falling off, and his last scarcely deserves naming; this however we scarce believe to be an indication of exhaustion. Keats says beautifully in his preface to *Endymion*, that "The imagination of a boy is healthy, and the mature imagination of a man is healthy, but there is a space of life between, in which the soul is in a ferment, the character undecided, the way of life uncertain, the ambition thick-sighted."

Just at present we believe the author of *Pierre* to be in this state of ferment. *Typee*, his first book, was healthy; *Omoo* nearly so; after that came *Mardi*, with its excusable wildness; then came *Moby Dick,* and *Pierre* with its inexcusable insanity. We trust that these rhapsodies will end the interregnum of nonsense to which Keats refers, as forming a portion of every man's life; and that Mr. Melville will write less at random and more at leisure, than of late.

—Fitz-James O'Brien, "Our Young Authors— Melville," *Putnam's Monthly,* February 1853, p. 163

"Sir Nathaniel" "American Authorship: IV. Herman Melville" (1853)

This anonymous essay, which first appeared in 1853 in England and was later reprinted several times in American periodicals, ends by saying almost "nothing" of *Pierre*, because the author can think of nothing good to say about it. The author builds in no biography, and while judging each of Melville's works, becomes strangely preoccupied with assessing Melville's cast of characters. *Mardi* has too much "romance and adventure," while *Redburn* has too little. Having stated such, the author then lapses into a series of appreciations of *Redburn* that belie the assertion of the book being "singularly free from excitement, and . . . incident." *Moby-Dick* only glancingly has merit, and is "distressingly marred," finally coming off as "a huge dose of hyperbolic slang, maudlin sentimentalism, and tragicomic bubble and squeak." This review of Melville is significant as representative of prerevival attitudes that would remain mostly intact for decades.

The Muses, it was once alleged by Christopher North, have but scantly patronised sea-faring verse: they have neglected ship-building, and deserted the dockyards,—though in Homer's days they kept a private yacht, of which he was captain. "But their attempts to reestablish anything like a club, these two thousand years or so, have miserably failed; and they have never quite recovered their nerves since the loss of poor Falconer, and their disappointment at the ingratitude shown to Dibdin." And Sir Kit adds, that though they do indeed now and then talk of the "deep blue sea," and occasionally, perhaps, skim over it like sea-plovers, yet they avoid the quarter-deck and all its discipline, and decline the dedication of the cat-o'-nine-tails, in spite of their number.

By them, nevertheless, must have been inspired—in fitful and irregular afflatus—some of the prose-poetry of Herman Melville's sea-romances.

Ocean breezes blow from his tales of Atlantic and Pacific cruises. Instead of landsman's grey goose quill, he seems to have plucked a quill from skimming curlew, or to have snatched it, a fearful joy, from hovering albatross, if not from the wings of the wind itself. The superstition of life on the waves has no abler interpreter, unequal and undisciplined as he is—that superstition almost inevitably engendered among men who live, as it has been said, "under a solemn sense of eternal danger, one inch only of plank (often worm-eaten) between themselves and the grave; and who see for ever one wilderness of waters."[1] His intimacy with the sights and sounds of that wilderness, almost entitles him to the reversion of the mystic "blue cloak" of Keats's submarine greybeard, in which

> every ocean form
> Was woven with a black distinctness; storm,
> And calm, and whispering, and hideous roar
> Were emblem'd in the woof; with every shape
> That skims, or dives, or sleeps 'twixt cape and cape. [2]

A landsman, somewhere observes Mr. Tuckerman, can have no conception of the fondness a ship may inspire, before he listens, on a moonlight night, amid the lonely sea, to the details of her build and workings, unfolded by a complacent tar. Moonlight and midseas are much, and a complacent tar is something; but we "calculate" a landsman *can* get some conception of the true-blue enthusiasm in question, and even become slightly inoculated with it in his own *terra firma* person, under the tuition of a Herman Melville. This graphic narrator assures us, and there needs no additional witness to make the assurance doubly sure, that his sea adventures have often served, when spun as a yarn, not only to relieve the weariness of many a night-watch, but to excite the warmest sympathies of his shipmates. Not that we vouch for the fact of his having experienced the adventures in literal truth, or even of being the pet of the fo'castle as yarn-spinner extraordinary. But we do recognise in him and in his narratives (the earlier ones, at least) a "capital" fund of even untold "interest," and so richly veined a nugget of the *ben trovato* as to "take the shine out of" many a golden *vero*. Readers there are, who, having been enchanted by a perusal of *Typee* and *Omoo,* have turned again and rent the author, when they heard a surmise, or an assertion, that his tales were more or less imagination. Others there are, and we are of them, whose enjoyment of the history was little affected by a suspicion of the kind during perusal (which few can evade), or an affirmation of it afterwards. "And if a little more romantic than truth may warrant, it will be no harm," is

Miles Coverdale's morality, when projecting a chronicle of life at Blithedale. Miles *a raison*.

Life in the Marquesas Islands!—how attractive the theme in capable hands! And here it was treated by a man "out of the ordinary," who had contrived, as Tennyson sings,

> To burst all links of habit—there to wander far away,
> On from island unto island at the gateways of the day.
> Larger constellations burning, mellow moons and happy skies,
> Breadths of tropic shade and palms in cluster, knots of Paradise,—
> Droops the heavy-blossom'd bower, hangs the heavy-fruited tree—
> Summer isles of Eden lying in dark-purple spheres of sea.

"The Marquesas! what strange visions of outlandish things," exclaims *Tommo* himself, "does the very name spirit up! Lovely houris—cannibal banquets—groves of cocoa-nuts—coral reefs—tattooed chiefs, and bamboo temples; sunny valleys planted with bread-fruit trees—carved canoes dancing on the flashing blue waters—savage woodlands guarded by horrible idols—heathenish rites and human sacrifices." And then the zest with which Tommo and Toby, having deserted the ship, plunge into the midst of these oddly-assorted charms—cutting themselves a path through cane-brakes—living day by day on a stinted tablespoonful of "a hash of soaked bread and bits of tobacco"—shivering the livelong night under drenching rain—traversing a fearful series of dark chasms, separated by sharp-crested perpendicular ridges—leaping from precipice above to palm-tree below—and then their entrance into the Typee valley, and introduction to King Mehevi, and initiation into Typee manners, and willy-nilly experience of Typee hospitality. Memorable is the portrait-gallery of the natives: Mehevi, towering with royal dignity above his faithful commons; Marnoo, that all-influential Polynesian Apollo, whose tattooing was the best specimen of the Fine Arts in that region, and whose eloquence wielded at will that fierce anthropophagic *demos;* Marheyo, paternal and warm-hearted old savage, a time-stricken giant—and his wife, Tinor, genuine busybody, most notable and exacting of housewives, but no termagant or shrew for all that; and their admirable son, Kory-Kory—his face tattoed with such a host of pictured birds and fishes, that he resembled a pictorial musuem of natural history, or an illuminated copy of Goldsmith's *Animated Nature*—and whose devotion to the stranger no time could wither nor custom stale. And poor Fayaway, olive-cheeked nymph, with sweet blue eyes of placid yet unfathomable depth, a child of nature with easy unstudied graces, breathing from infancy an atmosphere of perpetual summer—whom, deserted by the roving Tommo, we are led to compare (to *his* prejudice) with Frederika forsaken by Goethe—an episode in the many-sided Baron's life which we have not yet come to regard so tolerantly as Mr. Carlyle.

Omoo, the Rover, keeps up the spirit of *Typee* in a new form. Nothing can be livelier than the sketches of ship and ship's company. "Brave *Little Jule*, plump *Little Jule*," a very witch at sailing, despite her crazy rigging and rotten bulwarks—blow high, blow low, always ready for the breeze, and making you forget her patched sails and blistered hull when she was dashing the waves from her prow, and prancing, and pawing the sea—flying before the wind—rolling now and then, to be sure, but in very playfulness—with spars erect, looking right up into the wind's eye, the pride of her crew; albeit they had their misgivings that this playful craft, like some vivacious old mortal all at once sinking into a decline, might, some dark night, spring a leak, and carry them all to the bottom. The Captain, or "Miss Guy,"—essentially a cockney, and no more meant for the sea than a hairdresser. The bluff mate, John Jermin, with his squinting eye, and rakishly-twisted nose, and grey ringleted bullet head, and generally pugnacious looks, but with a heart as big as a bullock—obstreperous in his cups, and always for having a fight, but loved as a brother by the very men he flogged, for his irresistibly good-natured way of knocking them down. The ship's carpenter, "Chips," ironically styled "Beauty" on strict *lucus à non lucendo* principles—as ugly in temper as in visage. Bungs, the cooper, a man after a bar-keeper's own heart; who, when he felt, as he said, "just about right," was characterised by a free lurch in his gait, a queer way of hitching up his waistbands, and looking unnecessarily steady at you when speaking. Bembo, the harpooner, a dark, moody savage—none of your effeminate barbarians, but a shaggy-browed, glaring-eyed, crisp-haired fellow, under whose swart, tattooed skin the muscles worked like steel rods. Rope Yarn, or Ropey, the poor distraught land-lubber—a forlorn, stunted, hook-visaged creature, erst a journeyman baker in Holborn, with a soft and underdone heart, whom a kind word made a fool of. And, best of all, Doctor Long Ghost, a six-feet tower of bones, who quotes Virgil, talks of Hobbes of Malmesbury, and repeats poetry by the canto, especially *Hudibras;* and who sings mellow old songs, in a voice so round and racy, the real juice of sound; and who has seen the world from so many angles, the acute of civilisation and the obtuse of savagedom; and who is as inventive as he is incurable in the matter of practical jokes—all effervescent with animal spirits and tricksy good-humour. Of the Tahiti folks, Captain Bob is an amusing personage, a corpulent giant, of three-alderman-power in gormandising feats, and so are

Po-po and his family, and the irreverently-ridiculed court of Queen Pomare. It is uncomfortable to be assured in the preface, that "in every statement connected with missionary operations, a strict adherence to facts has, of course, been scrupulously observed"—and the satirist's rather flippant air in treating this subject makes his protestation not unnecessary, that "nothing but an earnest desire for truth and good has led him to touch upon it at all." Nevertheless, there is mournful emphasis in these revelations of *mickonaree* progress—and too much reason to accept the tenor of his remarks as correct, and to bewail the inapplicability to modern missionaries in general, of Wordsworth's lines—

> Rich conquest waits them:—the tempestuous sea
> Of Ignorance, that ran so rough and high
> These good men humble by a few bare words,
> And calm with awe of God's divinity.

For does not even so unexceptionable a pillar of orthodoxy as Sir Archibald Alison, express doubt as to the promise of Missions, in relation to any but European ethnology? affirming, indeed,[3] that had Christianity been adapted to man in his rude and primeval state, it would have been revealed at an earlier period, and would have appeared in the age of Moses, not in that of Caesar:—a dogmatic assertion, by the way, highly characteristic of the somewhat peremptory baronet, and not very harmonious, either in letter or spirit, with the broad text on which worldwide missionary enterprise is founded, and for which Sir Archibald must surely have an *ethnic* gloss of his own private interpretation: Πορευθέντες μαθητεύσατε πάντα τὰ ἐθνή.

But to Mr. Melville. And in a new, and not improved aspect. Exit Omoo; enter Mardi. And the cry is, *Heu! quantum mutatus ab illo*—

> Alas, how changed from him,
> This vein of Ercles, and this soul of whim—

changed enough to threaten an *exeunt omnes* of his quondam admirers. The first part of *Mardi* is worthy of its antecedents; but too soon we are hurried whither we would not, and subjected to the caprices, *velut agri somnia*, of one who, of malice aforethought,

> Delphinum silvis appingit, fluctibus aprum—

the last clause signifying that he *bores* us with his "sea of troubles," and provokes us to take arms against, and (if possible) by opposing, end them. Yet do some prefer his new shade of marine blue, and exult in this his "sea-change into something rich and strange." And the author of *Nile Notes* defines *Mardi*, as a whole, to be unrhymed poetry, rhythmical and measured—the swell of its sentences having a low, lapping cadence, like the dip of the sun-stilled, Pacific waves,—and sometimes the grave music of Bacon's Essays! Thou wert right, O Howadji, to add, "Who but an American could have written them." Alas, Cis-Atlantic criticism compared them to Foote's "What, no soap? So he died, and she very imprudently married the barber,"—with the wedding concomitants of the Picninnies and Great Panjandrum and gunpowder-heeled terpsichorics—Foote being, moreover, preferred to Melville, on the score of superiority in sense, diversion, and brevity. Nevertheless, subsequent productions have proved the author of *Mardi* to plume himself on his craze, and love to have it so. And what will he do in the end thereof?

In tone and taste *Redburn* was an improvement upon *Mardi*, but was as deficient as the latter was overfraught with romance and adventure. Whether fiction or fact, this narrative of the first voyage of Wellingborough Redburn,[4] a New York merchant's son, as sailor-boy in a merchant-vessel, is even prosy, bald, and eventless; and would be dull beyond redemption, as a story, were not the author gifted with a scrutinising gaze, and a habit of taking notes as well as "prenting" them, which ensures his readers against absolute common-place. It is true, he more than once plunges into episodic extravaganzas—such as the gambling-house frenzy of Harry Bolton—but these are, in effect, the dullest of all his moods; and tend to produce, what surely they are inspired by, blue devils. Nor is he over chary of introducing the repulsive,—notwithstanding his disclaimer, "Such is the fastidiousness of some readers, that, many times, they must lose the most striking incidents in a narrative like mine:"[5] for not only some, but most readers, are too fastidious to enjoy such scenes as that of the starving, dying mother and children in a Liverpool cellar, and that of the dead mariner, from whose lips darted out, when the light touched them, "threads of greenish fire, like a forked tongue," till the cadaverous face was "crawled over by a swarm of worm-like flames"—a hideous picture, as deserving of a letter of remonstrance on aesthetic grounds, as Mr. Dickens' spontaneous combustion case (Krook) on physical.[6] Apart from these exceptions, the experiences of Redburn during his "first voyage" are singularly free from excitement, and even incident. We have one or two "marine views" happily done, though not in the artist's *very* happiest style. The picture of a wreck may be referred to—that of a dismantled, water-logged schooner, that had been drifting about for weeks; her bulwarks all but gone—the bare stanchions, or posts, left standing here and there, splitting in two the waves which broke clear over the deck—her open main-hatchway yawning into view every time she rolled in the trough of the sea, and submerged again, with a rushing, gurgling sound of many waters; the relic of a jacket nailed atop of the broken mainmast, for a signal; and, sad, stern sight—most strange and most unnatural—"three dark, green, grassy objects," lashed, and leaning over sideways against the taffrail—slowly swaying with every roll, but otherwise motionless! There is a spirited sketch, too, of the sailor-boy's first ascent to "loose the mainskysail"—not daring to look down, but keeping his eyes glued to the shrouds—panting and breathing hard before he is half-way up—reaching the "Jacob's ladder," and at last, to his own amazement, finding himself hanging on the skysail yard, holding on might and main to the mast, and curling his feet round the rigging, as if they were another pair of hands; thence gazing at length, mute and awe-stricken, on the dark midnight sea beneath, which looks like a great, black gulf, hemmed in all round by beetling black cliffs—the ship below, seeming like a long narrow plank in the water—the boy above, seeming in utter loneliness to tread the swart night clouds, and every second expecting to find himself falling—falling—falling, as he used to feel when the nightmare was on him. Redburn managed his first ascent deftly, and describes it admirably. Sir Nathaniel, indeed, never has been sedentary διὰ νυκτός on a main skysail; but he is pretty sure, from these presents, that Mr. Melville *has*. Equally sure, in his own case, is Sir N., that *had* he attained that giddy eminence, not only should he have expected to find himself falling—falling—falling, but would have found himself, or been found, fallen: which Redburn was *not*. Gallant boy—clear-headed, light-hearted, fast-handed, nimble-footed!—he deserved to reach the top of the tree, and, having reached, to enjoy the sweet peril, like blossom that hangs on the bough: and that in time he did come to enjoy it we find from his record of the wild delirium there is about it—the fine rushing of the blood about the heart—the glad thrilling and throbbing of the whole system, to find yourself tossed up at every pitch into the clouds of a stormy sky, and hovering like a judgment angel between heaven and earth; both hands free, with one foot in the rigging, and one somewhere behind you in the air.

The crew, again, are sketched by a true draughtsman—though one misses the breadth and finish of his corresponding descriptions in *Omoo*. There is Captain Riga, all soft-sawder ashore, all vinegar and mustard at sea—a gay Lothario of all inexperienced, sea-going youths, from the capital or the country—who condoles and sympathises with them in dock, but whom they will not know again when he gets out of sight of land, and mounts his cast-off clothes, and adjusts his character to the shabbiness of his coat, and holds the perplexed lads a little better than his boots, and will no more think of addressing them than of invoking wooden Donald, the figure-head at the ship's bows. There is Jackson—a meagre, consumptive, overbearing bully—squinting, broken-nosed, rheumatic—the weakest body and strongest will on board—"one glance of whose squinting eye was as good as a knock-down, for it was the most subtle, deep, infernal-looking eye ever lodged in a human head," and must have once belonged to a wolf, or starved tiger,—no oculist could ever "turn out a glass eye half so cold, and snaky, and deadly"—fit symbol of a man who, "though he could not read a word, was spontaneously an atheist," and who, during the long night-watches, would enter into arguments to prove that there was nothing to be believed, or loved, or worth living for, but everything to be hated, in the wide world: in short, "a Cain afloat; branded on his yellow brow with some inscrutable curse; and going about corrupting and searing every heart that beat near him." There is Jack Blunt, the "Irish Cockney," with his round face like a walrus, and his stumpy figure like a porpoise standing on end—full of dreams and marine romance—singing songs about susceptible mermaids—and holding fast a comfortable creed that all sailors are saved, having plenty of squalls here below, but fair weather aloft. There is Larry, the whaleman, or "blubber-boiler," ever extolling the delights of the free and easy Indian Ocean, and deprecating civilised life, or, as he styles it, "snivelisation," which has "spiled him complete, when he might have been a great man in Madagasky." There is Dutch Max, stolid and seemingly respectable, but a systematic bi-(if not poly-gamist). And there is the black cook, serious, metaphysical, "and given to talk about original sin"—sitting all Sunday morning over his boiling pots, and reading grease-spotted good books; yet tempted to use some bad language occasionally, when the sea dashes into his stove, of cold, wet, stormy mornings. And, to conclude, there is the steward, a dandy mulatto, yclept Lavender; formerly a barber in West-Broadway, and still redolent of Cologne water and relics of his stock-in-trade there—a sentimental darky, fond of reading *Charlotte Temple,* and carrying a lock of frizzled hair in his waistcoat pocket, which he volunteers to show you, with his handkerchief to his eyes. Mr. Melville is perfectly *au fait* in nautical characterisation of this kind, and as thoroughly vapid when essaying revelations of English aristocratic life, and rhapsodies about Italian organ-boys, whose broken English resembles a mixture of "the potent wine of Oporto with some delicious syrup," and who discourse transcendentally and ravishingly about their mission, and impel the author to affirm that a Jew's-harp hath power to awaken all the fairies in our soul, and make them dance there, "as on a moonlit sward of violets;" and that there is no humblest thing with music in it, not a fife, not a negro-fiddle, that is not to be reverenced[7] as much as the grandest organ that ever rolled its flood-tide of harmony down a cathedral nave! What will Mr. Melville think of our taste, when we own to a delight in the cathedral organ, but also to an incurable irreverance towards street-organ, vagrant fiddle, and perambulatory fife?—against which we have a habit of shutting the window, and retiring to a back room. That we are *moved* by their concord of sweet sounds, we allow; but it is to a wish that *they* would "move on," and sometimes to a mental invocation of the police. Whence, possibly, Mr. Melville will infer, on Shakspearian authority, that we are met only for

> Treasons, stratagems, and spoils;

and will demand, *quoad* our critical taste,

> Let no such man be trusted.

Next came *White Jacket; or, the World in a Man-of-War*. The hero's *soubriquet* is derived from his—shirt, or "white duck frock," his only wrap-rascal—a garment patched with old socks and old trouser-legs, bedarned and bequilted till stiff as King James's cotton-stuffed and dagger-proof doublet—provided, moreover with a great variety of pockets, pantries, clothes-presses, and cupboards, and "several unseen recesses behind the arras,"—insomuch, exclaims the proud, glad owner, "that my jacket, like an old castle, was full of winding stairs, and mysterious closets, crypts, and cabinets; and like a confidential writingdesk, abounded in snug little out-of-the-way lairs and hiding-places, for the storage of valuables." The adventures of the adventurous proprietor of this encyclopaedic toga, this cheap magazine of a coat, are detailed with that eager vivacity, and sometimes that unlicensed extravagance, which are characteristic of the scribe. Some of the sea-pictures are worthy of his highest mood—when a fine imagination overrides and represses the chaos of a wanton fancy. Give him to describe a storm on the wide waters—the gallant ship labouring for life and against hope—the gigantic masts snapping almost under the strain of the top-sails—the ship's bell dismally tolling, and this at murk midnight—the rampant billows curling their crests in triumph—the gale flattening the mariners against the rigging as they toil upwards, while a hurricane of slanting sleet and hail pelts them in savage wrath: and he will thrill us quiet landsmen who dwell at home at ease.

For so successful a trader in "marine stores" as Mr. Melville, *The Whale* seemed a speculation every way big with promise. From such a master of his harpoon might have been expected a prodigious hit. There was about blubber and spermaceti something unctuously suggestive, with him for whaleman. And his three volumes entitled *The Whale* undoubtedly contain much vigorous description, much wild power, many striking details. But the effect is distressingly marred throughout by an extravagant treatment of the subject. The style is maniacal—mad as a March hare—mowing, gibbering, screaming, like an incurable Bedlamite, reckless of keeper or strait-waistcoat. Now it vaults on stilts, and performs *Bombastes Furioso* with contortions of figure, and straining strides, and swashbuckler fustian, far beyond *Pistol* in that Ancient's happiest mood. Now it is seized with spasms, acute and convulsive enough to excite bewilderment in all beholders. When he pleases, Mr. Melville can be so lucid, straightforward, hearty, and unaffected, and displays so unmistakable a shrewdness, and satirical sense of the ridiculous, that it is hard to suppose that *he* can have indited the rhodomontade to which we allude. Surely the man is a Doppelganger—a dual number incarnate (singular though he be, in and out of all conscience):—surely he is two single gentlemen rolled into one, but retaining their respective idiosyncrasies—the one sensible, sagacious, observant, graphic, and producing admirable matter—the other maundering, drivelling, subject to paroxysms, cramps, and total collapse, and penning exceeding many pages of unaccountable "bosh." So that in tackling every new chapter, one is disposed to question it beforehand, "Under which king, Bezonian?"—the sane or the insane; the constitutional and legitimate, or the absolute and usurping? Writing of Leviathan, he exclaims, "Unconsciously my chirography expands into placard capitals. Give me a condor's quill! Give me Vesuvius' crater for an inkstand! Friends, hold my arms!" Oh that his friends had obeyed that summons! They might have saved society from a huge dose of hyperbolical slang, maudlin sentimentalism, and tragi-comic bubble and squeak.

His Yankeeisms are plentiful as blackberries. "I am tormented," quoth he, "with an everlasting itch for things remote." Remote, too frequently, from good taste, good manners, and good sense. We need not pause at such expressions as "looking a sort of diabolically funny;"—"beefsteaks done rare;"—"a speechlessly quick chaotic bundling of a man into eternity;"—"bidding adieu to circumspect life, to exist only in a delirious throb." But why wax fast and furious in a thousand such paragraphs as these:—"In landlessness alone resides the highest truth, indefinite as the Almighty ... Take heart, take heart, O Bulkington! Bear thee grimly, demi-god! Up from the spray of thy ocean-perishing—straight up, leaps thy apotheosis!"—"Thou [*scil*. Spirit of Equality] great God! who didst not refuse to the swart convict, Bunyan, the pale, poetic pearl; Thou who didst clothe with doubly hammered leaves of finest gold the stumped and paupered arm of old Cervantes; Thou who didst pick up Andrew Jackson from the pebbles; who didst hurl him upon a war-horse; who didst thunder him higher than a throne!"—"If such a furious trope may stand, his [Capt. Ahab's] special lunacy stormed his general sanity, and carried it, and turned all its concentrated cannon upon its own mad mark . . . then it was, that his torn body and gashed soul bled into one another; and so interfusing made him mad."—"And the miser-merman, Wisdom, revealed [to a diving negro] his hoarded heaps; and among the joyous, heartless, ever-juvenile eternities, Pip saw the multitudinous, God-omnipresent, coral insects, that out of the firmament of waters heaved the colossal orbs. He saw God's foot upon the treadle of the loom, and spoke it; and therefore his shipmates called him mad."

The story itself is a strange, wild, furibund thing—about Captain Ahab's vow of revenge against one Moby Dick. And who is Moby Dick? A fellow of a whale, who has made free with the captain's leg; so that the captain now stumps on ivory, and goes circumnavigating the globe in quest of the old offender, and raves by the hour in a lingo borrowed from Rabelais, Carlyle, Emerson, newspapers transcendental and transatlantic, and the magnificent proems of our Christmas pantomimes. Captain Ahab is introduced with prodigious efforts at preparation; and there is really no lack of rude power and character about his presentment—spoiled, however, by the Cambyses' vein in which he dissipates his vigour. His portrait is striking—looking "like a man cut away from the stake, when the fire has overrunningly wasted all the limbs without consuming them, or taking away one particle from their compacted aged robustness"—a man with a brow gaunt and ribbed, like the black sand beach after some stormy tide has been gnawing it, without being able to drag the firm thing from its place. Ever since his fell encounter with Moby Dick, this impassioned veteran has cherished a wild vindictiveness against the whale, frantically identifying with him not only all his bodily woes, but all his feelings of exasperation—so that the White Whale swims before him "as the monomaniac incarnation of all those malicious agencies which some deep men feel eating in them, till they are left living on with half a heart and half a lung." The amiable cannibal Queequeg occasions some stirring and some humorous scenes, and is probably the most reasonable and cultivated creature of the ship's company. Starbuck and Stubb are both tiresome, in different ways. The book is rich with facts connected with the natural history of the whale, and the whole art and process of whaling; and with spirited descriptions of that process, which betray an intense straining at effect. The climax of the three days' chase after Moby Dick is highly wrought and sternly exciting—but the catastrophe, in its whirl of waters and fancies, resembles one of Turner's later nebulous transgressions in gamboge.

Speaking of the passengers on board Redburn's ship *Highlander*, Mr. Melville significantly and curtly observes, "As for the ladies, I have nothing to say concerning them; for ladies are like creeds; if you cannot speak well of them, say nothing." He will pardon us for including in this somewhat arbitrary classification of forms of beauty and forms of faith, his own, last, and worst production, *Pierre; or, the Ambiguities*.

O author of *Typee* and *Omoo*, we admire so cordially the proven capacity of your pen, that we entreat you to doff the "non-natural sense" of your late lucubrations—to put off your worser self—and to do your better, real self, that justice which its "potentiality" deserves.

Notes
1. Thomas De Quincey.
2. *Endymion*, Book III.
3. See Alison's *History of Europe* (New Series), vol. i., p. 74.
4. The hero himself is a sort of amalgam of Perceval Keene and Peter Simple—the keenness strangely antedating the simplicity.
5. *Redburn* vol. ii., ch. 27.
6. See G. H. Lewes' Two Letters.
7. No parallel passage is that fine saying of Sir Thomas Browne in *Religio Medici*, ii., 9.

—"Sir Nathaniel," "American Authorship: IV. Herman Melville" *New Monthly Magazine*, July 1853, pp. 300–308

W. Clark Russell "Sea-Stories" (1884)

W. Clark Russell, in his attention to Melville "only as a seafarer," typifies another way the complexity of Melville was often categorized and reduced. Students considering the Melville revival, a period that stretched approximately from 1917 to the 1930s, will want to remember that Russell was an inspiration for Archibald MacMechan's important attempt to revise Melville's reputation, an entry included in the Works section of this volume.

Whoever has read the writings of Melville must I think feel disposed to consider *Moby Dick* as his finest work. It is indeed all about the sea, whilst *Typee* and *Omoo*, are chiefly famous for their lovely descriptions of the South Sea Islands, and of the wild and curious inhabitants of those coral strands;

but though the action of the story is altogether on shipboard, the narrative is not in the least degree nautical in the sense that Cooper's and Marryat's novels are. The thread that strings a wonderful set of fancies and incidents together, is that of a whaler, whose master, Captain Ahab, having lost his leg by the teeth of a monstrous white whale, to which the name of Moby Dick has been given, vows to sail in pursuit of his enemy. The narrator embarks in the ship that is called the *Pequod,* which he describes as having an "old-fashioned, claw-footed look about her."

> She was apparelled like any barbaric Ethiopic Emperor, his neck heavy with pendants of polished ivory. She was a thing of trophies. A cannibal of a craft, tricking herself forth in the chased bones of her enemies. All round her unpanelled, open bulwarks were garnished like one continuous jaw, with the long sharp teeth of the sperm-whale, inserted there for pins to fasten her old hempen thews and tendons to. Those thews ran not through base blocks of land wood, but deftly travelled over sheaves of ivory. Scorning a turnstile wheel at her reverend helm she sported there a tiller; and that tiller was in one mass, curiously carved from the long narrow jaw of her hereditary foe. The helmsman, who steered by that tiller in a tempest, felt like the Tartar when he holds back his fiery steed by clutching its jaw. A noble craft, but somehow a most melancholy! All noble things are touched with that.

Melville takes this vessel, fills her full of strange men, and starts her on her insane quest, that he may have the ocean under and around him to muse upon, as though he were in a spacious burial-ground, with the alternations of sunlight and moonlight and deep starless darkness to set his thoughts to. *Moby Dick* is not a sea-story—one could not read it as such—it is a medley of noble impassioned thoughts born of the deep, pervaded by a grotesque human interest, owing to the contrast it suggests between the rough realities of the cabin and the forecastle, and the phantasms of men conversing in rich poetry, and strangely moving and acting in that dim weatherworn Nantucket whaler. There is a chapter where the sailors are represented as gathered together on the forecastle; and what is made to pass among them, and the sayings which are put into their mouths, might truly be thought to have come down to us from some giant mind of the Shakspearean era. As we read, we do not need to be told that seamen don't talk as those men do; probabilities are not thought of in this story. It is like a drawing by William Blake, if you please; or, better yet, it is of the *Ancient Mariner* pattern, madly fantastic in places, full of extraordinary thoughts, yet gloriously coherent—the work of a hand which, if the desire for such a thing had ever been, would have given a sailor's distinctness to the portrait of the solemn and strange Miltonic fancy of a ship built in the eclipse and rigged with curses dark. In *Typee,* and *Omoo,* and *Redburn,* he takes other ground, and writes—always with the finest fancy—in a straight-headed way. I am concerned with him only as a seafarer. In *Redburn* he tells a sailor's yarn, and the dream-like figures of the crew of the *Pequod* make place for Liverpool and Yankee seamen, who chew tobacco and use bad language. His account of the sufferings of the emigrants in this book leaves a deep impression upon the mind. His accuracy is unimpeachable here, for the horrors he relates were as well known thirty and forty years ago as those of the middle passages were in times earlier still. In *Omoo,* again, he gives us a good deal of the sea, and presumably relates his own experiences on board a whaler. He seems proud of his calling, for in *Moby Dick* he says:—

> And as for me, if by any possibility there be any as yet undiscovered prime thing in me; if I shall ever deserve any real repute in that small but high-hushed world which I might not be unreasonably ambitious of; if hereafter I shall do anything that, upon the whole, a man might rather have done than left undone; if at my death my executors, or more properly my creditors, find any precious MSS. in my desk, then here I prospectively ascribe all the honour and the glory to whaling; for a whale-ship was my Yale College and my Harvard.

He returns to the whaleman in *Omoo,* and in his barque, the *Little Jule,* charms the nautical reader with the faithfulness of his portraiture, and the humour and the poetry he puts into it. There is some remarkable character-drawing in this book: notably John Jermin, the mate of the *Little Jule,* and Doctor Long Ghost, the nickname given by the sailors to a man who shipped as a physician, and was rated as a gentleman and lived in the cabin, until both the captain and he falling drunk, he drove home his views on politics by knocking the skipper down, after which he went to live forward. He is as quaint, striking, and original a personage as may be found in English fiction, and we find him in the dingy and leaky forecastle of the *Little Jule,* where he is surrounded by coarse and worn whalemen in Scotch caps and ragged clothes quoting Virgil, talking of Hobbes, "besides repeating poetry by the canto, especially *Hudibras.*" Yet his portrait does not match that of John Jermin, the mate, whom, in spite of his love of rum and homely method of reasoning with a man by means of a handspike, one gets to heartily like and to follow about with laughter as, intoxicated, he chases the sun all over the deck at noon with an old quadrant at his eye, or tumbles into the forecastle after a seaman who has enraged him by contemptuous remarks.

—W. Clark Russell, "Sea-Stories," Contemporary Review, September 1884, pp. 356–58

Robert Buchanan "Socrates in Camden, with a Look Round" (1885)

Meantime my sun-like music-maker,
Shines solitary and apart;
Meantime the brave sword-carrying Quaker
Broods in the peace of his great heart,—
While Melville, sea-compelling man,
Before whose wand Leviathan
Rose hoary white upon the Deep,
With awful sounds that stirred its sleep,
Melville, whose magic drew Typee,
Radiant as Venus, from the sea,
Sits all forgotten or ignored,
While haberdashers are adored!
He, ignorant of the drapers' trade,
Indifferent to the art of dress,
Pictured the glorious South-sea maid
Almost in mother nakedness—
Without a hat, or boot, or stocking,
A want of dress to most so shocking,
With just one chemisette to dress her
She *lives*,—and still shall live, God bless her!
 Long as the sea rolls deep and blue,
While heaven repeats the thunder of it,
Long as the White Whale ploughs it through,
The shape my sea-magician drew
Shall still endure, or I'm no prophet!

—Robert Buchanan, "Socrates in Camden, with a Look Round," Academy, August 15, 1885, p. 103

Edwin P. Whipple
"American Literature" (1886)

Herman Melville, after astonishing the public with a rapid succession of original novels, the scene of which was placed in the islands of the Pacific, suddenly dropped his pen, as if in disgust of his vocation.

—Edwin P. Whipple, "American Literature" (1886),
American Literature and Other Papers, 1887, p. 125

Charles F. Richardson (1887)

At this period English and American literature (of course including poetry and prose fiction) were beginning to feel the scientific and economic influence of the age,—an age which on its superficial side was searching for facts rather than dreams or fancies. [. . .] response was made by Herman Melville in his brisk and stirring tales of the sea or sketches of travel, in which fact and fancy were mingled by the nervously impatient author, in the proportion desired by his immediate public. Melville's own adventures had been those of a modern Captain John Smith in the Pacific islands and waters; so that the *pars magna fui* of his lively books gave them the needed fillip of personality, and duly magnified their elements of wonder. That brilliant power of delineation which, in Melville's conversation, so charmed his warm friends the Hawthornes, is apparently not heightened in his books, but would seem to be rather diminished by the exigencies of writing. But the personal narrative or fiction of *Typee, Omoo,* and *Moby Dick,* with their adventurous rapidity of description of Pacific seas, ships, savages and whales, represented the restless facility which has always been an American trait, and which occasionally develops into some enduring literary success.

—Charles F. Richardson, *American Literature,
1607–1885*, 1887, Vol. 2, pp. 403–04

Robert Louis Stevenson (1888)

Robert Louis Stevenson's acid outburst labeling Melville a "howling cheese" is perhaps rivaled in the history of critical summary judgment only by James Russell Lowell's measurement of Poe as "two-fifths sheer fudge." Why is Stevenson so dismissive of a literary precursor to whom he is often compared? His comedic dismissal of *Typee* is potentially useful to writers considering either masculinity and literature or the influence of Melville on later authors. Students wishing to explore genre through Melville might want to look beyond the outburst to why Stevenson, writing in the era of realism, saw falseness in Melville's romantic productions. Recent critics have begun to explore how Stevenson grew away from Western myths of the South Seas, such as the myth of cross-cultural love we encounter in Melville's *Typee* and *Moby-Dick*. Stevenson instead became quite critical of romantic assessments of Pacific exoticism, so his simple condemnation of Melville may indeed carry much more significance. Students might read Stevenson in the context of the short remarks by Conrad and London collected in the final section of this volume.

I shall have a fine book of travels, I feel sure; and will tell you more of the South Seas after very few months than any other writer has done—except Herman Melville perhaps, who is a howling cheese.

—Robert Louis Stevenson,
Letter to Charles Baxter (September 6, 1888)

ANONYMOUS (1891)

This October 1891 *New York Times* article is less remarkable for its celebration of the "romance" and "pictorial power" of Melville's work than for its tone of perplexed inquiry when discussing how Melville could have died "an absolutely forgotten man." In this respect, the article foreshadows the future correction of Melville's reputation. Students exploring the history of Melville's reputation or reception may find it noteworthy that at his death *Moby-Dick* can be assessed not only as a lesser work, but also as purportedly the "authentic . . . story of a whaling voyage." Students might also compare this piece to the short Stevenson piece that immediately precedes it, as Stevenson's sentiments run counter to those expressed in this anonymous article.

There has died and been buried in this city, during the current week, at an advanced age, a man who is so little known, even by name, to the generation now in the vigor of life that only one newspaper contained an obituary account of him, and this was but of three or four lines. Yet forty years ago the appearance of a new book by Herman Melville was esteemed a literary event, not only throughout his own country, but so far as the English-speaking race extended. To the ponderous and quarterly British reviews of that time, the author of *Typee* was about the most interesting of literary Americans, and men who made few exceptions to the British rule of not reading an American book not only made Melville one of them, but paid him the further compliment of discussing him as an unquestionable literary force. Yet when a visiting British writer a few years ago inquired at a gathering in New-York of distinctly literary Americans what had become of Herman Melville, not only was there not one among them who was able to tell him, but there was scarcely one among them who had ever heard of the man concerning whom he inquired, albeit that man was then living within a half mile of the place of the conversation. Years ago the books by which Melville's reputation had been made had long been out of print and out of demand. The latest book, now about a quarter of a century old, *Battle Pieces and Aspects of the War,* fell flat, and he has died an absolutely forgotten man.

In its kind this speedy oblivion by which a once famous man so long survived his fame is almost unique, and it is not easily explicable. Of course, there are writings that attain a great vogue and then fall entirely out of regard or notice. But this is almost always because either the interest of the subject matter is temporary, and the writings are in the nature of journalism, or else the workmanship to which they owe their temporary success is itself the produce or the product of a passing fashion. This was not the case with Herman Melville. Whoever, arrested for a moment by the tidings of the author's death, turns back now to the books that were so much read and so much talked about forty years ago has no difficulty in determining why they were then read and talked about. His difficulty will be rather to discover why they are read and talked about no longer. The total eclipse now of what was then a literary luminary seems like a wanton caprice of fame. At all events, it conveys a moral that is both bitter and wholesome to the popular novelists of our own day.

Melville was a born romancer. One cannot account for the success of his early romances by saying that in the Great South Sea he had found and worked a new field for romance, since evidently it was not his experience in the South Sea that had led him to romance, but the irresistible attraction that romance had over him that led him to the South Sea. He was able not only to feel but to interpret that charm, as it never had been interpreted before, as it never has been interpreted since. It was the romance and the mystery of the great ocean and its groups of islands that made so alluring to his own generation the series of fantastic tales in which these things were celebrated. *Typee* and *Omoo* and *Mardi* remain for readers of English the poetic interpretation of the Polynesian Islands and their surrounding seas. Melville's pictorial power was very great, and it came, as such power always comes, from his feeling more intensely than others the charm that he is able to present more vividly than others. It is this power which gave these romances the hold upon readers which it is surprising that they have so completely lost. It is almost as visible in those of his books that are not professed romances, but purport to be accounts of authentic experiences—in *White Jacket,* the story of life before the mast in an American man-of-war; in *Moby Dick,* the story of a whaling voyage. The imagination that kindles at a touch is as plainly shown in these as in the novels, and few readers who have read it are likely to forget Melville's poetizing of the prosaic process of trying out blubber in his description of the old whaler wallowing through the dark and "burning a corpse." Nevertheless, the South Pacific is the field that he mainly made his own, and that he made his own, as those who remember his books will acknowledge, beyond rivalry. That this was a very considerable literary achievement there can be no question. For some months a contemporaneous writer, of whom nobody will dispute that he is a romancer and a literary artist, has been working in the same field, but it cannot seriously be pretended that Mr. Stevenson has taken from Herman Melville the laureateship of the Great South Sea. In fact, the readers of Stevenson abandon as quite unreadable what he has written from that quarter.

—Unsigned, *New York Times,* October 2, 1891, p. 4

Richard Henry Stoddard (1891)

Richard Henry Stoddard was a contemporary of Melville's, and his take on the author's work and temperament is notable for its unbridled confidence. He overlooks the author's arguable proficiency in verse (as displayed particularly in *Battlepieces*), and he simply deems Melville's language "unliterary." Students may want to account for this type of attitude toward Melville's writing, for it is an enduring critical summary and judgment that finds the structure and language in Melville's unorthodox work to be uneven, unexamined, rushed, and even "chaotic." Students exploring these facets of Melville's art may wish to compare Stoddard's sentiments to those expressed by William Trent later in this section.

There was a wealth of imagination in the mind of Mr. Melville, but it was an untrained imagination, and a world of the stuff out of which poetry is made, but no poetry, which is creation and not chaos. He saw like a poet, felt like a poet, thought like a poet, but he never attained any proficiency in verse, which was not among his natural gifts. His vocabulary was large, fluent, eloquent, but it was excessive, inaccurate and unliterary. He wrote too easily, and at too great length, his pen sometimes running away with him, and from his readers. There were strange, dark, mysterious elements in his nature, as there were in Hawthorne's, but he never learned to control them, as Hawthorne did from the beginning, and never turned their possibilities into actualities.

—Richard Henry Stoddard, *Critic,* November 14, 1891, p. 272

HENRY S. SALT "MARQUESAN MELVILLE" (1892)

Henry S. Salt's "Marquesan Melville" captures the fact that the author was remembered and celebrated by readers (and perhaps not only British readers) well after the mythical lapse into silence, and well before the revival. Salt points the way to the reawakening of serious interest in Melville. This is an important piece for students focusing on a growing critical concern—appreciation of Melville across the Atlantic. Salt's mostly generous words were written on the occasion of Melville's death and attempt a general assessment of Melville's major works, except for *Billy Budd*, which was left unpublished and in manuscript in 1892. Salt once considered writing a biography of Melville, so it is no surprise that his overview contains a detailed synopsis of the life of Melville. Students investigating the myth and fact of Melville's life may want to compare assertions in this early work to later, more authoritative biographies such as those of Hershel Parker or Laurie Robertson-Lorant. Salt's essay is also important for its agreement with Carl Van Doren that Melville and George Borrow might be usefully compared. Also, Salt explores in some detail the myth of the noble savage as it pertains to *Typee*. Melville's handling of the difference between savagery and civilization is a critical commonplace still, and students exploring this issue in more recent scholarship have in Salt's words an accurate representation of how the topic was viewed in his time. Students examining Melville's language might want to compare Salt's treatment of the subject to the comments concerning *Moby-Dick* in the Duyckinck, Lawrence, and Olson essays in the Works section of this volume. Salt finds a movement between the *Typee* era, when a "limpid simplicity" reigns in the author's language, to the *Moby-Dick* era, when readers encounter "a habit of gorgeous and fantastic word-painting." Students might also compare the brief recognition of and general aversion to *Pierre* that Salt registers to the exuberant hatchet job the book suffers in the poisoned pen reviews collected later in this volume.

———— ———— ————

Has America a literature? I am inclined to think it a grave mistake to argue seriously with those afflicted persons who periodically exercise themselves over this idlest of academic questions. It is wiser to meet them with a practical counter-thrust, and pointedly inquire, for example, whether they are familiar with the writings of Herman Melville. Whereupon, confusion will in most cases ensue, and you will go on to suggest that to criticise *Hamlet,* with the prince's part omitted, would be no whit more fatuous than to demonstrate the non-existence of an American literature, while taking no account of its true intellectual giants. When it was announced, a few months ago, that "Mr. Herman Melville, the author," had just died in New York at the age of seventy-two, the news excited but little interest on this side of the Atlantic; yet, forty years ago, his name was familiar to English, as to American readers, and there is little or no exaggeration in Robert Buchanan's remark, that he is "the one great imaginative writer fit to stand shoulder to shoulder with Whitman on that continent."

It was in 1846 that Melville fairly took the world by storm with his *Typee: the Narrative of a four months' residence in the Marquesas Islands,* the first of a brilliant series of volumes of adventure, in which reality was so deftly encircled with a halo of romance that readers were at once captivated by the force and freshness of the style and puzzled as to the personality of the author. Who and what was this mysterious sojourner in the far islands of the Pacific— this "Marquesan Melville," as a writer in *Blackwood* denominated him? Speculation was rife, and not unaccompanied by suspicion; for there were some critics who not only questioned the veracity of Herman Melville's "Narratives," but declared his very name to be fictitious. "Separately," remarked one sagacious reviewer, "the names are not uncommon; we can urge no valid reason against their juncture; yet in this instance they fall suspiciously on our ear."

Herman Melville, however, was far from being a mythical personage, though in his early life, as in his later, he seems to have instinctively shrunk from any other publicity than that which was brought him by his books. He was a genuine child of nature, a sort of nautical George Borrow, on whom the irresistible sea-passion had descended in his boyhood, and won him away from the ordinary routine of respectable civilised life, until, to quote his own words, to travel had become a necessity of his existence, "a way of driving off the spleen and regulating the circulation." The son of a cultured American merchant, of Scotch extraction, he had early imbibed from his father's anecdotes a romantic attachment to the sea. "Of winter evenings," he says, "by the well-remembered sea-coal fires in old Greenwich Street, New York, he used to tell my brother and me of the monstrous waves at sea, mountain-high, and of the masts bending like twigs." At the age of eighteen, his father having died in bankruptcy, he found himself unexpectedly face to face with poverty and disappointment, and was forced to embark as a common seaman in a merchant vessel bound to Liverpool, a voyage of disillusionment and bitter experience, of which he has left us what is apparently an authentic record in one of his early volumes.[1]

Returned from this expedition, he essayed for a time to gain a quiet livelihood as a teacher. But destiny and his natural genius had willed it otherwise; it was no academic lecture-room, but the deck of a whale-ship, that was to be "his Yale College and his Harvard." "Oh, give me again the rover's life," he exclaims, "the joy, the thrill, the whirl! Let me feel thee again, old sea! Let me leap into thy saddle once more! I am sick of these *terra firma* toils and cares, sick of the dust and reek of towns. Let me snuff thee up, sea-breeze, and whinny in thy spray!" So in 1841 the child of nature was again aboard, and off to the Pacific on a whaler; and it was the adventures that befell him, during this absence of nearly four years' duration, that subsequently furnished the material for the chief series of his volumes. In *Typee* he related the story of his romantic captivity among a tribe of noble savages in the Marquesas; in *Omoo* we have his further wanderings in the Society and Sandwich Islands; in *White Jacket,* his return voyage as a common sailor in a man-of-war. *Mardi,* on the other hand, is a phantasy, in which the imaginative element, having slipped from the control of the narrative, runs riot in the wildest and most extravagant luxuriance.

Typee must be regarded as, on the whole, the most charming of Melville's writings, and the one which may most surely count on lasting popularity; it is certainly the masterpiece of his earlier period, during which the artistic sense was still predominant over those transcendental tendencies which characterised his later volumes. Coming at a time when men's minds were filled with a vague, undefined interest in the wonders of the Pacific, and when the French annexation of Tahiti, of which Melville was an eyewitness, had drawn universal attention to that quarter of the globe, it gained an instantaneous and wide-spread success, both in America and England, and was quickly translated into several European tongues. Alike in the calm beauty of its descriptive passages, and in the intense vividness of its character-sketches, it was, and is, and must ever be, a most powerful and fascinating work. Indeed, I think I speak within the mark in saying that nothing better of its kind is to be found in English literature, so firm and clear is it in outline, yet so dreamily suggestive in the dim mystic atmosphere which pervades it. Here is a passage from one of the early chapters, itself as rhythmical as the rhythmical drifting of the whaler *Dolly* under the trade-winds of the Pacific:

> The sky presented a clear expanse of the most delicate blue, except along the skirts of the horizon, where you might see a thin drapery of pale clouds which never varied their form or colour. The long, measured, dirge-like swell of the Pacific came rolling along with its surface broken by little tiny waves, sparkling in the sunshine. Every now and then a shoal of flying fish, scared from the water under the bows, would leap into the air, and fall the next moment like a shower of silver into the sea. Then you would see the superb albicore, with his glittering sides, sailing aloft, and, often describing an arc in his descent, disappear on the surface of the water. Far off, the lofty jet of the whale might be seen, and nearer at hand the prowling shark, that villainous foot-pad of the seas, would come skulking along, and at a wary distance regard us with his evil eye. At times some shapeless monster of the deep, floating on the surface, would, as we approached, sink slowly into the blue waters, and fade away from the sight. But the most impressive feature of the scene was the almost unbroken silence that reigned over sky and water. Scarcely a sound could be heard but the occasional breathing of the grampus and the rippling at the cutwater.

And Typee itself, the scene of Melville's detention, when he and a companion sailor had deserted from the whale-ship—what a fairyland of tropical valleys, and crystal streams, and groves of cocoa-palms and bread-fruit trees, is here magically depicted for us! How life-like the portraiture of the innocent, placid, happy islanders, who, albeit cannibals at times, were yet far superior to civilised nations in many of the best qualities by which civilisation is supposed to be distinguished! And Fayaway—surely never was Indian maiden so glorified by poet or romancer[2] as is the gentle, beautiful, faithful Fayaway in Melville's marvellous tale! The strongest and tenderest pictures that George Borrow has drawn for us of his friendly relations with the wandering gipsy-folk by roadside or dingle are not more strong and tender than Melville's reminiscences of this "peep at Polynesian life." As Borrow possessed the secret of winning the confidence of the gipsies, so Melville, by the same talisman of utter simplicity and naturalness, was able to fraternise in perfect good fellowship with the so-called savages of the Pacific.

It is, furthermore, significant that Melville's familiarity with these "noble savages" was productive of a feeling the very opposite of contempt; he bears repeated and explicit testimony to the enviable healthfulness and happiness of the uncivilised society in which he sojourned so long. "The continual happiness," he says, "which, so far as I was able to judge, appeared to prevail in the valley, sprung principally from that all-pervading sensation which Rousseau has told us he at one time experienced, the mere buoyant sense of a healthful, physical existence. And indeed, in this particular, the Typees had ample reason to felicitate themselves, for sickness was almost unknown. During the whole period of my stay, I saw but one invalid among them; and on their smooth, clear skins you observed no blemish or mark of disease." Still more emphatic is his tribute to their moral qualities. "Civilisation does not engross all the virtues of humanity: she has not even her full share of them. If truth and justice, and the better principles of our nature, cannot exist unless enforced by the statute-book, how are we to account for the social condition of the Typees? So pure and upright were they in all the relations of life, that entering their valley, as I did, under the most erroneous impressions of their character, I was soon led to exclaim in amazement: Are these the ferocious savages, the blood-thirsty cannibals, of whom I have heard such frightful tales! . . . I will frankly declare that after passing a few weeks in this valley of the Marquesas, I formed a higher estimate of human nature than I had ever before entertained. But, alas! since then I have been one of the crew of a man-of-war, and the pent-up wickedness of five hundred men has nearly overturned all my previous theories."

But here it may be asked by later, as by earlier readers, "Was Melville's narrative a true one? Is his testimony on these subjects a testimony of any scientific value?" The answer to this question, despite the suspicion of the critics, is a decided affirmative. Not only is Melville's account of Typee in close agreement with that of earlier voyagers, as, for example, Captain Porter's *Journal of a Cruise to the Pacific Ocean,* published in 1822, but it has been expressly corroborated by later adventurers. "I cannot resist," wrote an American naval officer,[3] "paying the faint tribute of my own individual admiration to Mr. Melville. Apart from the innate beauty and charming tone of his narratives, the delineations of island life and scenery, from my own personal observation, are most correctly and faithfully drawn." Another witness, who has recently been cited, was the Rev. Titus Coan, of the Hawaiian

Islands, who "had personally visited the Marquesas group, found the Typee valley, and verified in every detail the romantic descriptions of the gentle but man-devouring islanders."[4]

After the publication of *Typee,* Melville married the daughter of Chief Justice Shaw, to whom the book was dedicated, and made his home, from 1850 to 1863, in an old spacious farmhouse at Pittsfield, Massachusetts, commanding picturesque views of Greylock and the other Berkshire mountains. He was here a neighbour of Nathaniel Hawthorne, who was then living at Lenox, and there are records of many friendly intimacies between the two authors, whose intellects were in many ways akin. We read in the Hawthorne diaries of "Mr. Omoo's visits," and how he came accompanied by "his great dog," and how he held transcendental conversations with Hawthorne "about time and eternity, things of this world and of the next, and books, and publishers, and all possible and impossible matters, that lasted pretty deep into the night." It is during this residence at Pittsfield, the adventurous struggles of his early life being now concluded, that we note the commencement of the second, the transcendental period of Melville's literary career. It has been truly said of him that "he had all the metaphysical tendencies which belong so eminently to the American mind;" and it is interesting to observe in this, as in other cases, the conjunction of the practical with the metaphysical temperament. "The chief characteristic of Herman Melville's writings"—so I have elsewhere remarked[5]—"is this attempted union of the practical with the ideal. Commencing with a basis of solid fact, he loves to build up a fantastic structure, which is finally lost in the cloudland of metaphysical speculation."

As *Typee* is the best production of the earlier and simpler phase of Melville's authorship, so undoubtedly is *The Whale* (or *Moby Dick,* as it is sometimes styled) the crown and glory of the later phase; less shapely and artistic than *Typee,* it far surpasses it in immensity of scope and triumphant energy of execution.[6] It is in *The Whale* that we see Melville casting to the winds all conventional restrictions, and rioting in the prodigality of his imaginative vigour. It is in *The Whale* that we find the fullest recognition of that magical influence of the sea—the "image of the ungraspable phantom of life"—which from first to last was the most vital inspiration of his restless and indomitable genius. ("The ocean," he finely wrote in a later volume, "brims with natural griefs and tragedies; and into that watery immensity of terror man's private grief is lost like a drop.") Ostensibly nothing more than a wild story of a strange voyage of vengeance, a "quenchless feud" between a fierce old sea-captain and a particular white sperm-whale of renowned strength and audacity, the book, which abounds with real facts concerning the details of the whale-fishery, has a mystic esoteric significance which lifts it into a wholly different category. In the character of Captain Ahab, who "looked like a man cut away from the stake when the fire has overrunningly wasted all the limbs without consuming them," we see a lurid personification of the self-destructive spirit of Hatred and Revenge, while Moby Dick, the white whale, "swam before him as the monomaniac incarnation of all those malicious agencies which some deep men feel eating in them." To quote detached passages from a work of such ambitious conception and colossal proportions would be worse than useless; I must therefore content myself with saying that *The Whale,* faulty as it is in many respects, owing to the turgid mannerisms of Melville's transcendental mood, is nevertheless the supreme production of a master mind—let no one presume to pass judgment on American literature unless he has read, and re-read, and wonderingly pondered, the three mighty volumes of *The Whale.*

The increasing transcendentalism of Melville's later thought was accompanied and reflected by a corresponding complexity of language, the limpid simplicity so remarkable in *Typee,* and *Omoo,* and *White Jacket* being now succeeded by a habit of gorgeous and fantastic word-painting, which, though brilliantly effective at its best, degenerated, at its worst, into mere bombast and rhetoric, a process which had already been discernible in the concluding portions of *Mardi,* while in *Pierre* (or *The Ambiguities,* as it was appropriately designated) it reached the fatal climax of its development. This unfortunate book, published in 1852, was to a great extent the ruin of its author's reputation; for the critics not unfairly protested against the perversity of "a man born to create, who resolves to anatomise; a man born to see, who insists upon speculating." Of *The Confidence Man* (1857), and Melville's later books in general, it is not necessary to speak; though it is noticeable that in his narrative of *Israel Potter* (1855), and one or two of the short stories in *The Piazza Tales* (1856), he partly recovered his old firmness of touch and delicacy of workmanship.

For, in spite of all the obscurities and mannerisms which confessedly deform his later writings, it remains true that *naturalness* is, on the whole, Melville's prime characteristic, both in the tone and in the style of his productions. His narratives are as racy and vigorous as those of Defoe or Smollett or Marryat; his character-sketches are such as only a man of keen observation, and as keen a sense of humour, could have realised and depicted. His seamen and his sea-captains all, his savages ashore or aboard, from the noble unsophisticated Mehevi in *Typee* to the semi-civilised comical Queequeg in *The Whale, are* admirably vivid and impressive, and the reader who shall once have made their acquaintance will thenceforward in no wise be persuaded that they are not real and living personages. Moreover, there is a large-souled humanity in Melville—the direct outcome of his generous, emotional, yet uniformly sane temperament—which differentiates him entirely from the mere artist or *litterateur*. "I stand for the heart," he writes, in one of his letters to Nathaniel Hawthorne, a statement fully substantiated by the many humane sentiments that find expression in his pages, whether on the subject of modern warfare, or negro slavery, or the barbarities of naval discipline, or the cruel treatment of the harmless "savages" of the Pacific by the more savage apostles of "civilisation." For the rest of it, Melville appears as a frank, simple believer in common human nature, and so little a respecter of persons that his democracy was described by Hawthorne as "ruthless." "With no son of man," says Melville, "do I stand upon any etiquette or ceremony, except the Christian ones of charity and honesty. A thief in jail is as honourable a personage as General George Washington."

It may be surmised that this uncompromising attitude was scarcely calculated to win the favour of society. A friend who visited Melville at Pittsfield described him as an Ishmael who was "apparently considered by the good people of Pittsfield as little better than a cannibal or a beach-comber." "In vain," he says,[7] "I sought to hear of Typee and those Paradise islands; he preferred to pour forth his philosophy and his theories of life. The shade of Aristotle arose like a cold mist between myself and Fayaway. But what a talk it was! Melville is transformed from a Marquesan to a gipsy student, the gipsy element still remaining strong in him. And this contradiction gives him the air of one who has suffered from opposition, both literary and social."

There is no doubt that Melville's characteristic reticence on personal matters, together with his increasing love of retirement, was in large measure the cause of his otherwise unaccountable loss of literary fame; for even the well-merited failure of such books as *Pierre* and *The Confidence Man* would be in itself insufficient to explain the neglect of his genuine masterpieces. It is true that for a few years he was induced to lecture, in various parts of the States, on the subject of his voyages to the South Seas; but, as a rule, he could not, or would not, cultivate the indispensable art of keeping his name before the public. The man who could win the affections of a cannibal community in the Pacific was less at home in the intricacies of self-advertisement and "business." "Dollars damn me," he remarks in one of his letters. "When I feel most moved to write, that is banned—it will not pay. Yet, altogether, write the *other* way I cannot. So the product is a final hash, and all my books are botches." That he felt keenly mortified at the ill success *of Pierre,* is beyond question. When, on the occasion of a tour in Europe, in 1856, he visited Hawthorne at the Liverpool consulate, he told his friend that "the spirit of adventure had gone out of him." He is described by Hawthorne as looking "a little paler, perhaps, and a little sadder, and with his characteristic gravity and reserve of manner. He has suffered from too constant literary occupations, pursued without much success latterly; and his writings, for a long while past, have indicated a morbid state of mind."

In 1863, Melville found it necessary, for the better education of his children, to leave his home at Pittsfield, and to take up his quarters at New York, where for many years he held an inspectorship in the custom-house. His life became now altogether one of quietude and retirement; content to let the noisy world go by, he made no attempt to recover the fame which had once been his, and to which he still possessed an inalienable title. During these years, however, he published two volumes of poetry; *Battle Pieces,* which deals mainly with incidents of the civil war, and *Clarel, a Pilgrimage in the Holy Land,* described by Melville himself, in a letter to an English correspondent, as "a metrical affair, a pilgrimage or what not, of several thousand lines, eminently adapted for unpopularity." More interesting than these is a little story, *John Man and Other Sailors,* issued in 1888, and limited to twenty-five copies—a limitation which affords a pathetic and significant comment on the acumen of a "reading public" which had allowed itself to become almost entirely oblivious of the author of *Typee* and *The Whale.* We need not doubt, however, that Melville found ample compensation for this neglect in that assurance of ultimate and lasting recognition which is seldom denied to men of genius. "His tall, stalwart figure," says Mr. Stedman,[8] "until recently could be seen almost daily, tramping through the Fort George district or Central Park; his roving inclination leading him to obtain as much out-door life as possible. His evenings were spent at home, with his books, his pictures, and his family, and usually with them alone."

His love of literature was fully sustained to the end. I have before me a most interesting batch of letters, dated between 1884 and 1888, addressed by him to Mr. James Billson, of Leicester, and mostly dealing with the poems of James Thomson ("B.V."), of which he was a great admirer. Some of these comments and appreciations are in Melville's best style. "*Sunday up the River,*" he writes, "contrasting with the *City of Dreadful Night,* is like a Cuban humming-bird, beautiful in faery tints, flying against the tropic thundercloud. Your friend was a sterling poet, if ever one sang. As to pessimism, although neither pessimist nor optimist myself, nevertheless I relish it in the verse, if for nothing else than as a counterpoise to the exorbitant hopefulness, juvenile and shallow, that makes such a muster in these days—at least in some quarters."

"Exorbitant hopefulness" could indeed have been hardly otherwise than distasteful to one who, like his own *John Marr* (a retired sailor whose fate it was to live on a "frontier-prairie," among an unresponsive inland people who cared nothing for the sea), had so long experienced the solitude of disappointed genius. But it is impossible to believe that this undeserved neglect can be permanent. The opinion of those competent judges who are students of Melville's works is so clear and emphatic in his favour,[9] that it is not too much to say that to read his books is generally to appreciate them; nor is it only those who have what is called an "educated taste" who are thus impressed, for I have been told of instances in which English working-men became his hearty admirers. It is satisfactory to know that a new edition of his best books is forthcoming, both in America and England, and that the public will thus have an opportunity, I will not say of repairing a wrong done to a distinguished writer, for, as I have already shown, the decay of his fame was partly due to circumstances of his own making, but at least of rehabilitating and confirming its earlier and truer judgment. Herman Melville will then resume his honourable place in American literature (for, to end as I began, I hold that the existence of an American literature is a fact and not a supposition), as the prose-poet of the Pacific—

> the sea-compelling man,
> Before whose wand Leviathan
> Rose hoary-white upon the deep,
> With awful sounds that stirred its sleep;
> Melville, whose magic drew Typee,
> Radiant as Venus, from the sea.[10]

Notes
1. *Redburn, His First Voyage: Being the Sailor-boy Confessions and Reminiscences of the Son of a Gentleman in the Merchant Service,* 1849.
2. Unless it be Paquita, in Joaquin Miller's *Life among the Modocs.*
3. Lieut. Wise, in *Los Gringos,* a volume of travels published in 1849.
4. For this and other particulars I am indebted to the courtesy of Mr. Arthur Stedman of New York, the friend and literary executor of Herman Melville.
5. *Art Review,* November 1889.
6. *The Whale* was dedicated to Hawthorne, and is referred to in his *Wonder-Book.* "On the hither side of Pittsfield sits Herman Melville, shaping out

the gigantic conception of his 'White Whale,' while the gigantic shadow of Greylock looms upon him from his study window."
7. Dr. Titus Coan's letter, quoted in the *New York World's* obituary notice of Melville.
8. New York *Tribune,* October 1, 1891.
9. I may instance Mr. William Morris, Mr. Theodore Watts, Mr. R. L. Stevenson, Mr. Robert Buchanan, and Mr. W. Clark Russell.
10. Robert Buchanan's *Socrates in Camden.*

—Henry S. Salt, "Marquesan Melville,"
Gentleman's Magazine, March 1892, pp. 248–57

John St. Loe Strachey
"Herman Melville" (1893)

John St. Loe Strachey, writing from England a few years after Melville's death, praises him as a "literary artist," while remarking that he "was apt to let the last great master of style he had been reading run away with him." Melville, for Strachey, is an American imitator of great English writers—of Thomas Browne and Carlyle. Students examining Melville's transatlantic influences may find the harsh judgments of this politically radical British critic useful.

With this renaissance of the South Seas, it was inevitable that there should come a demand for the republication *of Typee* and *Omoo,*—those wonderful "real romances" in which the inspired usher, who passed his time between keeping school at Green Bush, N.Y., and sailing among the islands, told the world how he had lived under the shadow of the bread-fruit trees, a life which, as far as sensuous delight and physical beauty were concerned, could only be compared to that of ancient Hellas. There, in vales lovelier than Tempe, and by waters brighter than those of the Aegean, he had seen the flower-crowned and flower-girdled Maenads weave the meshes of their rhythmic dance; had sat at feasts with youths whose forms might have inspired Lysippus and Praxiteles; had watched in amazement and delight the torches gleaming through the palm-groves, while the votaries of mysteries, like those of Demeter or Dionysus, performed their solemn rites and meet oblations; and yet, in spite of all, had yearned with a passionate yearning for the pleasant fields of New England and the wholesome prose of modern life,—the incomparable charities of hearth and home.

Though Melville has not the literary power of Mr. Stevenson, the description in *Typee* of the life he led among a cannibal tribe in the Marquesas islands has a charm beyond the charm of *The Wrecker,* the *Island Nights,* or those studies of the Marquesas which Mr. Stevenson contributed to the earlier numbers of *Black and White. Typee* is the "document" *par excellence* of savage life, and a document written by one who knew how to write as well as to look. We have said that Mr. Melville does not write as well as Mr. Stevenson, but this does not mean that he is not a literary artist. Mr. Melville is no mean master of prose, and had his judgment been equal to his feeling for form, he might have ranked high in English literature on the ground of style alone. Unfortunately, he was apt to let the last great master of style he had been reading run away with him. For example, in *Moby Dick*—one of the best and most thrilling sea-stories ever written—Mr. Melville has "hitched to his car" the fantastic Pegasus of Sir Thomas Browne. With every circumstance of subject favourable, it would be madness to imitate the author of *Urne Burial.* When his style is made the vehicle for describing the hunting of sperm-whales in the Pacific, the result cannot but be disastrous. Yet so great an artist is Mr. Melville and so strong are the fascinations of his story, that we defy any reader of sense to close this epic of whaling without the exclamation,—"With all its faults I would not have it other than it is." Discovering a right line in obliquity and by an act of supreme genius forcing his steed to run a pace for which he was not bred, Mr. Melville contrives, in spite of Sir Thomas Browne, to write a book which is not only enchanting as a romance, but a genuine piece of literature. No one who has read the chapter on "Nantucket" and its seafarers, and has learned how at nightfall the Nantucketer, like "the landless gull that at sunset folds her wings and is rocked to sleep between billows," "furls his sails and lays him to his rest, while under his very pillow rush herds of walruses and whales," will have the heart to cavil at Melville's style. In *White Jacket*—a marvellous description of life on a man-of-war—we see yet another deflection given to Mr. Melville's style, and with still worse results. He had apparently been reading Carlyle before he wrote it; and Carlylisms, mixed with the dregs of the *Religio Medici,* every now and then crop up to annoy the reader. In spite, however, of this heavy burden, *White Jacket* is excellent reading, and full of the glory of the sea and the spirit of the Viking. And here we may mention a very pleasant thing about Mr. Melville's books. They show throughout a strong feeling of brotherhood with the English. The sea has made him feel the oneness of the English kin, and he speaks of Nelson and the old Admirals like a lover or a child. Though Mr. Melville wrote at a time when English insolence and pig-headedness, and Yankee bumptiousness, made a good deal of ill-blood between the two peoples, he at heart feels that, on the sea at least, it is the English kin against the world.

—John St. Loe Strachey, "Herman Melville," Spectator, June 24, 1893, pp. 858–59

WILLIAM P. TRENT (1903)

William Trent was originally a southerner who, by the time he wrote this entry in 1903, was teaching at Columbia University in New York. He had caused an uproar earlier in his career with his critique of the novelist and slavery apologist William Gilmore Simms. This is why Trent draws a line from Melville to Simms. His essay points again to the advocacy of the author by Stevenson. Trent pronounces *Moby-Dick* a "masterpiece" and a "work of genius," if he does so with significant reservations. Students examining the reception of Melville's work after the author's death might note that Trent underestimates the force of the coming Melville revival.

Fortune, which seemed not long since to have deserted Herman Melville as completely as (William Gilmore) Simms, has at last smiled again upon the former since a generation fond of narratives full of not too improbable adventure and of tropical glow has accepted, with at least fair complacency, the republication of books that won the warm commendation of Robert Louis Stevenson. The author of *Typee* was born in New York, and ultimately died there, after a long period of seclusion. He had no special incentive save his own love of adventure to desert farming at an early age and go to sea as a cabin-boy. He then tried teaching, but shipped again in 1841, this time on a whaler bound for the South Seas. The cruelty of his captain caused him—with a companion, the Toby of *Typee*—to desert the ship as she lay in a harbour in the Marquesas. Then followed the adventures so interestingly told in *Typee*, which was published in 1846, soon after Melville's return to civilization. His book was very successful in both England and America, although some persons refused to give credence to it or to *Omoo*, which immediately followed it. Marriage and literary success then transformed the adventurer into a fairly prolific man of letters. But as early as 1848 the quasi-speculative, chaotic romance entitled *Mardi* gave premonition of aberration and of the eventual frustration of a promising career. Melville's greatest achievement still awaited him, however, for after two other fair books of adventure he published, in 1851, his masterpiece, *Moby Dick, or the White Whale*. If it were not for its inordinate length, its frequently inartistic heaping up of details, and its obvious imitation of Carlylean tricks of style and construction, this narrative of tremendous power and wide knowledge might be perhaps pronounced the greatest sea story in literature. The breath of the sea is in it and much of the passion and charm of the most venturous of all the venturous callings plied upon the deep. It is a cool reader that does not become almost as eager as the terrible Captain Ahab in his demoniacal pursuit of Moby Dick, the invincible whale, a creation of the imagination not unworthy of a great poet. In this uneven, but on the whole genuine, work of genius, Melville probably overtasked himself. He published several other books while, like his friend Hawthorne, attending to his duties in the customhouse, but nothing comparable to his earlier works. One, *Israel Potter*, deserved Hawthorne's praise because of its spirited portraits of Franklin and Paul Jones, but no revival of their author's fame will justify the republication of these productions of his decline.

—William P. Trent, *A History of American Literature*, 1903, pp. 389–91

Carl Van Doren (1917)

This terse account of Melville's entire career belongs with the other overviews contained in this section, but differs in its extreme sketchiness. Van Doren calls the writer "disappointing," and stands in near total and almost dismissive opposition to Salt's previously expressed enthusiasm for a revival in Melville appreciation.

Herman Melville, grandson of the conservative old gentleman upon whom Holmes wrote *The Last Leaf*, and son of a merchant of New York, was born there, 1 August, 1819. The early death of his father and the loss of the family fortune having narrowed Melville's chances for higher schooling to a few months in the Albany Classical School, he turned his hand to farming for a year, shipped before the mast to Liverpool in 1837, taught school from 1837–40, and in January, 1841, sailed from New Bedford on a whaling voyage into the Pacific. Upon the experiences of that voyage his principal work is founded. The captain of the *Acushnet*, it seems, treated the crew badly, and

Melville, with the companion whom he calls Toby, escaped from the ship to the Island of Nukuheva [Nukahiva] in the Marquesas and strayed into the cannibal valley Typee [Taipi], where the savages kept them for four months in an "indulgent captivity." Rescued by an Australian whaler, Melville visited Tahiti and other islands of the Society group, took part in a mutiny, and once more changed ship, this time setting out for Honolulu. After some months as a clerk in Hawaii, he joined the crew of the frigate *United States* and returned by the Horn to Boston, October, 1844. "From my twenty-fifth year," he told Hawthorne, "I date my life." Why he held 1844 so important is not clear; he may then first have turned to authorship. Though he had kept no notes of his journeying, within a year he had completed his first book, *Typee,* the record of his captivity. This was followed the next year by *Omoo,* which completes his island adventures. In 1849 came *Redburn,* based on his earlier voyage to Liverpool, and in 1850 *White-Jacket,* an account of life on a man-of-war.

The first two had a great vogue and aroused much wonder as to the proportion of fiction and fact which might have gone to their making. Murray published *Typee* in England in the belief that it was pure fact. There were others to rank it with Richard Henry Dana's *Two Years before the Mast* (1841) as a transcript of real events. But though little is known of Melville's actual doings in the South Seas, it is at least clear that *Typee* and *Omoo* are no more as truthful as *Two Years before the Mast* than they are as crisp and nautical as that incomparable classic of the sea. Melville must be ranked less with Dana than with George Borrow. If he knew the thin boundary between romance and reality, he was still careless of nice limits, and his work is a fusion which defies analysis. *White-Jacket,* of these four books, is probably nearst a plain record; *Redburn* has but few romantic elements. *Omoo,* as a sequel, has not the freshness of *Typee,* nor has it such unity. *Typee,* indeed, is Melville at all but his best, and must be classed with the most successful narrations of the exotic life; after seventy years, when the South Pacific seems no longer another world, the spell holds. The valley of Taipi becomes, in Melville's handling, a region of dreams and languor which stir the senses with the fragrance and colour of the landscape and the gay beauty of the brown cannibal girls. And yet Melville, thoroughly sensitive to the felicities of that life, never loses himself in it but remains the shrewd and smiling Yankee.

The charge that he had been writing romance led Melville to deserve the accusation, and he wrote *Mardi* (1849), certainly one of the strangest, maddest books ever composed by an American. As in *Typee,* two sailors escape from a tyrannical captain in the Pacific and seek their fortune on the open sea, where they finally discover the archipelago of Mardi, a paradise more rich and sultry than the Marquesas, which becomes, as the story proceeds, a crazy chaos of adventure and satirical allegory. In *Mardi* for the first time appear those qualities which made a French critic call Melville "un Rabelais americain," his welter of language, his fantastic laughter, his tumultuous philosophies. He had turned, contemporaries said, from the plain though witty style of his first works to the gorgeous manner of Sir Thomas Browne; he had been infected, say later critics, with Carlylese. Whatever the process, he had surely shifted his interest from the actual to the abstruse and symbolical, and he never recovered from the dive into metaphysics which proved fatal to him as a novelist. It was, however, while on this perilous border that he produced the best of his, and one of the best of American, romances; it is the peculiar mingling of speculation and experience which lends *Moby Dick* (1851) its special power.

Married in 1847, Melville lived for three years in New York and then for thirteen years in a farmhouse near Pittsfield, Massachusetts. Although he did not cease to write at once, *Moby Dick* seems to have exhausted him. *Pierre* (1852) is hopelessly frantic; *Israel Potter* (1855) is not markedly original; neither are *The Piazza Tales* (1856), and *The Confidence Man* (1857). The verses which he wrote in his later years, his sole output, are in a few instances happy, but far more often jagged and harsh. Whatever the causes of his loss of power, he fretted under it and grew more metaphysical, tortured, according to Hawthorne, his good friend, by uncertainty as to a future life. That way, for Melville, was madness; his earlier works should have taught him that he was lost without a solid basis in fact. He moved restlessly about, lecturing on the South Seas during the years 1857–1860 in many cities of the United States and Canada. He visited Europe and Palestine. Finally, having returned to New York, he was appointed to a place in the Custom House in 1866, and served there for twenty years, living a private life of almost entire, though voluntary and studious, seclusion. His death, 28 September, 1891, after nearly forty silent years, removed from American literature one of its most promising and most disappointing figures. Of late his fame has shown a tendency to revive.

—Carl Van Doren, *The Cambridge History of American Literature,* 1917, pp. 320–23

WORKS

TYPEE

If *Typee* raised the ire of missionary interests, it also stands alone among Melville's works as a commercial success in its own day. These seven brief considerations of *Typee* chart the book's happy course. Melville's first release set up a readership for *Omoo*, and, as that novel appealed to a wide and sometimes young readership, it later made Melville fear that he would be remembered only as someone who had "lived among the cannibals." In 1846 Hawthorne and Melville were strangers; Hawthorne's influence had not yet helped elicit a complex change in Melville's prose. Avoiding the politics of the book, Hawthorne finds it "lightly but vigorously written" and "worthy" from "a literary point of view." Conversely, Margaret Fuller, transcendentalist and critic of normative religious practice, immediately addresses what she views as the scandalous politics in *Typee*. She judges Melville's reproach of missionary endeavor "strictly correct" and urges "sewing societies" to read *Typee* before sending another penny to the Pacific.

Thomas Low Nichols claims his due in championing the book, recalling that it was he who had advised "the diplomatic brother" to carry the book to John Murray in England. Gansevoort Melville, Herman's brother, had recently been granted a sinecure as secretary of the American legation in London. Even James Russell Lowell's brief comment speaks to the popularity of the book in the years immediately following its initial release.

Nathaniel Hawthorne (1846)

It records the adventures of a young American who ran away from a whale ship at the Marquesas, and spent some months as the guest, or captive, of a native tribe, of which scarcely anything had been hitherto known to the civilized world.—The book is lightly but vigorously written; and we are acquainted with no work that gives a freer and more effective picture of barbarian life, in that unadulterated state of which there are now so few specimens remaining. The gentleness of disposition that seems akin to the delicious climate, is shown in contrast with traits of savage fierceness;—on one page, we read of manners and modes of life that indicate a whole system of innocence and peace; and on the next, we catch a glimpse of a smoked human head, and the half-picked skeleton of what had been (in a culinary sense) a *well-dressed* man. The author's descriptions of the native girls are voluptuously colored, yet not more so than the exigencies of the subject appear to require. He has that freedom of view—it would be too harsh to call it laxity of principle—which renders him tolerant of codes or morals that may be little in accordance with our own; a spirit proper enough to a young and adventurous sailor, and which makes his book the more wholesome to our staid landsmen. The narrative is skillfully managed, and in a literary point of view, the execution of the work is worthy of the novelty and interest of its subject.

—Nathaniel Hawthorne, *Salem Advertiser,* March 25, 1846

MARGARET FULLER (1846)

Typee would seem, also, to be the record of imaginary adventures by someone who had visited those regions. But it is a very entertaining and pleasing narrative, and the Happy Valley of the gentle cannibals compares very well the best contrivances of the learned Dr Johnson to produce similar impressions. Of the power of this writer to make pretty and spirited pictures as well [as] of his quick and arch manner generally, a happy specimen may be seen in the account of the savage climbing the cocoa-tree, p. 273, vol. 2d. Many of the observations and narratives we suppose to be strictly correct. Is the account given of the result of the missionary enterprises in the Sandwich Islands of this number? We suppose so from what we have heard in other ways. With a view to ascertaining the truth, it would be well if the sewing societies, now engaged in providing funds for such enterprises would read the particulars, they will find in this book beginning p. 249, vol. 2d, and make inquiries in consequence, before going on with their efforts. Generally, the sewing societies of the country villages will find this the very book they wish to have read while assembled at their work. Othello's hairbreadth 'scapes were nothing to those by this hero in the descent of the cataracts, and many a Desdemona might seriously incline her care to the descriptions of the lovely Fay-a-way.

—Margaret Fuller, New York *Tribune,* April 4, 1846

HENRY WADSWORTH LONGFELLOW (1846)

In the evening we finished the first volume of *Typee,* a curious and interesting book with glowing descriptions of life in the Marquesas.

—Henry Wadsworth Longfellow, *Journal* (July 29, 1846),
cited in Samuel Longfellow, *Life of
Henry Wadsworth Longfellow,* 1891, Vol. 2, p. 52

James Russell Lowell (1848)

... for my part, I am heartily sick *of Typee.*

—James Russell Lowell, Letter to Sydney H. Gay
(September 1848)

Thomas Low Nichols (1864)

I read *Typee* at one sitting, and had, of course, no doubt of its success; but the better to assure it, I advised the diplomatic brother to take a copy to London, and have it issued there simultaneously with its publication in New York. I felt sure that the reviewers of the English press would make its American success, and I was not at all sure that the process could be reversed. It was accordingly brought out by Mr. Murray, in London, as *Life in the Marquesas,* and Harper Brothers in New York, and made at once a brilliant reputation for the author. It was one of the few instances of the first work of an unknown literary adventurer making for him a very desirable reputation. I met Herman Melville often, after I had read *Typee* before and after its publication. He was a simple-hearted, enthusiastic man of genius, who wrote with the consciousness of an impelling force, and with great power and beauty.

—Thomas Low Nichols, *Forty Years of American Life,*
1821–1861, 1864, Ch. 25

Katharine Lee Bates (1897)

Cooper outgoes all American competitors in extravagant fabrications of salt-water adventure. Herman Melville's South Sea stories are more direct and convincing, his *Typee,* especially, having the realistic shudder of an author who barely escaped a dishing up for cannibals.

—Katharine Lee Bates, *American Literature,* 1897, p. 276

Jack London "Typee" (1910)

"Taipi" the chart spelled it, and spelled it correctly, but I prefer "Typee," and I shall always spell it "Typee." When I was a little boy, I read a book spelled in that manner—Herman Melville's *Typee;* and many long hours I dreamed over its pages. Nor was it all dreaming. I resolved there and then, mightily, come what would, that when I had gained strength and years, I, too, would voyage to Typee. For the wonder of the world was penetrating to my tiny consciousness—the wonder that was to lead me to many lands, and that leads and never palls. The years passed, but Typee was not forgotten.

—Jack London, "Typee" (1910),
The Cruise of the Snark, 1911, pp. 154–55

OMOO

WALT WHITMAN (1847)

At the time Whitman wrote this review, several years before the initial publication of *Leaves of Grass,* he was the editor of the *Brooklyn Daily Eagle*. Notice that he sidesteps the debate over narrative authenticity and the morality of missions, preferring *Omoo* as "thorough entertainment."

Omoo, the new work (Harpers, pub.) by Mr Melville, author of *Typee*, affords two well printed volumes of the most readable sort of reading. The question whether these stories be authentic or not has, of course, not so much to do with their interest. One can revel in such richly good natured style, if nothing else. We therefore recommend this 'narrative of adventures in the south seas,' as thorough entertainment—not so light as to be tossed aside for its flippancy, nor so profound as to be tiresome. All books have their office—and this a very side one.

—Walt Whitman, *Daily Eagle,* New York, May 5, 1847

CHARLES GORDON GREENE (1847)

Charles Greene reviewed *Omoo* from Boston on the same day. He outstrips Whitman's modest praise, but reserves concern over the "heathenish" title. The line about Melville being "chary," of holding back, will be relevant for students exploring how the author may have been influenced by the uproar over his purported indelicacy in *Typee*.

The readers of *Typee* will need no invitation to read *Omoo*, in spite of its heathenish and *cattle-ish* appellation, which we are told signifies a 'rover' in the Tahitian language. Whether or not Mr Melville has ever visited the places which he describes, it is unnecessary to discuss, but if he have not, his books are worthy a place with Robinson Crusoe and Gulliver. If he have, it must be owned that he has the descriptive power in greater abundance than any traveller of the age. That *all* in his book is actually trite we can hardly believe, but he imparts a great deal of information tallying with the reports of former voyagers, and in addition, gives an array of characters as interesting as those of romance with acuteness and power. *Omoo* pictures the life of a rover in a whale ship and on the Society Islands for the space of several months. Columns on columns of pleasant extracts might be given, but we are forced to refer our readers to the volumes themselves. They will find them filled with stirring incident and beautiful description, and here and there a touch of the genuine comic. The long doctor is an actual creation, while the Tahitian girls are sprites of fun, softness and beauty. One wishes that Mr Melville had not been quite so chary of relating his own adventures with the fair Tahitians. We hope his next book may have a Christian title.

—Charles Gordon Greene, *Boston Post*, May 5, 1847

HORACE GREELEY (1847)

Horace Greeley was an important New York editor and journalist, an ever-aspiring politician, a Whig reformer, and a respected cultural critic. Greeley's *New York Tribune* barred tastelessness and scandal from its pages, which perhaps helps explain why this review of *Omoo* cuts two ways. On one hand, Greeley labels Melville a "born genius," a narrativist truthful "in the main" and comparable to the greatest of preceding generations. On the other hand, Greeley sets the pleasure he clearly takes in reading Melville at odds with his higher, public office—his responsibility to upbraid the author for his "defective" or "diseased ... moral tone."

Students discussing Melville's scathing critique of Pacific missions, which begins in *Typee*, and continues in *Omoo*, will find Greeley useful, for he does not "bid adieu to," or dismiss, *Omoo* altogether, but rather limits his negative comments to the vagaries of moral tone. The chief fault, he suggests, is that Melville's aggressive tone might prevent the book's political "Truth" from ever reaching the complacent "friends of Missions." Greeley here writes something potentially damaging to his own economic interests, as the "friends of Missions" certainly bought his paper. Students could compare this review to an entirely approving 1851 Greeley review of *Moby-Dick*, included later in this section.

Omoo, by Herman Melville, is replete alike with the merits and the faults of its forerunner, *Typee*. All of us were mistaken who thought the fascination of *Typee* owing mainly to its subject, or rather to the novel and primitive state of human existence it described. *Omoo* dispels all such illusions and proves the author a born genius, with few superiors either as a narrator, a describer, or a humorist. Few living men could have invested such scenes, incidents and persons as figure in *Omoo* with anything like the charm they wear in Melville's graphic pages; the adventures narrated might have occurred to any one, as others equally exciting have done to thousands of voyagers in the South Seas; but who has ever before described any so well? *Typee* and *Omoo*, doubtless in the main true narratives, are worthy to rank in interest with Robinson Crusoe and in vivacity with the best of Stephens's *Travels*.—Yet they are unmistakably defective if not positively diseased in moral tone, and will very fairly be condemned as dangerous reading for those of immature intellects and unsettled principles. Not that you can often put your finger on a passage positively offensive; but the *tone* is bad, and incidents of the most objectionable character are depicted with a racy lightness which would once have been admired but will now be justly condemned. A *penchant* for bad liquors is everywhere boldly proclaimed, while a hankering after loose company not always of the masculine order, is but thinly disguised and perpetually protruding itself throughout the work. This is to be deplored not alone for the author's sake, nor even for that of the last class which it will deter from perusing his adventures. We regret it still more because it will prevent his lucid and apparently candid testimony with regard to the value, the effect and the defects of the missionary labors among the South Sea Islanders from having its due weight with those most deeply interested. It is needless here to restate the hackneyed question as to the proper mode of effecting the desired renovation of savage, heathen tribes.—'Preach the Gospel to them,' say the devout: 'convert them to Christianity, and their Civilization follows of course.'—'Nay,' interposes another class: 'you must civilize them, to some extent, before they can even comprehend Christianity, much less truly embrace and adhere to it.'—The Truth obviously lies between these assertions, or rather, embraces them both. A Christianity which does not include Civilization, a Civilizing which does not involve Christianizing, will not answer. Above all, alike to their conversion and their civilization a change in their Social condition and habits—a change from idleness and inefficiency to regular and well directed industry—is absolutely essential.—Without this, the convert of to-day is constantly in danger of relapsing into avowed and inveterate heathenism.

This is the moral of Mr Melville's facts, as indeed of all other impartial testimonies on the subject. Reiterating my regret that he has chosen so to write that his statements will not have that weight with the friends of Missions which the interest of Truth requires, I bid adieu to *Omoo*.

—Horace Greeley, *Weekly Review*, New York,
June 23, 1847, p. 5

MARDI

Henry Cood Watson (1849)

Henry Cood Watson's conceit in this early review of *Mardi* is that he has been tricked by a confidence man into picking up a novel only to find "an undigested mass of rambling metaphysics." He then condemns the rhetorical payoff of having followed Melville on his figurative and wildly allegorizing world travels as "indifferent." But Watson reserves special dislike for the occasional poem embedded in *Mardi*, wondering how such a successful prose stylist could fail so completely at verse. Then he springboards into general and sustained condemnation of "contemporary experimentalists" in poetry, leaving Melville relatively unscathed for a paragraph and more.

We proceed to notice this extraordinary production with feelings anything but gentle towards its gifted but eccentric author. The truth is, that we have been deceived, inveigled, entrapped into reading a *work* where we have been led to expect only a *book*. We were flattered with the promise of an account of travel, amusing, though fictitious; and we have been compelled to pore over an undigested mass of rambling metaphysics. We had hoped for a pleasant boat-ride among the sunny isles of the tropics; instead of which, we were taken bodily, and immersed into the fathomless sea of Allegory, from which we have just emerged, gasping for breath, with monstrous Types, Myths, Symbols and such like fantastic weeds tangled in our vestments and hair. True, it is the province of the hapless critic to peruse all kinds of books—the good and the bad, or, worse yet, the indifferent—the serious and the grave. But, in his distribution of his task, it is his consoling privilege to appropriate a different season for each class of works—reserving dull trash and all manner of figurative strictures for his hours of penance. There was nothing in the appearance of this work, or the reputation of its author, to cause us to take it up as one of that class. And yet its perusal has proven to us a most unmitigated 'mortification of the flesh.'

For *Mardi* is the world—partly the actual world parabolically presented, piece-meal—and partly an imaginative world, whereof the original type never existed anywhere save in the fancy of Mr Melville. Let the reader, therefore, expect, when he opens this book. first to peruse the life-like incidents of an agreeable sea-romance; and then, just as his interest is fairly enlisted in behalf of its heroes, to be plunged into a cold bath of symbolical ethics, metaphysics and political economy. He will travel figuratively through England, France, Scotland, Italy, etc., and, if he succeed in studying out the riddles under which the author's meaning is disguised, he will be treated to—indifferent rhetoric in the premises. He will be accompanied in his travel by a Demi-God—the only sensible man in the book—a philosopher, a historian and a poet, all discussing various topics by the way; sometimes in a very pleasing, sometimes in a very prolix and tedious manner. He will be often tempted to address the author in the language of one of his own personages: 'I beseech thee, instruct me in thy dialectics that I may embrace thy more recondite lore.' He will often have occasion to admire the genius of our author; and oftener still, he will painfully realize—that to use Mr Melville's own words: 'Genius is full of trash.'

We do not propose to enter any further into the plan of the work—if it had a plan. Its execution alone, saves it from contemptuous oblivion. Style is its sole redeeming feature. Mr Melville possesses many of the essentials of poetry—a store of images, a readiness at perceiving analogies and felicitous expressions. Poetic thoughts and turns of phrase occur at every page. Nevertheless, although so poetic in his prose, he is remarkably unfortunate in his verse. The specimens in the work before us are not worth quoting. Whence this anomaly? The explanation which occurs to us might be addressed, in the shape of a warning, to several authors of undoubted talent in our age and country, who strive for originality of metre, and whose unsaleable works throng the shelves of their publishers. The English tongue no longer admits of such experiments; its genius has reached its culminating point; it has nothing to do but to remain at its level or descend. To climb higher is impracticable. After the great works of any language have made their appearance, a certain standard is obtained, from which to depart is to sink. The head waters of composition flowing from a certain ascertained height, there is no principle in the hydraulics of Art that will carry them to a more elevated point. All that subsequent endeavours can compass, is to make them reach the stated altitude. In the age of Virgil—the culminating age of

Latin literature—Horace was successful in importing new metres from the poets of Greece. But the Claudians of after periods ventured no such license; or, if they did, just posterity has buried their attempts in the merited oblivion, which will soon cover the works of our cotemporary experimentalists.

Do these writers imagine that metre was instituted by arbitrary rule? No! when the heart of a nation first begins to beat, that nation spontaneously cadences its speech according to its hidden genius. That cadence is metre. Let poets cease contriving new combinations or resuscitating the buried measures of other tongues. Let them study the cadence of their own language as noted down in its earliest works.

Mr Melville is hard upon the critics. We somewhat question the good taste of his remarks on that topic. The only difference between critics and other readers is that the former *print* their opinions. Oral and published criticisms generally agree, except when injudicious friends abuse the privilege of criticism to write up a book, or when malicious enemies attempt the reverse. In speaking of critics, he says: 'Like mules too from their dunghill, they trample down gardens of roses and deem that crushed fragrance their own.' We will take care not to bring ourselves within the scope of that reproach. Flowers there are many and beautiful in the garden of *Mardi*; but we refrain even from culling a bouquet for the benefit of our readers, partly for want of space, and partly because we shrink from the labor of again toiling through the rank vegetation that hides the roses. Let us not, therefore, be accused of trampling the flowers of Mr Melville, when we beseech him to weed out the noxious plants whose offensive luxuriance chokes up the fragrant spots in his garden.

—Henry Cood Watson, *Saroni's Musical Times*,
New York, September 1849, p. 6

REDBURN

GEORGE RIPLEY (1849)

George Ripley, author of the first two *Tribune* pieces, is right to note that *Redburn* "has something about it which savours more of the bookmaker by profession." Students of Melville's life will discover that he wrote this particular book in part for money, more out of situational than "innate necessity," and that he sought to capitalize on autobiographical matter not yet transformed into prose. Consider in this context the words he wrote to Hawthorne in early June 1851, included later in this section. Ripley's relief is palpable that *Redburn* returns Melville to "a genuine tale of the sea." He delights that Melville's "pictures of life . . . are drawn from nature" and not from "monstrous" imaginings.

Mr Melville has not worked himself entirely free from the affectations and pretentious spirit by which *Mardi* has gained such an unlucky notoriety. Nor does this work exhibit the freshness, the gayety, the natural frolicsomeness, which gave such a charm to the fragrant descriptions of *Typee*, and to a certain extent, to the off-hand, picturesque sketches of *Omoo*. It has something about it which savours more of the bookmaker by profession, and shows that it is not the product of any innate necessity. The writer never seems to be entirely at his ease, never so much lost in the reality of his story as to be indifferent to the effect of his readers. He reminds us of a certain facetious gentleman of our acquaintance, who, after saying a good thing, always looks round for the laugh. Still, this book is a decided improvement on *Mardi*. Mr Melville shows his good sense, or his respect for public opinion, by leaving the vein of mystic allegory and this transcendental, glittering soap-bubble speculation which he has 'done to death' in that ambitious composition.

Redburn is a genuine tale of the sea. It has the real briny flavor. The writer is equally at home on the deck or in the forecastle. His pictures of life on the ocean are drawn from nature, and no one can doubt their identity. His pages smell of tarred ropes and bilge water. With some occasional exaggerations, his descriptions have all the fidelity of a Dutch painting. Nor is he less skillful in his delineations of a sailor's life in port. The interior of the boarding house in Liverpool, the scenes of destitution and misery about the docks, the impressions of low life in a commercial city on the mind of an untrammelled rustic just landing from his first voyage are depicted with a minute fidelity of touch that is hardly surpassed by the dark and lurid coloring of Crabbe.

Redburn can scarcely fail of an extensive popularity. It is idle to compare its author with Defoe or even with some modern writers in the same line. But he is an artist of unparalleled merit in his own right. He has the true kind of 'stuff' in him, and writes with an original power, when in his best vein, that will always keep his production before the public eye. If he would trust more entirely to the natural play of his own fine imagination without goading it on to a monstrous activity, his work would stand a better chance of obtaining a healthy and lasting reputation.

—George Ripley, New York *Tribune*, December 1, 1849

WHITE-JACKET

George Ripley (1850)

In this review of *White-Jacket*, Ripley registers concern that the author may be slipping back to the sinful voice of *Mardi*, which he labels "metaphysical . . . Carlylese." The review is most notable, however, for the forcefulness with which it approves of Melville's attack on the U.S. Navy's "gigantic humbug"—flogging.

Never has there been a more memorable White Jacket than this which gives the name to Mr Melville's glowing log-book of a year's cruise in a United States frigate. . . .

The White jacket is made the emblem and 'sweet remembrancer' of all Mr Melville's perilous and comic experiences, while immured in the floating prison—to use the mildest term—of a public man-of-war. He here finds ample materials for an entertaining book, and has worked them up into a narrative of great power and interest. He always tells a story well, and a plenty are related in this volume. If he had confined himself to repeating what he had heard and seen, his book would have been more valuable, for the moral and metaphysical reflections he sets forth in bad Carlylese, are only incumbrances to the narrative, and often become intolerable.

Mr Melville has performed an excellent service in revealing the secrets of his prison-house, and calling the public attention to the indescribable abominations of the naval life, reeking with the rankest corruption, cruelty, and blood.

He writes without ill-temper, or prejudice, with no distempered, sentimental philanthropy, but vividly portraying scenes of which he was the constant witness, and in many instances suggesting a judicious remedy for the evils which he exhibits. His remarks on the discipline of our public vessels, are entitled to great consideration, and coincide with the prevailing tendencies of the public mind. It is not often that an observer of his shrewdness and penetration is admitted behind the scenes, and still less often that the results of personal experience are presented in such high-wrought pictures. A man of Melville's brain and pen is a dangerous character in the presence of a gigantic humbug, and those who are interested in the preservation of rotten abuses had better stop that 'chief from taking notes.'

—George Ripley, New York *Tribune*, April 5, 1850

FREDERICK SWARTWOUT COZZENS (1850)

Frederick Cozzens's review of *White-Jacket* is remarkable for its expression of the popular desire that books draw from nature. Students of visual culture may be interested in his appreciation of the book's "daguerreotype-like naturalness of description." Here Cozzens reflects the recent impact of photography on literary art and its criticism. Like Ripley, Cozzens registers the important social critique present in *White-Jacket*, so students investigating the varieties of direct or indirect social criticism in Melville's long writing career have key documents to cite in these two reviews.

Well, we are glad to find the author of *Typee* on the right ground at last. When we read his *Mardi*, or rather tried to read it, for we never could get quite through it, we feared that the author had mistaken his bent, like a comic actor with a 'penshong' for tragedy, and that we were thenceforth to hear from him in a pseudo-philosophical *rifacciamento* of Carlyle and Emerson. *Redburn* reassured us; and now comes *White-Jacket*, to reinstate the author in the best good-graces of the reading public. Not a page of this last work has escaped us; and so strong was the *continuous* interest which it excited, a quality not always encountered even in the most popular works of our time, that we accomplished its perusal in two 'sittings,' unavoidably protracted, we may remark, for we could not leave the work, while there was yet a page unread. Without the aid of much imagination, but with a daguerreotype-like naturalness of description of all which the writer saw and felt himself, and all which he saw others feel, Mr Melville has given us a volume which, in its evident truthfulness and accuracy of personal and individual delineation, reminds us continually of that admirable and justly popular work, the *Two Years Before the Mast* of the younger Dana. A vein of sly humor percolates through the book; and a sort of unctuous toying with verbal double-meanings, is once in a while to be met with, which go far to indicate, that if the author had lived in the 'City of *Brotherly Love*,' (church-burners, firemen-fighters, assassins, and rowdies, excuse the implied exceptional) he might, with a little proper instruction, have become as celebrated as 'a Philadelphia lawyer,' that preeminent model of a pun-hunter. We had intended to present several extracts from *White-Jacket*, which we had pencilled for that purpose in the perusal; but the universal prevalence of the book itself, at this late period, would doubtless make them 'twice-told tales' to the great majority of our readers. We would call especial attention, as a matter of present public interest, to the chapters descriptive of an instance of almost indiscriminate flogging on board a man-of-war, and the consequences of such inconsistent punishment, in the case of each offender. The force of public opinion, and the example of certain humane officers in the highest rank of the American navy, would seem to indicate that the time is not distant when corporeal punishment, if not mainly abolished, will at least be hereafter less frequently resorted to than formerly, and greatly lessened in its severity. The 'signs of the times' would seem to point unerringly to this result.

—Frederick Swartwout Cozzens,
Knickerbocker, 35, May 1850, p. 448

MOBY-DICK

HERMAN MELVILLE (1851)

The three letters that Melville wrote to Hawthorne in summer and fall 1851 remain remarkably important documents for both new and old students of Melville. In them, "The Whale," or *Moby-Dick*, is charted to completion and then to its early reception by Hawthorne. In these excerpts, we get an invaluable one-way mirror (as we have none of Hawthorne's replies) into what many deem the most important literary friendship captured in American letters. Melville, in writing to his associate, takes measure of his recent exposure to ideas that had changed his mind as well as his prose. The first letter, sent to Hawthorne in early June reveals Melville ready to "slave on [his] 'Whale'" in New York, readying it for the presses. Melville haltingly feels safe in confiding in Hawthorne. He opens up to his author friend about the trials of his own writing life. He faces poverty ("Dollars damn me"); he faces marketplace realities conflicting with his conception of literary "truth" ("What I feel most moved to write, that is banned,—it will not pay. Yet, altogether, write the other way I cannot."); he is even pressed by physical necessity at his farm, Arrowhead ("But see my hand!—four blisters on this palm"). These factors and more compromise the "silent grass-growing mood in which a man *ought* always to compose." But there is much more in this first letter. Melville is "unfold[ing] within [him]self," having encountered Shakespeare, Solomon, Hawthorne, and Goethe. Students investigating this change in Melville will want to start here and then go on to read "Hawthorne and His Mosses," Melville's 1850 *Literary World* review of Hawthorne's *Mosses from an Old Manse*. Students considering Melville's relation to writers such as Ralph Waldo Emerson have an ideal document to work with in this letter, especially in the closing, prevaricating consideration of the *"all* feeling." How does Melville's assessment differ from Emerson's earlier discussions of the oversoul? How is what Melville says here put into rhetorical practice in the novels and poems, especially in chapters from *Moby-Dick* such as "The Mast Head" or "A Squeeze of the Hand"?

My Dear Hawthorne,—I should have been rumbling down to you in my pine-board chariot a long time ago, were it not that for some weeks past I have been more busy than you can well imagine,—out of doors,—building and patching and tinkering away in all directions. Besides, I had my crops to get in,—corn and potatoes (I hope to show you some famous ones by and by),—and many other things to attend to, all accumulating upon this one particular season. I work myself; and at night my bodily sensations are akin to those I have so often felt before, when a hired man, doing my day's work from sun to sun. But I mean to continue visiting you until you tell me that my visits are both supererogatory and superfluous. With no son of man do I stand upon any etiquette or ceremony, except the Christian ones of charity and honesty. I am told, my fellow-man, that there is an aristocracy of the brain. Some men have boldly advocated and asserted it. Schiller seems to have done so, though I don't know much about him. At any rate, it is true that there have been those who, while earnest in behalf of political equality, will accept the intellectual estates. And I can well perceive, I think, how a man of superior mind can, by its intense cultivation, bring himself, as it were, into a certain spontaneous aristocracy of feeling,—exceedingly nice and fastidious,—similar to that which, in an English Howard, conveys a torpedo-fish thrill at the slightest contact with a social plebian. So, when you see or hear of my ruthless democracy on all sides, you may possibly feel a touch of a shrink, or something of that sort. It is but nature to be shy of a mortal who boldly declares that a thief in jail is as honorable a personage as Gen. George Washington. This is ludicrous. But Truth is the silliest thing under the sun. Try to get a living by the Truth—and go to the Soup Societies. Heavens! Let any clergyman try to preach the Truth from its very stronghold, the pulpit, and they would ride him out of his church on his own pulpit bannister. It can hardly be doubted that all Reformers are bottomed upon the truth, more or less; and to the world at large are not reformers almost universally laughingstocks? Why so? Truth is ridiculous to men. Thus easily in my room here do I, conceited and garrulous, reverse the test of my Lord Shaftesbury.

It seems an inconsistency to assert unconditional democracy in all things, and yet confess a dislike to all mankind—in the mass. But not so.—But it's an endless sermon,—no more of it. I began by saying that the reason I have not been to Lenox is this,—in the evening I feel completely done up, as the phrase is, and incapable of the long jolting to get to your house and back. In a week or so, I go to New York, to bury myself in a third-story room, and work and slave on my "Whale" while it is driving through the press. *That* is the only way I can finish it now,—I am so pulled hither and thither by circumstances. The calm, the coolness, the silent grass-growing mood in which a man *ought* always to compose,—that, I fear, can seldom be mine. Dollars damn me; and the malicious Devil is forever grinning in upon me, holding the door ajar. My dear Sir, a presentiment is on me,—I shall at last be worn out and perish, like an old nutmeg-grater, grated to pieces by the constant attrition of the wood, that is, the nutmeg. What I feel most moved to write, that is banned,—it will not pay. Yet, altogether, write the *other* way I cannot. So the product is a final hash, and all my books are botches. I'm rather sore, perhaps, in this letter, but see my hand!—four blisters on this palm, made by hoes and hammers within the last few days. It is a rainy morning; so I am indoors, and all work suspended. I feel cheerfully disposed, and therefore I write a little bluely. Would the Gin were here! If ever, my dear Hawthorne, in the eternal times that are to come, you and I shall sit down in Paradise, in some little shady corner by ourselves; and if we shall by any means be able to smuggle a basket of champagne there (I won't believe in a Temperance Heaven), and if we shall then cross our celestial legs in the celestial grass that is forever tropical, and strike our glasses and our heads together, till both musically ring in concert,—then, O my dear fellow-mortal, how shall we pleasantly discourse of all the things manifold which now so distress us,—when all the earth shall be but a reminiscence, yea, its final dissolution an antiquity. Then shall songs be composed as when wars are over; humorous, comic songs,—"Oh, when I lived in that queer little hole called the world," or, "Oh, when I toiled and sweated below," or, "Oh, when I knocked and was knocked in the fight"—yes, let us look forward to such things. Let us swear that, though now we sweat, yet it is because of the dry heat which is indispensable to the nourishment of the vine which is to bear the grapes that are to give us the champagne hereafter.

But I was talking about the "Whale." As the fishermen say, "he's in his flurry" when I left him some three weeks ago. I'm going to take him by his jaw, however, before long, and finish him up in some fashion or other. What's the use of elaborating what, in its very essence, is so short-lived as a modern book? Though I wrote the Gospels in this century, I should die in the gutter.—I talk all about myself, and this is selfishness and egotism. Granted. But how help it? I am writing to you; I know little about you, but something about myself so I write about myself,—at least, to you. Don't trouble yourself, though, about writing; and don't trouble yourself about visiting; and when you *do* visit, don't trouble yourself about talking. I will do all the writing and visiting and talking myself—By the way, in the last "Dollar Magazine" I read "The Unpardonable Sin." He was a sad fellow, that Ethan Brand. I have no doubt you are by this time responsible for many a shake and tremor of the tribe of "general readers." It is a frightful poetical creed that the cultivation of the brain eats out the heart. But it's my *prose* opinion that in most cases, in those men who have fine brains and work them well, the heart extends down to hams. And though you smoke them with the fire of tribulation, yet, like veritable hams, the head only gives the richer and the better flavor. I stand for the heart. To the dogs with the head! I had rather be a fool with a heart, than Jupiter Olympus with his head. The reason the mass of men fear God, and *at bottom dislike* Him, is because they rather distrust His heart, and fancy Him all brain like a watch. (You perceive I employ a capital initial in the pronoun referring to the Deity; don't you think there is a slight dash of flunkeyism in that usage?) Another thing. I was in New York for four-and-twenty hours the other day, and saw a portrait of N.H. And I have seen and heard many flattering (in a publisher's point of view) allusions to the "Seven Gables." And I have seen "Tales," and "A New Volume" announced, by N.H. So upon the whole, I say to myself, this N.H. is in the ascendant. My dear Sir, they begin to patronize. All Fame is patronage. Let me be infamous: there is no patronage in *that*. What "reputation" H.M. has is horrible. Think of it! To go down to posterity is bad enough, any way; but to go down as a "man who lived among the cannibals"! When I speak of posterity, in reference to myself, I only mean the babies who will probably be born in the moment immediately ensuing upon my giving up the ghost. I shall go down to some of them, in all likelihood. *Typee* will be given to them, perhaps, with their gingerbread. I have come to regard this matter of Fame as the most transparent of all vanities. I read Solomon more and more, and every time see deeper and deeper and unspeakable meanings in him. I did not think of Fame, a year ago, as I do now. My development has been all within a few years past. I am like one of those seeds taken out of the Egyptian Pyramids, which, after being three thousand years a seed and nothing but a seed, being planted in English soil, it developed itself, grew to greenness, and then fell to mould. So I. Until I was twenty-five, I had no development at all. From my twenty-fifth year I date my life. Three weeks have scarcely passed, at any time between then and now, that I have not unfolded within myself. But I feel that I am now come to the inmost leaf of the bulb, and that shortly the flower must fall to the mould. It seems to be now that Solomon was the truest man who ever spoke, and yet that he a little *managed* the truth with a view to popular conservatism; or else there have been many corruptions and interpolations of the text.—In reading some of Goethe's sayings, so worshipped by his votaries, I came across this, *"Live in the all."* That is to say, your separate identity is but a wretched one,—good; but get out of yourself, spread and expand yourself, and bring to yourself the tinglings of life that are felt in the flowers and the woods, that are felt in the planets Saturn and Venus, and the Fixed Stars. What nonsense! Here is a fellow with a raging toothache. "My dear boy," Goethe says to him, "you are sorely afflicted with that tooth; but you must *live in the all*, and then you will be happy!" As with all great genius, there is an immense deal of flummery in Goethe, and in proportion to my own contact with him, a monstrous deal of it in me.

H. Melville.

P.S. "Amen!" saith Hawthorne.

N.B. This "all" feeling, though, there is some truth in. You must often have felt it, lying on the grass on a warm summer's day. Your legs seem to send out shoots into the earth. Your hair feels like leaves upon your head. This is the *all* feeling. But what plays the mischief with the truth is that men will insist upon the universal application of a temporary feeling or opinion.

P.S. You must not fail to admire my discretion in paying the postage on this letter.

—Herman Melville, Letter to Nathaniel Hawthorne, early June 1851

Herman Melville (1851)

In this letter, Melville turns again to his neighbor at "Tanglewood" near Lenox, Massachusetts. Here Melville projects confidence and appears at the height of his powers as a writer. Though *Moby-Dick* is only "half through the press," and though he has returned to his farm, Arrowhead, to work on it, he says he can glimpse a "less bustling time." Melville reaches out to Hawthorne again, admitting his vulnerability ("This is rather a crazy letter . . ."). Students investigating the friendship between the two authors will find this an important document. Those considering the significance of the last, Latin line, or looking into Melville's religious beliefs more generally, will want to track down the fuller exposition of those words both in chapter 113 of *Moby-Dick*, "The Forge," and in Melville's sketch, "Devil as Quaker," handwritten in the margin of his seventh Shakespeare volume.

My dear Hawthorne—The clear air and open window invite me to write to you. For some time past I have been so busy with a thousand things that I have almost forgotten when I wrote you last, and whether I received an answer. This most persuasive season has now for weeks recalled me from certain crotchetty and over doleful chimearas, the like of which men like you and me and some others, forming a chain of God's posts round the world, must be content to encounter now and then, and fight them the best way we can. But come they will,—for, in the boundless, trackless, but still glorious wild wilderness through which these outposts run, the Indians do sorely abound, as well as the insignificant but still stinging mosquitoes. Since you have been here, I have been building some shanties of houses (connected with the old one) and likewise some shanties of chapters and essays. I have been plowing and sowing and raising and painting and printing and praying,—and now begin to come out upon a less bustling time, and to enjoy the calm prospect of things from a fair piazza at the north of the old farm house here.

Not entirely yet, though, am I without something to be urgent with. The "Whale" is only half through the press; for, wearied with the long delay of the printers, and disgusted with the heat and dust of the babylonish brick-kiln of New York, I came back to the country to feel the grass—and end the book reclining on it, if I may.—I am sure you will pardon this speaking all about myself, for if I *say* so much on that head, be sure all the rest of the world are thinking about themselves ten times as much. Let us speak, although we show all our faults and weaknesses,—for it is a sign of strength to be weak, to know it, and out with it,—not in [a] set way and ostentatiously, though, but incidentally and without premeditation.—But I am falling into my old foible—preaching. I am busy, but shall not be very long. Come and spend a day here, if you can and want to; if not, stay in Lenox, and God give you long life. When I am quite free of my present engagements, I am going to treat myself to a ride and a visit to you. Have ready a bottle of brandy, because I always feel like drinking that heroic drink when we talk ontological heroics together. This is rather a crazy letter in some respects, I apprehend. If so, ascribe it to the intoxicating effects of the latter end of June operating upon a very susceptible and peradventure feeble temperament.

Shall I send you a fin of the *Whale* by way of a specimen mouthful? The tail is not yet cooked—though the hell-fire in which the whole book is broiled might not unreasonably have cooked it all ere this. This is the book's motto (the secret one),—Ego non baptiso te in nomine—but make out the rest yourself.

H.M.

—Herman Melville, Letter to Nathaniel Hawthorne,
late June 1851

HERMAN MELVILLE (1851)

Melville writes this third letter in an ecstatic, Socratic, "pantheistic" mood, having heard from Hawthorne that he had "understood [his] book." What had Hawthorne understood? What does Melville mean when he writes that he has "written a wicked book, and feel[s] spotless as the lamb"? Students exploring *Moby-Dick*, masculinity in fiction, male friendship, or Melville's sexuality will want to pay special attention to the extremely sensual language in this letter. Whereas in the first letter readers encounter the remarkable fantasy of the two authors crossing their "celestial legs" in paradise, here we get even more extreme communion. Note that Melville's "spontaneous and instantaneous" prose outburst of "divine magnanimities" toward Hawthorne relate to the first Hawthorne letter's discussion of the "all" feeling. Melville here makes a distinction between "temporary" or "incidental" affective transport and the more profound feeling in him as he explores being *"One"* with Hawthorne's "divine magnet." The letter is essential for students considering the relationship between transcendentalism and skepticism, for one is led to question how "atmospheric skepticisms" are so closely wed here to spiritual elation. Finally, this letter points the way to Melville's continued growth as a writer, for his assertion that "truth is ever incoherent," and his notice that he has "heard of Krakens," yields a first reference to *Pierre; or, the Ambiguities*.

My Dear Hawthorne,—People think that if a man has undergone any hardship, he should have a reward; but for my part, if I have done the hardest possible day's work, and then come to sit down in a corner and eat my supper comfortably—why, then I don't think I deserve any reward for my hard day's work—for am I not now at peace? Is not my supper good? My peace and my supper are my reward, my dear Hawthorne. So your joy-giving and exultation-breeding letter is not my reward for my ditcher's work with that book, but is the good goddess's bonus over and above what was stipulated—for not one man in five cycles, who is wise, will expect appreciative recognition from his fellows, or any one of them. Appreciation! Recognition! Is love appreciated? Why, ever since Adam, who has got to the meaning of this great allegory—the world? Then we pygmies must be content to have our paper allegories but ill comprehended. I say your appreciation is my glorious gratuity. In my proud, humble way,—a shepherd-king,—I was lord of a little vale in the solitary Crimea; but you have now given me the crown of India. But on trying it on my head, I found it fell down on my ears, notwithstanding their asinine length—for it's only such ears that sustain such crowns.

Your letter was handed me last night on the road going to Mr. Morewood's, and I read it there. Had I been at home, I would have sat down at once and answered it. In me divine magnanimities are spontaneous and instantaneous—catch them while you can. The world goes round, and the other side comes up. So now I can't write what I felt. But I felt pantheistic then—your heart beat in my ribs and mine in yours, and both in God's. A sense of unspeakable security is in me this moment, on account of your having understood the book. I have written a wicked book, and feel spotless as the lamb. Ineffable socialities are in me. I would sit down and dine with you and all the gods in old Rome's Pantheon. It is a strange feeling—no hopefulness is in it, no despair. Content—that is it; and irresponsibility; but without licentious inclination. I speak now of my profoundest sense of being, not of an incidental feeling.

Whence come you, Hawthorne? By what right do you drink from my flagon of life? And when I put it to my lips—lo, they are yours and not mine. I feel that the Godhead is broken up like the bread at the Supper, and that we are the pieces. Hence this infinite fraternity of feeling. Now, sympathizing with the paper, my angel turns over another page. you did not care a penny for the book. But, now and then as you read, you understood the pervading thought that impelled the book—and that you praised. Was it not so? You were archangel enough to despise the imperfect body, and embrace the soul. Once you hugged the ugly Socrates because you saw the flame in the mouth, and heard the rushing of the demon,—the familiar,—and recognized the sound; for you have heard it in your own solitudes.

My dear Hawthorne, the atmospheric skepticisms steal into me now, and make me doubtful of my sanity in writing you thus. But, believe me, I am not mad, most noble Festus! But truth is ever incoherent, and when the big hearts strike together, the concussion is a little stunning. Farewell. Don't write a word about the book. That would be robbing me of my miserly delight. I am heartily sorry I ever wrote anything about you—it was paltry. Lord, when shall we be done growing? As long as we have anything more to do, we have done nothing. So, now, let us add Moby Dick to our blessing, and step from that. Leviathan is not the biggest fish;—I have heard of Krakens.

This is a long letter, but you are not at all bound to answer it. Possibly, if you do answer it, and direct it to Herman Melville, you will missend it—for the very fingers that now guide this pen are not precisely the same that just took it up and put it on this paper. Lord, when shall we be done changing? Ah! it's a long stage, and no inn in sight, and night coming, and the body cold. But with you for a passenger, I am content and can be happy. I shall leave the world, I feel, with more satisfaction for having come to know you. Knowing you persuades me more than the Bible of our immortality.

What a pity, that, for your plain, bluff letter, you should get such gibberish! Mention me to Mrs. Hawthorne and to the children, and so, good-by to you, with my blessing.

Herman.

P.S. I can't stop yet. If the world was entirely made up of Magians, I'll tell you what I should do. I should have a paper-mill established at one end of the house, and so have an endless riband of foolscap rolling in upon my desk; and upon that endless riband I should write a thousand—a million—billion thoughts, all under the form of a letter to you. The divine magnet is on you, and my magnet responds. Which is the biggest? A foolish question—they are *One*.

H.

P.P.S. Don't think that by writing me a letter, you shall always be bored with an immediate reply to it—and so keep both of us delving over a writing-desk eternally. No such thing! I sh'n't always answer your letters, and you may do just as you please.

—Herman Melville, Letter to Nathaniel Hawthorne,
November 1851

Anonymous (1851)

The opening line of this review from *The Spectator* gives the reader first notice of the "singular" composite structure of Melville's most famous book. Melville "repels" here; he is guilty of "wordmongering," prolixity, and recourse to "marvellous" yarns that erode what is usefully "probable" in the narrative. Here we have mention of reckless social satire in Melville's book, and students considering the evolution of Melville's tenuous engagement with reform culture will want to pay particular attention to those passages. Students comparing the difference between the British and American first editions have essential reading here as well, for the closing lines of this review famously expose the awkward fact that the Bentley edition contains no epilogue—no Ishmael as a Jobian messenger who survives the wreck.

This sea novel is a singular medley of naval observation, magazine article writing, satiric reflection upon the conventionalisms of civilized life, and rhapsody run mad. So far as the nautical parts are appropriate and unmixed, the portraiture is truthful and interesting. Some of the satire, especially in the early parts, is biting and reckless. The chapter-spinning is various in character; now powerful from the vigorous and fertile fancy of the author, now little more than empty though sounding phrases. The rhapsody belongs to wordmongering where ideas are the staple; where it takes the shape of narrative or dramatic fiction, it is phantasmal—an attempted description of what is impossible in nature and without probability in art; it repels the reader instead of attracting him.

The elements of the story are a South Sea whaling voyage, narrated by Ishmael, one of the crew of the ship Pequod, from Nantucket. Its 'probable' portions consist of the usual sea matter in that branch of the industrial marine; embracing the preparations for departure, the voyage, the chase and capture of whale, with the economy of cutting up, &c., and the peculiar discipline of the service. This matter is expanded by a variety of digressions on the nature and characteristics of the sperm whale, the history of the fishery, and similar things, in which a little knowledge is made the excuse for a vast many words. The voyage is introduced by several chapters in which life in American seaports is rather broadly depicted.

The 'marvellous' injures the book by disjointing the narrative, as well as by its inherent want of interest, at least as managed by Mr Melville. In the superstition of some whalers, (grounded upon the malicious foresight which occasionally characterizes the attacks of the sperm fish upon the boats sent to capture it,) there is a *white* whale which possesses supernatural power. To capture or even to hurt it is beyond the art of man; the skill of the whaler is useless; the harpoon does not wound it; it exhibits a contemptuous strategy in its attacks upon the boats of its pursuers; and happy is the vessel where only loss of limb, or of a single life, attends its chase. Ahab, the master of the Pequod—a mariner of long experience, stern resolve and indomitable courage, the high hero of romance, in short, transferred to a whale-ship—has lost his leg in a contest with the white whale. Instead of daunting Ahab, the loss exasperates him; and by long brooding over it his reason becomes shaken. In this condition he undertakes the voyage; making the chase of his fishy antagonist the sole object of his thoughts, and, so far as he can without exciting overt insubordination among his officers, the object of his proceedings.

Such a groundwork is hardly natural enough for a regular-built novel, though it might form a tale, if properly managed. But Mr Melville's mysteries provoke wonder at the author rather than terror at the creation; the soliloquies and dialogues of Ahab, in which the author attempts delineating the wild imaginings of monomania, and exhibiting some profoundly speculative views of things in general, induce weariness or skipping; while the whole scheme mars, as we have said, the nautical continuity of story—greatly assisted by various chapters of a bookmaking kind.

Perhaps the earliest chapters are the best, although they contain little adventure. Their topics are fresher to English readers than the whale-chase, and they have more direct satire. One of the leading personages in the voyage is Queequeg, a South Sea Islander, that Ishmael falls in with at New Bedford, and with whom he forms a bosom friendship. . . .

The strongest point of the book is its 'characters.' Ahab, indeed, is a melodramatic exaggeration, and Ishmael is little more than a mouthpiece; but the harpooners, the mates, and several of the seamen, are truthful portraitures of the sailor as modified by the whaling service. The persons ashore are equally good, though they are soon lost sight of. The two Quaker owners are the author's means for a hit at the religious hypocrisies. Captain Bildad, an old sea-dog, has got rid of everything pertaining to the meeting-house save an occasional 'thou' and 'thee.' Captain Peleg, in American phrase 'professes religion.' . . .

It is a canon with sonic critics that nothing should be introduced into a novel which it is physically impossible for the writer to have known: thus, he must not describe the conversation of miners in a pit if they *all* perish. Mr Melville hardly steers clear of this rule, and he continually violates another by beginning in the autobiographical form and changing ad libitum into the narrative. His catastrophe overrides all role: not only is Ahab, with his boat's-crew, destroyed in his last desperate attack upon the white whale, but the Pequod herself sinks with all on board into the depths of the illimitable ocean. Such is the go-ahead method.

—Anonymous, *The Spectator*, October 25, 1851, pp. 1026–27

HENRY CHORLEY (1851)

Moby-Dick was published in England (in three volumes as *The Whale*) by Richard Bentley. Less than a month later, the first American version appeared from Harper and Brothers, titled *Moby-Dick; or, The Whale*. The first British reviews, from *The Spectator* and *Athenaeum*, were coeval and quite critical. While Chorley credits Melville with flashes of brilliance, he finds that the book's "patchiness" and internal difference land the author among those "incorrigibles who occasionally tantalize us with indications of genius." The negative portrayal of internal difference in the book is a hallmark of the early criticism, and students analyzing the composition of the book will want to look from the early reviews to Lincoln Colcord's "Notes on *Moby-Dick*"; there they will find substantial reconsideration of this critical concern. Where Chorley closes his assessment in condemnation, Colcord closes in praise. What accounts for the difference? For answers, students might consider the complex of spatial, temporal, literary, and cultural alterations that separate the two reviews.

This is an ill-compounded mixture of romance and matter-of-fact. The idea of a connected and collected story has obviously visited and abandoned its writer again and again in the course of composition. The style of his tale is in places disfigured by mad (rather than bad) English; and its catastrophe is hastily, weakly, and obscurely managed. The second title—'Moby Dick'—is the name given to a particular sperm whale, or white sea monster, more malignant and diabolical even than the sperm whale in general is known to be. This ocean fiend is invested with especial horrors for our ship's crew;—because, once upon a time, a conflict with him lost their Captain a limb. Captain Ahab had an ivory leg made,—took an oath of retribution,—grew crazy,—lashed himself up into a purpose of cruising in quest of his adversary,—and bound all who sailed with him to stand by him in his wrath. With this cheerful Captain, on such a wise and Christian voyage of discovery, went to sea Ishmael, the imaginary writer of this narrative.

Frantic though such an invention seems to be, it might possibly have been accepted as the motive and purpose of an extravaganza had its author been consistent with himself. Nay, in such a terrible cause—when Krakens and Typhoons and the wonders of Mid-Ocean, &c. &c. were the topics and toys to be arranged and manoeuvred—we might have stretched a point in admission of electrical verbs and adjectives as hoarse as the hurricane. There is a time for everything in imaginative literature;—and, according to its order, a place—for rant as well as for reserve; but the rant must be good, honest, shameless rant, without flaw or misgiving. The voice of 'the storm wind Euroclydon' must not be interrupted by the facts of Scoresby and the figures of Cocker. Ravings and scraps of useful knowledge flung together salad-wise make a dish in which there may be much surprise, but in which there is little savour. The real secret of this patchiness in the present case is disclosed in Mr Melville's appendix; which contains such an assortment of curious quotations as Southey might have wrought up into a whale-chapter for 'The Doctor,'—suggesting the idea that a substantial work on the subject may have been originally contemplated. Either Mr Melville's purpose must have changed, or his power must have fallen short. The result is, at all events, a most provoking book,—neither so utterly extravagant as to be entirely comfortable, nor so instructively complete as to take place among documents on the subject of the Great Fish, his capabilities, his home and his capture. Our author must be henceforth numbered in the company of the incorrigibles who occasionally tantalize us with indications of genius, while they constantly summon us to endure monstrosities, carelessnesses, and other such harassing manifestations of bad taste as daring or disordered ingenuity can devise....

We have little more to say in reprobation or in recommendation of this absurd book,—having detailed its leading incident. Mr Melville has been on former occasions characterized by us as one who thoroughly understands the tone of sea superstition. There is a wild humorous poetry in some of his terrors which distinguishes him from the vulgar herd of fustian-weavers. For instance, his interchapter on 'The Whiteness of the Whale' is full of ghostly suggestions for which a Maturin or a Monk Lewis would have been thankful. Mr Melville has to thank himself only if his horrors and his heroics are flung aside by the general reader, as so much trash belonging to the worst school of Bedlam literature,—since he seems not so much unable to learn as disdainful of learning the craft of an artist.

—Henry Chorley, *Athenaeum,* October 25, 1851, pp. 1112–13

Anonymous (1851)

This excerpt echoes the other two early British critiques of eccentricity and formal problems in *The Whale*, but mentions more of merit. Dispensing vagaries, the anonymous reviewer asserts that Melville projects "knowledge of the human heart" as well as "versatility of talent." This is the first critical voice to appreciate Melville's crew of "all countries and all coulors." Students considering Melville as a social critic, or taking the general measure of his "Americanness" may find it useful to compare this review with other pieces in this volume, especially Karl E. Zink's "Herman Melville and the Forms," in which the significance of "the crew" also makes an appearance.

The Whale is a most extraordinary work. There is so much eccentricity in its style and in its construction, in the original conception and in the gradual development of its strange and improbable story, that we are at a loss to determine in what category of works of amusement to place it. It is certainly neither a novel nor a romance, although it is made to drag its weary length through three closely printed volumes, and is published by Bentley, who, *par excellence*, is the publisher of the novels of the fashionable world, for who ever heard of novel or romance without a heroine or a single love scene? The plot of the narrative is scarcely worthy of the name, as it hangs entirely on the inveterate pursuit by a monomaniac old Captain after a certain humpbacked whale, who in some previous voyage had bitten off one of his legs, and whose destruction he had bound himself and his crew by terrible oaths to accomplish, in revenge for the injury he had himself sustained. The tragical catastrophe, which innumerable signs, omens, and superstitious warnings are constantly predicting to the infatuated commander, is the wreck of the ship, and the loss of the whole crew in the frantic attack that is made upon the invincible white whale.

The story has merit, but it is a merit *sui generis*, and does not consist in the work either when viewed as a whole or with reference to the arrangement of its separate parts. The plot is meagre beyond comparison, as the whole of the incident might very conveniently have been comprised in half of one of these three interminable volumes. Nevertheless, in his descriptions of character, in his analysis of the motives of actions, and in the novelty of the details of a whaling expedition, the author has evinced not only a considerable knowledge of the human heart, combined with a thorough acquaintance with the subject he is handling, but a rare versatility of talent. The crew of the Pequod, the inharmonious name given to the whaler, is composed of mariners of all countries and all colours, from the civilised British sailor to the savage and cannibal harpooner of the South Sea Islands. In describing the idiosyncrasies of all these different castes of men our author has evinced acuteness of observation and powers of discrimination, which would alone render his work a valuable addition to the literature of the day....

The first and second volumes are spun out with long descriptions of the various cetacious tribes, which do now, and have at different periods of time inhabited the ocean. The information these chapters convey may be important to naturalists or whalers, but will have little interest for the general reader. Bating a few Americanisms, which sometimes mar the perspicuity and the purity of the style, the language of the work is appropriate and impressive; and the stirring scenes with which the author concludes are abundant evidence of the power he possesses of making his narrative intensely interesting.

—Anonymous, *Britannia*, November 8, 1851, pp. 714–15

EVERT A. DUYCKINCK
"MELVILLE'S *MOBY DICK; OR, THE WHALE*" (1851)

Melville first met this important literary figure in 1847, when, after marrying Elizabeth Shaw, he moved to New York City and fell into the literary scene there. The relationship between Melville and Duyckinck was one of the most important in Melville's life. Duyckinck was an editor in New York at Wiley and Putnam, and then went on to purchase his own popular journal, before eventually establishing his longstanding and influential organ, *The Literary World*. He lent Melville books from his library, encouraged the author's career in journals, and reviewed his work. It was in the *World*, for example, that Melville published "Hawthorne and his *Mosses*," marking an important transformation in the author at the very time he was in the Berkshires drafting *Moby-Dick*. This change is also well captured by Charles Olson in the excerpt from *Call Me Ishmael* included later in this section.

Students exploring Melville's use of symbolism and allegory will find this review of note. George Ripley's positive comments on Melville and allegory usefully contrast with Duyckinck's more troubled observations on rhetorical practice in *Moby-Dick*.

Duyckinck's review is significant because, to Melville, he represented both high literary circles and a willingness to compromise—to appreciate popular tastes and a rapidly growing literary marketplace. Duyckinck's sentiments are useful to students exploring Melville's struggle to resolve the tension between his life and art—his early and pressing need for money and his desire to write in an environment free of commercial constraint. Students might usefully connect the significance of Duyckinck's review with the words Melville wrote to Hawthorne in June 1851, included earlier in this volume: "What I feel most moved to write, that is banned,—it will not pay. Yet, altogether, write the *other* way I cannot."

Every reader throughout the United States has probably perused in the newspapers the account of a recent incident in the whale fishery which would stagger the mind by its extent of the marvellous, were it not paralleled by a well known case—that of the Essex of Nantucket, still authenticated by living witnesses. It appears from a narrative published in the *Panama Herald* (an American newspaper in that region, itself one of the wonders of the age!), taken down from the lips of the captain of the vessel, John S. Deblois, that the ship Ann Alexander, of New Bedford, having left that port in June of last year with the usual vicissitudes of Cape Horn service, losing a New Hampshire man overboard in a storm at that point, had entered upon her Pacific hunting-grounds, and in the recent month of August was coursing within a few degrees of the Equator—a well known haunt of the whale. On the 20th of that month, nine in the morning, fish were discovered; two boats were lowered in pursuit, and by mid-day a particular sperm whale was struck and fast to the line. The first mate commanded the boat, thus far successful, and the Captain himself the other. After running some time, in the words of the narrative, the whale turned upon the boat to which he was attached, and rushing at it with tremendous violence, lifted open its enormous jaws, and taking the boat in, actually crushed it to fragments as small as a common-sized chair. Captain Deblois struck for the spot, and rescued the nine members of the boat's crew—a feat, we presume, which could only be accomplished among men hardy, resolute, and full of vitality as whalemen, strung at the moment by excitement to almost superhuman energy and superiority to the elements. The Captain, with his double boat's crew, proceeded to the ship, some six miles off. There the waist-boat was fitted out, the men divided, and both parties went again in pursuit of the whale, the mate again taking the lead. The whale perceived the coming renewal of the attack, made for the boat, crushed it with his jaw, the men again throwing themselves into the deep. The Captain once more rescuing them, was himself pursued by the whale, which passed the boat with distended jaw; but they reached the ship in safety. A boat was sent for the oars of the broken vessels floating on the water, which were secured. Sail was set on the ship, and it was determined to proceed after the whale. He was overtaken, and a lance thrown into his head! The ship passed on, when it was immediately discovered that the whale was in pursuit. The ship manoeuvred out of his way. *After he had fairly passed they kept off to overtake and attack him again.* The whale settled down deep below the surface. It was then near sundown. Capt. Deblois, continues the account, was at this time standing on the knight-heads on the larboard bow, with shaft in hand, ready to strike the monster a deadly blow should he appear, the ship moving about five knots, when looking over the side of the ship he discerned the whale rushing towards her at the rate of fifteen knots. In an instant the monster struck the ship with tremendous violence, shaking her from stem to stern. She quivered under the violence of the shock as if she had struck upon a rock. Captain Deblois descending to the forecastle, discovered that *the whale had struck the ship about two feet from the keel, abreast the foremast, knocking a great hole entirely through her bottom.* The ship was sinking rapidly. All hands were ordered into the boats, the captain leaving the deck last, throwing himself into the sea, and swimming to his comrades. That night was passed in the boats, with but twelve quarts of water saved, and no provisions for twenty-two men. In the morning the ship still lay on her beam-ends. Not a man would board her to cut away the masts, right the vessel, and procure provisions—fearing her sinking instantly—except the captain, who undertook the work with a single hatchet, and succeeded in getting the ship nearly on her keel. Nothing could be procured by cutting through the decks but some vinegar and a small quantity of wet bread, with which they abandoned the dangerous vessel. At the close of the next day they hailed the ship Nantucket of Nantucket, and were welcomed by its Captain, Gibbs, with the utmost hospitality. They were landed at Paita, where an authenticated protest of this extraordinary series of occurrences was made before the United States Consul.

By a singular coincidence this extreme adventure is, even to very many of the details, the catastrophe of Mr. Melville's new book, which is a natural-historical, philosophical, romantic account of the person, habits, manners, ideas of the great sperm whale; of his haunts and of his belongings; of his associations with the world of the deep, and of the not less remarkable individuals and combinations of individuals who hunt him on the oceans. Nothing like it has ever before been written of the whale; for no man who has at once seen so much of the actual conflict, and weighed so carefully all that has been recorded on the subject, with equal powers of perception and reflection, has attempted to write at all on it—the labors of Scoresby covering a different and inferior branch of the history. To the popular mind this book of Herman Melville, touching the Leviathan of the deep, is as much of a discovery in Natural History as was the revelation of America by Christopher Columbus in geography. Let any one read this book with the attention which it deserves, and then converse with the best informed of his friends and acquaintances who have not seen it, and he will notice the extent and variety of treatment; while scientific men must admit the original observation and speculation.

Such an infuriated, resolute sperm whale as pursued and destroyed the Ann Alexander is the hero, Moby Dick, of Mr. Melville's book. The vengeance with which he is hunted, which with Capt. Deblois was the incident of a single, though most memorable day, is the leading passion and idea of Captain Ahab of the Pequod for years, and throughout the seas of the world. Incidentally with this melo-dramatic action and spiritual development of the character of Ahab, is included a full, minute, thorough investigation, and description of the whale and its fishery. Such is a short-hand account of this bulky and multifarious volume.

It opens, after a dedication to Nathaniel Hawthorne, with a preliminary flourish in the style of Carlyle and the Doctor of etymology, followed by a hundred or so of extracts of "Old Burton," passages of a quaint and pithy character from Job and King Alfred to Miriam Coffin; in lieu of the old style of Scott, Cooper, and others, of distributing such flourishes about the heads of chapters. Here they are all in a lump, like the grace over the Franklin barrel of pork, and may be taken as a kind of bitters, a whet and fillip to the imagination, exciting it to the curious, ludicrous, sublime traits and contemplations which are to follow.

It is some time after opening with Chapter I. before we get fairly afloat, but the time is very satisfactorily occupied with some very strange, romantic, and, withal, highly humorous adventures at New Bedford and Nantucket. A scene at the Spouter Inn, of the former town, a night in bed with a Pacific Islander, and a mid-ocean adventure subsequently with a Frenchman over some dead whales in the Pacific, treat the reader to a laugh worthy of Smollet. . . .

A difficulty in the estimate of this, in common with one or two other of Mr. Melville's books, occurs from the double character under which they present themselves. In one light they are romantic fictions, in another statements of absolute fact. When to this is added that the romance is made a vehicle of opinion and satire through a more or less opaque allegorical veil, as particularly in the latter half of *Mardi,* and to some extent in this present volume, the critical difficulty is considerably thickened. It becomes quite impossible to submit such books to a distinct classification as fact, fiction, or essay. Something of a parallel may be found in Jean Paul's German tales, with an admixture of Southey's *Doctor*. Under these combined influences of personal observation, actual fidelity to local truthfulness in description, a taste for reading and sentiment, a fondness for fanciful analogies, near and remote, a rash daring in speculation, reckless at times of taste and propriety, again refined and eloquent, this volume of *Moby Dick* may be pronounced a most remarkable sea-dish—an intellectual chowder of romance, philosophy, natural history, fine writing, good feeling, bad sayings—but over which, in spite of all uncertainties, and in spite of the author himself, predominates his keen perceptive faculties, exhibited in vivid narration.

There are evidently two if not three books in *Moby Dick* rolled into one. Book No. 1 we could describe as a thorough exhaustive account admirably given of the great Sperm Whale. The information is minute, brilliantly illustrated, as it should be—the whale himself so generously illuminating the midnight page on which his memoirs are written—has its level passages, its humorous touches, its quaint suggestion, its incident usually picturesque and occasionally sublime. All this is given in the most delightful manner in *The Whale*. Book No. 2 is the romance of Captain Ahab, Queequeg, Tashtego, Pip & Co., who are more or less spiritual personages talking and acting differently from the general business run of the conversation on the decks of whalers. They are for the most part very serious people, and seem to be concerned a great deal about the problem of the universe. They are striking characters withal, of the romantic spiritual cast of the German drama; realities of some kinds at bottom, but veiled in all sorts of poetical incidents and expressions. As a bit of German melodrama, with Captain Ahab for the Faust of the quarter-deck, and Queequeg with the crew, for Walpurgis night revellers in the forecastle, it has its strong points, though here the limits as to space and treatment of the stage would improve it. *Moby Dick* in this view becomes a sort of fishy moralist, a leviathan metaphysician, a folio Ductor Dubitantium, in fact, in the fresh water illustration of Mrs. Malaprop, "an allegory on the banks of the Nile." After pursuing him in this melancholic company over a few hundred squares of latitude and longitude, we begin to have some faint idea of the association of whaling and lamentation, and why blubber is popularly synonymous with tears.

The intense Captain Ahab is too long drawn out; something more of *him* might, we think, be left to the reader's imagination. The value of this kind of writing can only be through the personal consciousness of the reader, what he brings to the book; and all this is sufficiently evoked by a dramatic trait or suggestion. If we had as much of Hamlet or Macbeth as Mr. Melville gives us of Ahab, we should be tired even of their sublime company. Yet Captain Ahab is a striking conception, firmly planted on the wild deck of the Pequod—a dark disturbed soul arraying itself with every ingenuity of material resources for a conflict at once natural and supernatural in his eye, with the most dangerous extant physical monster of the earth, embodying, in strongly drawn lines of mental association, the vaster moral evil of the world. The pursuit of the White Whale thus interweaves with the literal perils of the fishery—a problem of fate and destiny—to the tragic solution of which Ahab hurries on, amidst the wild stage scenery of the ocean. To this end the motley crew, the air, the sky, the sea, its inhabitants are idealized throughout. It is a noble and praiseworthy conception; and though our sympathies may not always accord with the train of thought, we would caution the reader against a light or hasty condemnation of this part of the work.

Book III., appropriating perhaps a fourth of the volume, is a vein of moralizing, half essay, half rhapsody, in which much refinement and subtlety, and no little poetical feeling, are mingled with quaint conceit and extravagant daring speculation. This is to be taken as in some sense dramatic; the narrator throughout among the personages of the Pequod being one Ishmael, whose wit may be allowed to be against everything on land, as his hand is against everything at sea. This piratical running down of creeds and opinions, the conceited indifferentism of Emerson, or the run-a-muck style of Carlyle is, we will not say dangerous in such cases, for there are various forces at work to meet more powerful onslaught, but it is out of place and uncomfortable. We do not like to see what, under any view, must be to the world the most sacred associations of life violated and defaced.

We call for fair play in this matter. Here is Ishmael, telling the story of this volume, going down on his knees with a cannibal to a piece of wood, in the second story fireplace of a New-Bedford tavern, in the spirit of amiable and transcendent charity, which may be all very well in its way; but why dislodge from heaven, with contumely, "long-pampered Gabriel, Michael and Raphael." Surely Ishmael, who is a scholar, might have spoken respectfully of the Archangel Gabriel, out of consideration, if not for the Bible (which might be asking too much of the school), at least for one John Milton, who wrote *Paradise Lost*.

Nor is it fair to inveigh against the terrors of priestcraft, which, skilful though it may be in making up its woes, at least seeks to provide a remedy for the evils of the world, and attribute the existence of conscience to "hereditary dyspepsias, nurtured by Ramadans"—and at the same time go about petrifying us with imaginary horrors, and all sorts of gloomy suggestions, all the world through. It is a curious fact that there are no more bilious people in the world, more completely filled with megrims and head shakings, than some of these very people who are constantly inveighing against the religious melancholy of priestcraft.

So much for the consistency of Ishmael—who, if it is the author's object to exhibit the painful contradictions of this self-dependent, self-torturing agency of a mind driven hither and thither as a flame in a whirlwind, is, in a degree, a successful embodiment of opinions, without securing from us, however, much admiration for the result.

With this we make an end of what we have been reluctantly compelled to object to this volume. With far greater pleasure, we acknowledge the acuteness of observation, the freshness of perception, with which the author brings home to us from the deep, "things unattempted yet in prose or rhyme," the weird influences of his ocean scenes, the salient imagination which connects them with the past and distant, the world of books and the life of experience—certain prevalent traits of manly sentiment. These are strong powers with which Mr. Melville wrestles in this book. It would be a great glory to subdue them to the highest uses of fiction. It is still a great honor, among the crowd of successful mediocrities which throng our publishers' counters, and know nothing of divine impulses, to be in the company of these nobler spirits on any terms.

—Evert A. Duyckinck, "Melville's *Moby Dick; or, The Whale*," *Literary World*, November 15, 1851, p. 381; November 22, 1851, pp. 403–04

HORACE GREELEY (1851)

Horace Greeley, who wrote the carefully complimentary review of *Omoo* also excerpted in this volume, here pronounces *Moby-Dick* the "best production which has yet come from [Melville's] seething brain." Greeley finds no fault in the hybrid nature of the book, but instead enjoys an "intensity of . . . plot . . . happily relieved by minute descriptions . . . of the whale fishery." He seems relieved to find more emphasis on the rough husk of maritime life, on the "odorous realities" of "oil and blubber" than on direct social critique as in *Typee* and *Omoo*, or on flights of political allegory as in *Mardi*. Students exploring the ways Melville's rhetorical and political stylistics changed in the span of his career might explore the accuracy of Greeley's measurement of *Moby-Dick*. Is he correct or not in finding only "occasional touches of . . . subtle mysticism" in the book? How might influential voices like Greeley's have contributed to the alteration of Melville's style and politics?

The present volume is a "Whaliad," or the Epic of that veritable old leviathan, who "esteemeth iron as straw, and laughs at the spear, the dart, and the habergeon," no one being able to "fill his skin with a barbed iron, or his head with fish-hooks." Mr. Melville gives us not only the romance of his history, but a great mass of instruction on the character and habits of his whole race, with complete details of the wily stratagems of their pursuers.

The interest of the work pivots on a certain Captain Ahab, whose enmity to Moby-Dick, the name of the whale-demon, has been aggravated to monomania. In one rencounter with this terror of the seas, he suffers a signal defeat; loses a leg in the contest; gets a fire in his brain; returns home a man with one idea; feels that he has a mission; that he is predestined to defy his enemy to mortal strife; devotes himself to the fulfillment of his destiny; with the persistence and cunning of insanity gets possession of another vessel; ships a weird, supernatural crew of which Ishmael, the narrator of the story, is a prominent member; and after a "wild huntsman's chase" through unknown seas, is the only one who remains to tell the destruction of the ship and the doomed Captain Ahab by the victorious, indomitable Moby-Dick.

The narrative is constructed in Herman Melville's best manner. It combines the various features which form the chief attractions of his style, and is commendably free from the faults which we have before had occasion to specify in this powerful writer. The intensity of the plot is happily relieved by minute descriptions of the most homely processes of the whale fishery. We have occasional touches of the subtle mysticism, which is carried to such an inconvenient excess in Mardi, but it is here mixed up with so many tangible and odorous realities, that we always safely alight from the excursion through mid-air upon the solid deck of the whaler. We are recalled to this world by the fumes of "oil and blubber," and are made to think more of the contents of barrels than of allegories. The work is also full of episodes, descriptive of strange and original phases of character. One of them is given in the commencement of the volume, showing how "misery makes a man acquainted with strange bedfellows." . . .

We part with the adventurous philosophical Ishmael, truly thankful that the whale did not get his head, for which we are indebted for this wildly imaginative and truly thrilling story. We think it the best production which has yet come from that seething brain, and in spite of its lawless flights, which put all regular criticism at defiance, it gives us a higher opinion of the author's originality and power than even the favorite and fragrant first-fruits of his genius, the never-to-be-forgotten *Typee.*

—Horace Greeley, *New York Daily Tribune,* November 22, 1851

WILLIAM T. PORTER
"MOBY DICK, OR THE WHALE" (1851)

The Porter review is generally positive and primarily memorable and novel in the way it explores Melville's writing as "valuable to the world." Porter charts Melville's social criticism through the early books to *Moby-Dick* and deems him in company with Charles Dickens. For Porter, *Moby-Dick* is "many-sided," less oddly composite and internally fractured as it is encyclopedic and all-encompassing. This marks a difference from the early British reviews and helped to establish a critical divide that has long persisted.

Our friend Melville's books begin to accumulate. His literary family increases rapidly. He had already a happy and smiling progeny around him, but lo! at the appointed time another child of his brain, with the accustomed signs of the family, claims our attention and regard. We bid the book a hearty welcome. We assure the "happy father" that his "labors of love" are no "love's labor lost."

We confess an admiration for Mr. Melville's books, which, perhaps, spoils us for mere criticism. There are few writers, living or dead, who describe the sea and its adjuncts with such true art, such graphic power, and with such powerfully resulting interest. *Typee, Omoo, Redburn, Mardi,* and *White Jacket,* are equal to anything in the language. They are things of their own. They are results of the youthful experience on the ocean of a man who is at once philosopher, painter, and poet. This is not, perhaps, a very unusual mental combination, but it is not usual to find such a combination "before the mast." So far Mr. Melville's early experiences, though perhaps none of the pleasantest to himself, are infinitely valuable to the world. We say *valuable* with a full knowledge of the terms used; and, not to enter into details, which will be fresh in the memory of most of Mr. Melville's readers, it is sufficient to say that the humanities of the world have been quickened by his works.

Who can forget the missionary *expose*—the practical good sense which pleads for "Poor Jack," or the unsparing but just severity of his delineations of naval abuses, and that crowning disgrace to our navy—flogging? Taken as matters of art these books are amongst the largest and the freshest contributions of original thought and observation which have been presented in many years. Take the majority of modern writers, and it will be admitted that however much they may elaborate and rearrange the stock of ideas pre-existant, there is little added to this "common fund." Philosophers bark at each other—poets sing stereotyped phrases—John Miltons re-appear in innumerable *Pollock's Courses of Time*—novelists and romances stick to the same overdone incidents, careless of the memories of defunct Scotts and Radcliffs, and it is only now and then when genius, by some lucky chance of youth, ploughs deeper into the soil of humanity and nature, that fresher experience—perhaps at the cost of much individual pain and sorrow—are obtained; and the results are books, such as those of Herman Melville and Charles Dickens. Books which are living pictures, at once of the practical truth, and the ideal amendment: books which mark epochs in literature and art.

It is, however, not with Mr. Melville generally as a writer that we have now to deal, but with *Moby Dick, or the Whale,* in particular; and at first let us not forget to say that in "taking titles" no man is more felicitous than our author. Sufficiently dreamy to excite one's curiosity, sufficiently explicit to indicate some main and peculiar feature. *Moby Dick* is perhaps a creation of the brain—*The Whale* a result of experience; and the whole title a fine polished result of both. A title may be a truth or a lie. It may be clap-trap, or true art. A bad book may have a good title, but you will seldom find a good book with an inappropriate name.

Moby Dick, or the Whale, is all whale. Leviathan is here in full amplitude. Not one of your museum affairs, but the real, living whale, a bona-fide, warm-blooded creature, ransacking the waters from pole to pole. His enormous bulk, his terribly destructive energies, his habits, his food, are all before us. Nay, even his lighter moods are exhibited. We are permitted to see the whale as a lover, a husband, and the head of a family. So to speak, we are made guests at his fire-side; we set our mental legs beneath his mahogany, and become members of his interesting social circle. No book in the world brings together so much whale. We have his history, natural and social, living and dead. But Leviathan's natural history, though undoubtedly valuable to science, is but a part of the book. It is in the personal adventures of his captors, their toils, and, alas! not unfrequently their wounds and martyrdom, that our highest interest is excited. This mingling of human adventure with new, startling, and striking objects and pursuits, constitute one of the chief charms of Mr. Melville's books. His present work is a drama of intense interest. A whale, *Moby Dick*—a dim, gigantic, unconquerable, but terribly destructive being is one of the persons of the drama. We admit a disposition to be critical on this character. We had doubts as to his admissibility as an actor into dramatic action, and so it would seem had our author, but his chapter, "The Affidavit," disarms us; all improbability or incongruity disappears, and *Moby Dick* becomes a living fact, simply doubtful at first, because he was so new an idea, one of those beings whose whole life, like the Palladius or the Sea-serpent, is a romance, and whose memoirs unvarnished are of themselves a fortune to the first analist or his publisher.

Moby Dick, or the Whale, is a "many-sided" book. Mingled with much curious information respecting whales and whaling there is a fine vein of sermonizing, a good deal of keen satire, much humor, and that too of the finest order, and a story of peculiar interest. As a romance its characters are so new and unusual that we doubt not it will excite the ire of critics. It is not tame enough to pass this ordeal safely. Think of a monomaniac whaling captain, who, mutilated on a former voyage by a particular whale, well known for its peculiar bulk, shape, and color—seeks, at the risk of his life and the lives of his crew, to capture and slay this terror of the seas! It is on this idea that the romance hinges. The usual staple of novelists is entirely wanting. We have neither flinty-hearted fathers, designing villains, dark caverns, men in armor, nor anxious lovers. There is not in the book any individual, who, at a certain hour, *"might have been seen"* ascending hills or descending valleys, as is usual. The thing is entirely new, fresh, often startling, and highly dramatic, and with those even, who, oblivious of other fine matters, scattered with profusest hand, read for the sake of the story, must be exceedingly successful. . . . we must conclude by strongly recommending *Moby Dick, or the Whale,* to all who can appreciate a work of exceeding power, beauty, and genius.

—William T. Porter, *"Moby Dick, or the Whale,"*
Spirit of the Times, December 6, 1851

WILLIAM A. BUTLER (1851)

This review from the *National Intelligence* quibbles at the outset over Melville's offense to "good taste" and "good morals" in chapter 40 ("Midnight, Forecastle") but then submits to overwhelmingly positive assessments of the book. Students exploring how Melville's writing proved offensive to some readers of the time will want to examine chapter 40 carefully for the "ribald orgies" Butler accuses Melville of crafting. Students discussing the comedic elements in Melville have an early consideration of the subject.

If we were disposed on the present occasion to follow the example thus set us by our betters, we should forthwith proceed, taking *Moby Dick or the Whale*, as our text, to indite a discourse on cetology. Such, however, is not our intention. Nor do we propose, like a veritable devil's advocate, to haul Mr Herman Melville over the coals for any offences committed against the code of Aristotle and Aristarchus: we have nothing to allege against his admission among the few writers of the present day who give evidence of some originality; but, while disposed to concede to Mr Melville a palm of high praise for his literary excellencies, we must enter our decided protest against the querulous and cavilling innuendoes which he so much loves to discharge, like barbed and poisoned arrows, against objects that should be shielded from his irreverent wit. On this point we hope it is necessary to enlarge in terms of reprehension, further than to say that there are many passages in his last work, as indeed in most that Mr Melville has written, which 'dying he would wish to blot.' Neither good taste nor good morals can approve the 'forecastle scene,' with its maudlin and ribald orgies, as contained in the 40th chapter of *Moby Dick*. It has all that is disgusting in Goethe's 'Witches' Kitchen,' without its genius.

Very few readers of the lighter literature of the day have forgotten, we presume, the impression produced upon their minds of Mr Melville's earlier publications—*Typee* and *Omoo*. They opened to all the circulating library readers an entirely new world. His 'Peep at Polynesian Life,' during a four months' residence in a valley of the Marquesas, as unfolded in *Typee*, with his rovings in the 'Little Jule' and his rambles through Tahiti, as detailed in *Omoo*, abound with incidents of stirring adventure and 'moving accidents by flood and field,' replete with all the charms of novelty and dramatic vividness. He first introduced us to cannibal banquets, feasts of raw fish and *poee-poee*; he first made us acquainted with the sunny glades and tropical fruits of the Typee valley, with its golden lizards among the spear-grass and many colored birds among the trees; with its groves of cocoa-nut, its tattooed savages, and temples of light bamboo. Borne along by the current of his limpid style, we sweep past bluff and grove, wooden glen and valley, and dark ravines lighted up far within by wild waterfalls, while here and there in the distance are seen the white huts of the natives, nestling like birds-nests in clefts gushing with verdure, while off the coral reefs of each sea-girt island the carved canoes of tattooed chieftains dance on the blue waters. Who has forgotten the maiden Fayaway and the faithful Kory-Kory, or the generous Marheyo, or the Doctor Long Ghost, that figure in his narratives? So new and interesting were his sketches of life in the South Sea islands that few were able to persuade themselves that his story of adventure was not authentic. We have not time at present to renew the inquiry into their authenticity, though we incline to suspect they were about as true as the sketches of adventures detailed by De Foe in his *Robinson Crusoe*. The points of resemblance between the inimitable novel of De Foe and the production of Mr Melville are neither few nor difficult to be traced. In the conduct of his narrative the former displays more of naturalness and *vraisemblance*; the latter more of fancy and invention; and while we rather suspect that Robinson's man Friday will always remain more of a favorite than Kory-Kory among all readers 'in their teens,' persons of maturer judgment and more cultivated taste will prefer the mingled *bonhommie*, quiet humor, and unstrained pathos which underlie and pervade the graphic narratives of Mr Melville. Still we are far from considering Mr Melville a greater artist than Daniel De Foe in the general design of his romantic pictures; for is it not a greater proof of skill in the use of language to be able so to paint the scenes in a narration as to make us forget the narrator in the interests of his subjects? In this, as we think, consists the charm of *Robinson Crusoe*—a book which every boy reads and no man forgets; the perfect naturalness of the narrative, and the transparent diction in which it is told, have never been equalled by any subsequent writer, nor is it likely that they will be in an age fond of point and pungency.

Mr Melville is not without a rival in this species of romance-writing, founded on personal adventure in foreign and unknown lands. Dr Mayo, the author of *Kaloolah* and other works, has opened to us a phantasmagorical view of life in Northern Africa similar to the 'peep' which Mr Melville has given us of the South Sea Islands through his kaleidoscope. Each author has familiarized himself with the localities in which his dramatic exhibition of men and things is enacted, and each have doubtless claimed for themselves a goodly share of that invention which produced the Travels of Gulliver and the unheard-of adventures and exploits of the Baron Munchausen. Framazugda, as painted by Dr Mayo, is the Eutopia of Negro-dom, just as the Typee valley has been called the Eutopia of the Pacific Islands, and Kaloolah is the 'counterfeit presentment' of Fayaway. *Moby-Dick, or the Whale* is the narrative of a whaling voyage; and, while we must beg permission to doubt its authenticity in all respects, we are free to confess that it presents a most striking and truthful portraiture of the whale and his perilous capture. We do not imagine that Mr Melville claims for this his latest production the same historical credence which he asserted was due to *Typee* and *Omoo*; and we do not know how we can better express our conception of his general drift and style in the work under consideration than by entitling it a prose Epic on Whaling. In whatever light it may be viewed, no one can deny it to be the production of a man of genius. The descriptive powers of Mr Melville are unrivalled, whether the scenes he paints reveal 'old ocean into tempest toss'd,' or are laid among the bright hillsides of some Pacific island, so warm and undulating that the printed page on which they are so graphically depicted seems almost to palpitate beneath the sun. Language in the hands of this master becomes like a magician's wand, evoking at will 'thick-coming fancies,' and peopling the 'chambers of imagery' with hideous shapes of terror or winning forms of beauty and loveliness. Mr Melville has a strange power to reach the sinuosities of a thought, if we may so express ourselves; he touches with his lead and line depths of pathos that few can fathom, and by a single word can set a whole chime of sweet or wild emotions into a pealing concert. His delineation of character is actually Shakespearean—a quality which is even more prominently evinced in *Moby Dick* than in any of his antecedent efforts. Mr Melville especially delights to limn the full-length portrait of a savage, and if he is a cannibal it is all the better; he seems fully convinced that the highest type of man is to be found in the forests or among the anthropophagi of the Fejee Islands. Brighter geniuses than even his have disported on this same fancy; for such was the youthful dream of Burke, and such was the crazy vision of Jean Jacques Rousseau.

The humor of Mr Melville is of that subdued yet unquenchable nature which spreads such a charm over the pages of Sterne. As illustrative of this quality in his style, we must refer our readers to the irresistibly comic passages scattered at irregular intervals through *Moby Dick*; and occasionally we find in this singular production the traces of that 'wild imagining' which throws such a weird-like charm about the Ancient Mariner of Coleridge; and many of the scenes and objects in *Moby Dick* were suggested, we doubt not, by this ghastly rhyme. . . .

On such a slender thread hangs the whole of this ingenious romance, which for variety of incident and vigor of style can scarcely be exceeded.

—William A. Butler, *National Intelligence*,
Washington, D.C., December 16, 1851

GEORGE RIPLEY "LITERARY NOTICES" (1852)

Ripley joins the voices in approval of the composite narrative structure of *Moby-Dick*, asserting that the "sudden and decided transitions" between narrative elements constitute no "fatal" flaw, but rather result in an "element of great power." This is early recognition of the organic power of Melville's masterpiece. Students investigating Melville's place in the evolution of the novel as a genre might find Ripley's comments about character in *Moby-Dick* useful. He celebrates in Melville's book "a unique picture gallery, which every artist must despair of rivaling." The allusion to paintings, to vibrant, yet essentially static portraits reminds us that Melville crafted his Ahab and Ishmael, indeed his entire cast of memorable characters, in the era before the realism we ascribe to writers such as Samuel Clemens and Stephen Crane predominated—a period when readers expected characters to be both representative and real. How static are Melville's characters? Where do Melvillean characters fit in the evolution of the novel as a genre?

A new work by Herman Melville, entitled *Moby Dick; or, The Whale,* has just been issued by Harper and Brothers, which, in point of richness and variety of incident, originality of conception, and splendor of description, surpasses any of the former productions of this highly successful author. *Moby Dick* is the name of an old White Whale; half fish and half devil; the terror of the Nantucket cruisers; the scourge of distant oceans; leading an invulnerable, charmed life; the subject of many grim and ghostly traditions. This huge sea monster has a conflict with one Captain Ahab; the veteran Nantucket salt comes off second best; not only loses a leg in the affray, but receives a twist in the brain; becomes the victim of a deep, cunning monomania; believes himself predestined to take a bloody revenge on his fearful enemy; pursues him with fierce demoniac energy of purpose; and at last perishes in the dreadful fight, just as he deems that he has reached the goal of his frantic passion. On this slight framework, the author has constructed a romance, a tragedy, and a natural history, not without numerous gratuitous suggestions on psychology, ethics, and theology. Beneath the whole story, the subtle, imaginative reader may perhaps find a pregnant allegory, intended to illustrate the mystery of human life. Certain it is that the rapid, pointed hints which are often thrown out, with the keenness and velocity of a harpoon, penetrate deep into the heart of things, showing that the genius of the author for moral analysis is scarcely surpassed by his wizard power of description.

In the course of the narrative the habits of the whale are fully and ably described. Frequent graphic and instructive sketches of the fishery, of sea-life in a whaling vessel, and of the manners and customs of strange nations are interspersed with excellent artistic effect among the thrilling scenes of the story. The various processes of procuring oil are explained with the minute, painstaking fidelity of a statistical record, contrasting strangely with the weird, phantom-like character of the plot, and of some of the leading personages, who present a no less unearthly appearance than the witches in *Macbeth*. These sudden and decided transitions form a striking feature of the volume. Difficult of management, in the highest degree, they are wrought with consummate skill. To a less gifted author, they would inevitably have proved fatal. He has not only deftly avoided their dangers, but made them an element of great power. They constantly pique the attention of the reader, keeping curiosity alive, and presenting the combined charm of surprise and alternation.

The introductory chapters of the volume, containing sketches of life in the great marts of Whalingdom, New Bedford and Nantucket, are pervaded with a fine vein of comic humor, and reveal a succession of portraitures, in which the lineaments of nature shine forth, through a good deal of perverse, intentional exaggeration. To many readers, these will prove the most interesting portions of the work. Nothing can be better than the description of the owners of the vessel, Captain Peleg and Captain Bildad, whose acquaintance we make before the commencement of the voyage. The character of Captain Ahab also opens upon us with wonderful power. He exercises a wild, bewildering fascination by his dark and mysterious nature, which is not at all diminished when we obtain a clearer insight into his strange history. Indeed, all the members of the ship's company, the three mates, Starbuck, Stubbs, and Flash, the wild, savage Gayheader, the case-hardened old blacksmith, to say nothing of the pearl of a New Zealand harpooner, the bosom friend of the narrator—all stand before us in the strongest individual relief, presenting a unique picture gallery, which every artist must despair of rivaling.

The plot becomes more intense and tragic, as it approaches toward the denouement. The malicious old Moby Dick, after long cruisings in pursuit of him, is at length discovered. He comes up to the battle, like an army with banners. He seems inspired with the same fierce, inveterate cunning with which Captain Ahab has followed the traces of his mortal foe. The fight is described in letters of blood. It is easy to foresee which will be the victor in such a contest. We need not say that the ill-omened ship is broken in fragments by the wrath of the weltering fiend. Captain Ahab becomes the prey of his intended victim. The crew perish. One alone escapes to tell the tale. Moby

Dick disappears unscathed, and for aught we know, is the same "delicate monster," whose power in destroying another ship is just announced from Panama.

—George Ripley, "Literary Notices,"
Harper's New Monthly Magazine, December 1852, p. 137

Archibald MacMechan
"The Best Sea Story Ever Written" (1899)

Archibald MacMechan was a prominent Canadian literary essayist and educator who had briefly corresponded with Melville a decade before publishing this piece in the *Queen's Quarterly* of October 1899. This essay is remarkable for how it sets the tone for how Melville will be appreciated in the revival years, beginning in 1917. MacMechan looks to "reverse [the] judgment in history" and provide "tardy justice" for a reputation fallen into neglect. Students should be careful when citing MacMechan, however, as he is not always right on the facts. For example, MacMechan gets Melville's age wrong. Several of the writers collected in this volume attempt to provide quick, thumbnail sketches of the literary output and life of the author before essential papers and facts were gathered in books such as Jay Leda's *The Melville Log*, an important 1951 documentary charting of the author's life. Students using these excerpts and critical commentaries are encouraged to cross-check facts with even more recent biographical sources, such as Hershel Parker's two-volume biography. MacMechan is important, though, primarily for focusing critical attention on *Moby-Dick*; he calls Melville "a man of one book," which, if a dangerously reductive assertion, is certainly an assessment that has had an impact on Melville's later reception. Students considering the ways Melville differs from other writers who took the sea and seafaring as their primary subject will also find this essay helpful. MacMechan also takes note early on of the absence of women in Melville, an issue with now a very long critical imprint. "There is hardly a flutter of petticoat from chapter first to last," he writes. Finally, students considering Melville's "Americanness" have in MacMechan an important document. Is he right that Melville is "completely detached from the land"? How can this be so if Melville's "large" and "expansive" ideas, "freedom from all scholastic rules and conventions," make him "a Walt Whitman of prose," kin to the good gray poet of democracy? Melville as a representative of America is a rich vein to tap through many of the writings collected here. Comparing

MacMechan's words to those of another non-native, D.H. Lawrence, would be a good place to start.

Anyone who undertakes to reverse some judgment in history or criticism, or to set the public right regarding some neglected man or work, becomes at once an object of suspicion. Nine times out of ten he is called a literary snob for his pains, or a prig who presumes to teach his betters, or a "phrase-monger," or a "young Osric," or something equally soul-subduing. Besides, the burden of proof lies heavy upon him. He preaches to a sleeping congregation. The good public has returned its verdict upon the case, and is slow to review the evidence in favour of the accused, or, having done so, to confess itself in the wrong. Still, difficult as the work of rehabilitation always is, there are cheering instances of its complete success; notably, the rescue of the Elizabethan dramatists by Lamb and Hazlitt and Leigh Hunt. Nor in such a matter is the will always free. As Heine says, ideas take possession of us and force us into the arena, there to fight for them. There is also the possibility of triumph to steel the raw recruit against all dangers. Though the world at large may not care, the judicious few may be glad of new light, and may feel satisfaction in seeing even tardy justice meted out to real merit. In my poor opinion much less than justice has been done to an American writer, whose achievement is so considerable that it is hard to account for the neglect into which he has fallen.

This writer is Herman Melville, who died in New York in the autumn of 1891, aged eighty-three. That his death excited little attention is in consonance with the popular apathy towards him and his work. The civil war marks a dividing line in his literary production as well as in his life. His best work belongs to the *ante-bellum* days, and is cut off in taste and sympathy from the distinctive literary fashions of the present time. To find how complete neglect is, one has only to put question to the most cultivated and patriotic Americans north or south, east or west, even professed specialists in the nativist literature, and it will be long before the Melville enthusiast meets either sympathy or understanding. The present writer made his first acquaintance with *Moby Dick* in the dim, dusty Mechanics' Institute Library (opened once a week by the old doctor) of an obscure Canadian village, nearly twenty years ago; and since that time he has seen only one copy of the book exposed for sale, and met only one person (and that not an American) who had read it. Though Kingsley has a good word for Melville, the only place where real appreciation of him is to be found of recent years is in one of Mr. Clark Russell's dedications.

There occurs the phrase which gives this paper its title. Whoever takes the trouble to read this unique and original book will concede that Mr. Russell knows whereof he affirms.

Melville is a man of one book, and this fact accounts possibly for much of his unpopularity. The marked inferiority of his work after the war, as well as changes in literary fashion, would drag the rest down with it. Nor are his earliest works, embodying personal experience like *Redburn* and *White Jacket*, quite worthy of the pen which wrote *Moby Dick*. *Omoo* and *Typee* are little more than sketches, legitimately idealized, of his own adventures in the Marquesas. They are notable works in that they are the first to reveal to civilized people the charm of life in the islands of the Pacific, the charm which is so potent in *Vailima Letters* and *The Beach of Falesá*. Again, the boundless archipelagos of Oceanica furnish the scenes of *Mardi*, his curious political satire. This contains a prophecy of the war, and a fine example of obsolete oratory in the speech of the great chief Alanno from Hio-Hio. The prologue in a whale-ship and the voyage in an open boat are, perhaps, the most interesting parts. None of his books are without distinct and peculiar excellences, but nearly all have some fatal fault. Melville's seems a case of arrested literary development. The power and promise of power in his best work are almost unbounded; but he either did not care to follow them up or he had worked out all his rifts of ore. The last years of his life he spent as a recluse.

His life fitted him to write his one book. The representative of a good old Scottish name, his portrait shows distinctively Scottish traits. The head is the sort that goes naturally with a tall, powerful figure. The forehead is broad and square; the hair is abundant; the full beard masks the mouth and chin; the general aspect is of great but disciplined strength. The eyes are level and determined; they have speculation in them. Nor does his work belie his blood. It shows the natural bent of the Scot towards metaphysics; and this thoughtfulness is one pervading quality of Melville's books. In the second place, his family had been so long established in the country (his grandfather was a member of the "Boston tea-party") that he secured the benefits of education and inherited culture: and this enlightenment was indispensable in enabling him to perceive the literary "values" of the strange men, strange scenes and strange events amongst which he was thrown. And then, he had the love of adventure which drove him forth to gather his material at the ends of the earth. He made two voyages; first as a green hand of eighteen in one of the old clipper packets to Liverpool and back; and next, as a young man of twenty-three, in a whaler. The latter was sufficiently adventurous. Wearying of sea-life, he deserted on one of the Marquesas Islands, and came near being killed and eaten by cannibal natives who kept him prisoner for four months. At last he escaped, and worked his way home on a U.S. man-o'-war. This adventure lasted four years and he went no more to sea.

After his marriage, he lived at Pittsfield for thirteen years, in close intimacy with Hawthorne, to whom he dedicated his chief work. My copy shows that it was written as early as 1851, but the title page is dated exactly twenty years later. It shows as its three chief elements this Scottish thoughtfulness, the love of literature and the love of adventure.

When Mr. Clark Russell singles out *Moby Dick* for such high praise as he bestows upon it, we think at once of other sea-stories,—his own, Marryatt's, Smollet's perhaps, and such books as Dana's *Two Years before the Mast.* But the last is a plain record of fact; in Smollet's tales, sea-life is only part of one great round of adventure; in Mr. Russell's mercantile marine, there is generally the romantic interest of the way of a man with a maid; and in Marryatt's the rise of a naval officer through various ranks plus a love-story or plenty of fun, fighting and prize-money. From all these advantages Melville not only cuts himself off, but seems to heap all sorts of obstacles in his self appointed path. Great are the prejudices to be overcome; but he triumphs over all. Whalers are commonly regarded as a sort of sea-scavengers. He convinces you that their business is poetic; and that they are finest fellows afloat. He dispenses with a love-story altogether; there is hardly a flutter of petticoat from chapter first to last. The book is not a record of fact; but of fact idealized, which supplies the frame for a terrible duel to the death between a mad whaling-captain and a miraculous white sperm whale. It is not a love-story but a story of undying hate.

In no other tale is one so completely detached from the land, even from the very suggestion of land. Though Nantucket and New Bedford must be mentioned, only their nautical aspects are touched on; they are but the steps of the saddle-block from which the mariner vaults upon the back of his sea-horse. The strange ship "Pequod" is the theatre of all the strange adventures. For ever off soundings, she shows but as a central speck in a wide circle of blue or stormy sea; and yet a speck crammed full of human passions, the world itself in little. Comparison brings out only more strongly the unique character of the book. Whaling is the most peculiar business done by man upon the deep waters. A war-ship is but a mobile fort or battery; a merchantman is but a floating shop or warehouse: fishing is devoid of any but the ordinary perils of navigation; but sperm-whaling, according to Melville, is the most exciting and dangerous kind of big game hunting. One part of the author's triumph consists in having made the complicated operations of this strange pursuit perfectly familiar to the reader; and that not in any dull, pedantic fashion, but touched with the imagination, the humor, the fancy, the reflection of a poet. His intimate knowledge of his subject and his intense interest in it make the whaler's life in all its details not only comprehensible but fascinating.

A bare outline of the story, though it cannot suggest its peculiar charm, may arouse a desire to know more about it. The book takes its name from a monstrous, invincible, sperm whale of diabolical strength and malice. In an encounter with this leviathan, Ahab, the captain of a Nantucket whaler, has had his leg torn off. The long illness which ensues drives him mad; and his one thought upon recovery is vengeance upon the creature that has mutilated him. He gets command of the "Pequod," concealing his purpose with the cunning of insanity until the fitting moment comes: then he swears the whole crew into his fatal vendetta. From this point on, the mad captain bears down all opposition, imposes his own iron will upon the ship's company, and affects them with like heat, until they are as one keen weapon fitted to his hand and to his purpose. In spite of all difficulties, in spite of all signs and portents and warnings, human and divine, he drives on to certain destruction. Everything conduces to one end, a three day's battle with the monster, which staves and sinks the ship, like the ill-fated "Essex."

For a tale of such length, *Moby Dick* is undoubtedly well constructed. Possibly the "Town-Ho's Story," interesting as it is, somewhat checks the progress of the plot; but by the time the reader reaches this point, he is infected with the leisurely, trade-wind, whaling atmosphere, and has no desire to proceed faster than at the "Pequod's" own cruising rate. Possibly the book might be shortened by excision, but when one looks over the chapters it is hard to decide which to sacrifice. The interest begins with the quaint words of the opening sentence: "Call me Ishmael"; and never slackens for at least a hundred pages. Ishmael's reasons for going to sea, his sudden friendship with Queequeg, the Fijian harpooneer, Father Mapple's sermon on Jonah, in the seamen's bethel, Queequeg's rescue of the country bumpkin on the way to Nantucket, Queequeg's Ramadan, the description of the ship "Pequod" and her two owners, Elijah's warning, getting under way and dropping the pilot, make up an introduction of great variety and picturesqueness. The second part deals with all the particulars of the various operations in whaling from manning the mast-heads and lowering the boats to trying out the blubber and cleaning up the ship, when all the oil is barrelled. In this part Ahab, who has been invisible in the retirement of his cabin, comes on deck and in various scenes different sides of his vehement, iron-willed, yet pathetic nature, are made intelligible. Here also is much learning to be found, and here, if anywhere, the story dawdles. The last part deals with the fatal three days' chase, the death of Ahab, and the escape of the White Whale.

One striking peculiarity of the book is its Americanism—a word which needs definition. The theme and style are peculiar to this country. Nowhere but in America could such a theme have been treated in such a style. Whaling is peculiarly an American industry; and of all whalemen, the Nantucketers were the keenest, the most daring, and the most successful. Now, though there are still whalers to be found in the New Bedford slips, and interesting as it is to clamber about them and hear the unconscious confirmation of all Melville's details from the lips of some old harpooneer or boat-header, the industry is almost extinct. The discovery of petroleum did for it. Perhaps Melville went to sea for no other purpose than to construct the monument of whaling in this unique book. Not in his subject alone, but in his style is Melville distinctly American. It is large in idea, expansive; it has an Elizabethan force and freshness and swing, and is, perhaps, more rich in figures than any style but Emerson's. It has the picturesqueness of the new world, and, above all, a free-flowing humour, which is the distinct *cachet* of American literature. No one would contend that it is a perfect style; some mannerisms become tedious, like the constant moral turn, and the curiously coined adverbs placed before the verb. Occasionally there is more than a hint of bombast, as indeed might be expected; but, upon the whole, it is an extraordinary style, rich, clear, vivid, original. It shows reading and is full of thought and allusion; but its chief charm is its freedom from all scholastic rules and conventions. Melville is a Walt Whitman of prose.

Like Browning he has a dialect of his own. The poet of *The Ring and the Book* translates the different emotions and thoughts and possible words of pope, jurist, murderer, victim, into one level uniform Browningese; reduces them to a common denominator, in a way of speaking, and Melville gives us not the actual words of American whalemen, but what they would say under the imagined conditions, translated into one consistent, though various Melvillesque manner of speech. The life he deals with belongs already to the legendary past, and he has us completely at his mercy. He is completely successful in creating his "atmosphere." Granted the conditions, the men and their words, emotions and actions, are all consistent. . . .

The humour has the usual tinge of Northern melancholy, and sometimes a touch of Rabelais. The exhortations of Stubb to his boat's crew, on different occasions, or such chapters as "Queen Mab," "The Cassock," "Leg and Arm," "Stubb's Supper," are good examples of his peculiar style.

But, after all, his chief excellence is bringing to the landsman the very salt of the sea breeze, while to one who has long known the ocean, he is as one praising to the lover the chiefest beauties of the Beloved. The magic of the ship and the mystery of the sea are put into words that form pictures for the dullest eyes. The chapter, "The Spirit Spout," contains these two aquarelles of the moonlit sea and the speeding ship side by side:

> It was while gliding through these latter waters that one serene and moonlight night, when all the waves rolled by like scrolls of silver; and by their soft, suffusing seethings all things made what seemed a silvery silence, not a solitude; on such a silent night a silvery jet was seen far in advance of the white bubbles at the bow. Lit up by the moon it looked celestial; seemed some plumed and glittering god uprising from the sea…
>
> Walking the deck, with quick, side-lunging strides, Ahab commanded the t'gallant sails and royals to be set, and every stunsail spread. The best man in the ship must take the helm. Then, with every mast-head manned, the piled-up craft rolled down before the wind. The strange, upheaving, lifting tendency of the taffrail breeze filling the hollows of so many sails made the buoyant, hovering deck to feel like air beneath the feet.

In the chapter called "The Needle," ship and sea and sky are blended in one unforgettable whole:

> Next morning the not-yet-subsided sea rolled in long, slow billows of mighty bulk, and striving in the "Pequod's" gurgling track, pushed her on like giants' palms outspread. The strong, unstaggering breeze abounded so, that sky and air seemed vast outbellying sails; the whole world boomed before the wind. Muffled in the full morning light, the invisible sun was only known by the spread intensity of his place; where his bayonet rays moved on in stacks. Emblazonings, as of crowned Babylonian kings and queens, reigned over everything. The sea was a crucible of molten gold, that bubblingly leaps with light and heat.

It would be hard to find five consecutive sentences anywhere containing such pictures and such vivid, pregnant, bold imagery: but this book is made up of such things.

The hero of the book is, after all, not Captain Ahab, but his triumphant antagonist, the mystic white monster of the sea, and it is only fitting that he should come for a moment at least into the saga. A complete scientific memoir of the Sperm Whale as known to man might be quarried from this book, for Melville has described the creature from his birth to his death, and even burial in the oil casks and the ocean. He has described him living, dead and anatomized. . . .

This book is at once the epic and the encyclopaedia of whaling. It is a monument to the honour of an extinct race of daring seamen; but it is a monument overgrown with the lichen of neglect. Those who will care to scrape away the moss may be few, but they will have their reward. To the class of gentleman-adventurer, to those who love both books and free life under the wide and open sky, it must always appeal. Melville takes rank with Borrow, and Jefferies, and Thoreau, and Sir Richard Burton; and his place in this brotherhood of notables is not the lowest. Those who feel the salt in their blood that draws them time and again out of the city to the wharves and the ships, almost without their knowledge or their will; those who feel the irresistible lure of the spring, away from the cramped and noisy town, up the long road to the peaceful companionship of the awaking earth and the untainted sky; all those—and they are many—will find in Melville's great book an ever fresh and constant charm.

—Archibald MacMechan, "The Best Sea Story Ever Written," *Queen's Quarterly*, October 1899, pp. 120–30

Joseph Conrad (1907)

Conrad is one of the great and prolific writers of sea literature. Student readers may know him best from *Heart of Darkness* and *Lord Jim*. Here, Conrad's seemingly offhand dismissal of Melville's importance allows an opportunity for students to scrutinize Conrad's word choice. Note that he merely "opens" Melville's books and then does not go "further." Did he give the books a chance? Also, is it fair to Melville to say that he takes "whaling" as his subject? Something more is going on here. On one hand, Conrad may prefer his own narrative strategies, his own complexly serious experimentation in narrative structure and voice. On the other hand, Conrad's dismissal of Melville seems a powerful, quasi-public example of one writer disavowing an influence—an example of one strong writer refusing to recognize an important precursor in the tradition. We actually do not know the depth of Conrad's real investment in Melville's writing, and students intent on measuring the veracity of these words should remember that the Melville revival is still a decade away. In 1907 Melville's book may not have been able to deliver anxiety to the author of *The Secret Sharer.*

Years ago I looked into *Typee* and *Omoo,* but as I didn't find there what I am looking for when I open a book I did go no further. Lately I had in my hand *Moby Dick.* It struck me as a rather strained rhapsody with whaling for a subject and not a single sincere line in the 3 vols of it.

—Joseph Conrad, Letter to Humphrey Milford
(January 15, 1907)

Frank Jewett Mather Jr. "Herman Melville" (1919)

Frank Jewett Mather Jr. lauds *Moby-Dick*, claiming that this "extraordinary work in morals" reveals Melville's strength emerging from "the interplay of fact and application." Fact, according to Mather, "betokens" for Melville the complexities of "our moral life." Students examining how Melville deploys commonplace (and fabulous) nautical occurrences in the service of symbolism and allegory will find Mather (and the Weaver excerpt that follows it) indispensable reading. Mather differs from many other early reviewers of Melville's prose in deeming "the preachments" to be inseparable from the value of the prose.

Moby Dick has the tremendous advantage of its concreteness. Captain Ahab's mad quest of the white whale imposes itself as real, and progressively enlists and appalls the imagination. Out of the mere stray episodes and minor characters of *Moby Dick* a literary reputation might be made. The retired Nantucket captains, Bildad and Peleg, might have stepped out of Smollett. Father Mapple's sermon on the Book of Jonah is in itself a masterpiece, and I know few sea tales which can hold their own with the blood feud of Mate Radney and sailor Steelkilt. The style still has the freshness and delicate power of *Typee*, but is subtler. Take the very modern quality of a passage which a Loti might envy:

> It was while gliding through these latter waters that one serene and moonlight night, when all the waves rolled by like scrolls of silver; and by their soft, suffusing seethings, made what seemed a

silvery silence, not a solitude; on such a silent night a silvery jet was seen far in advance of the white bubbles at the bow. Lit up by the moon, it looked celestial; seemed some plumed and glittering god uprising from the sea.

There is also a harsher note befitting the theme. The tang of it is in the passage with which this essay opened. The tragic and almost incredible motive of the quest of the demon whale gains credibility from the solid basis of fact, as mad captain Ahab himself is based, so to speak, on his ivory leg. The insane adventure itself grows real through the actuality of its participants: Was there ever such a trio as the savage harpooners? Their very names, Feddallah, Tashetego, Queequeg, are a guarantee of good faith. A reader instinctively hurrahs at the deeds of such mates as Starbuck and Stubbs while with them he cowers under the fateful eye of Captain Ahab. Throughout the book are shudders, sympathies, and laughs.

But *Moby Dick* is more than what it undisputedly is, the greatest whaling novel. It is an extraordinary work in morals and general comment. In the discursive tradition of Fielding and the anatomist of melancholy, Melville finds a suggestion or a symbol in each event and fearlessly pursues the line of association. As he and Queequeg plait a mat on the same warp, the differing woofs and resulting surfaces become a symbol for man's free will asserting itself against the background of fate. Such reflections are in a grave, slow-moving style in which Burton has counted for much and Carlyle for something. It is the interplay of fact and application that makes the unique character of the book. As for the Christian fathers the visible world was merely a similitude or foreshadowing of the eternal world, so for Melville the voyage of the Pequod betokens our moral life in the largest sense. . . .

Cut out the preachments, and you will have a great novel, some readers say. Yes, but not a great Melville novel. The preachments are the essence. The effect of the book rests on the blend of fact, fancy, and profound reflection, upon a brilliant intermingling of sheer artistry and moralizing at large. It is Kipling before the latter crossed with Sir Thomas Browne, it comprises all the powers and tastes of Herman Melville, is his greatest and most necessary work. So while no one is obliged to like *Moby Dick*—there are those who would hold against Dante his moralizing and against Rabelais his broad humor—let such as do love this rich and towering fabrique adore it wholeheartedly—from stem to stern, athwart ships and from maintruck to keelson.

In a sense *Moby Dick* exhausted Melville's vein. At thirty-two he had put into a single volume all that he had been in action, all that he was to be in thought.

—Frank Jewett Mather Jr., "Herman Melville,"
Review, 1, August 1919, pp. 276–78, 298–301

Raymond Weaver "Herman Melville" (1921)

Raymond Weaver wrote the first book-length literary biography of Melville in 1921, and in this excerpt from that groundbreaking and myth-making book we learn that Melville's allegorical genius in *Moby-Dick* was to slip conventionality and to strike at "the demonism at the cankered heart of nature." Weaver read Melville as a freethinking visionary. Like Mather and other critics in this era of celebrating organic form in *Moby-Dick*, a disconnection between, "literalness" or "fact," on one hand, and the "fantastic" or "the romantic," on the other, is read as a source of the book's power and not as evidence of its faulty or hurried construction. Students looking more closely at *Moby-Dick*'s composition (both the process of writing the book and the final form Melville achieves) have in Weaver and Mather two powerful commentaries on the book's synthetic force. Students might want to compare these two readings with the Lincoln Colcord review that follows.

Melville's third and supreme claim to distinction rests upon a single volume, which, after the order of Melchizedek, is without issue and without descent: 'a work which is not only unique in its kind, and a great achievement' to quote a recent judgment from England, 'but is the expression of an imagination that rises to the highest, and so is amongst the world's great works of art.' This book is, of course, *Moby-Dick*, Melville's undoubted masterpiece. 'In that wild, beautiful romance'—the words are Mr Masefield's—'Melville seems to have spoken the very secret of the sea, and to have drawn into his tale all the magic, all the sadness, all the wild joy of many waters. It stands quite alone; quite unlike any other book known to me. It strikes a note which no other sea writer has ever struck.'

The organising theme of this unparalleled volume is the hunt by the mad Captain Ahab after the great white whale which had dismembered him of his leg; of Captain Ahab's unwearied pursuit by rumour of its whereabouts; of the final destruction of himself and his ship by its savage onslaught. On the white hump of the ancient and vindictive monster Captain Ahab piles the sum of all the rage and hate of mankind from the days of Eden down.

Melville expresses an ironical fear lest his book be scouted 'as a monstrous fable, or still worse and more detestable, a hideous and intolerable allegory.' Yet fabulous allegory it is: an allegory of the demonism at the cankered heart of nature, teaching that 'though in many of its visible aspects the world seems formed in love, the invisible spheres were formed in fright.' Thou shalt know the truth, and the truth shall make you mad. To the eye of truth, so Melville would convince us, 'the palsied universe lies before us as a leper;' 'all deified Nature absolutely paints like a harlot, whose allurements cover nothing but the charnel house within.' To embody this devastating insight, Melville chooses as a symbol, an albino whale. 'Wonder ye then at the fiery hunt?'

An artist who goes out to find sermons in stones does so at the peril of converting his stone pile into his mausoleum. His danger is excessive, if, having his sermons all ready, he makes it his task to find the stones to fit them. Allegory justifies itself only when the fiction is the fact and the moral the induction; only when its representation is as imaginatively real as its meaning; only when the stones are interesting boulders in a rich and diversified landscape. So broadly and vividly is *Moby-Dick* based on solid foundation that even the most literal-minded, innocent of Melville's dark intent, have found this book of the soul's daring and the soul's dread a very worthy volume. One spokesman for this congregation, while admitting that 'a certain absorption of interest lies in the nightmare intensity and melodramatic climax of the tale,' finds his interest captured and held far more by

> the exposition of fact with which the story is loaded to the very gunwale. No living thing on earth or in the waters under the earth is so interesting as the whale. How it is pursued, from the Arctic to the Antarctic; how it is harpooned, to the peril of boat and crew; how, when brought to the side, 'cutting in' is accomplished; how the whale's anatomy is laid bare; how his fat is redeemed—to be told this in the form of a narrative, with all manner of dramatic but perfectly plausible incidents interspersed, is enough to make the book completely engrossing without the white whale and Captain Ahab's fatal monomania.

So diverse are the samples out of which *Moby-Dick* is compounded, yet so masterful is each of its samples, that there is still far from universal agreement as to the ground colour of this rich and towering fabric. Yet by this very disagreement is its miraculous artistry affirmed.

In *Moby-Dick*, all the powers and tastes of Melville's complex genius are blended. *Moby-Dick* is at once indisputably the greatest whaling novel, and 'a hideous and intolerable allegory.' As Mr Frank Jewett Mather, Jr has said, 'Out of the mere episodes and minor instances of *Moby-Dick*, a literary reputation might be made. The retired Nantucket captains Bildad and Peleg might have stepped out of Smollett. Father Mapple's sermon on the book of Jonah is in itself a masterpiece, and I know few sea tales that can hold their own with the blood feud of Mate Radney and sailor Steelkilt.' Captain Hook of *Peter Pan* is but Captain Boomer of *Moby-Dick* with another name: and this an identity founded not on surmise, but on Sir James Barrie's professed indebtedness to Melville. There are, in *Moby-Dick*, long digressions, natural, historical and philosophical, on the person, habits, manners and ideas of whales; there are long dialogues and soliloquies such as were never spoken by mortal man in his waking senses, conversations that for sweetness, strength and courage remind one of passages from Dekker, Webster, Massinger, Fletcher and the other old dramatists loved both by Melville and by Charles Lamb; in the discursive tradition of Fielding, Sir Thomas Browne and the anatomist of melancholy, Melville indulges freely in independent moralisings, half essay, half rhapsody; withal, scenes like Ishmael's experience at the 'Spouter-Inn' with a practising cannibal for bed-fellow, are, for finished humour, among the most competent in the language. When Melville sat down to write, always at his knee stood that chosen emissary of Satan, the comic spirit: a demoniac familiar never long absent from his pages.

There are those, of course, who would hold against Dante his moralising, and against Rabelais his broad humour. In like manner, peculiarity of temperament has necessarily coloured critical judgment of *Moby-Dick*. But though critics may mouth it as they like about digressions, improbability, moralising reflections, swollen talk, or the fetish of art now venerated with such articulate inveteracy, all wonderfully agree upon the elementary force of *Moby-Dick*, its vitality, its thrilling power. That it achieves the effect of illusion, and to a degree peculiar to the highest feats of the creative imagination, is incontestable. No writer has more. On this point it is simply impossible to praise Melville too highly. What defects *Moby-Dick* has are formal rather than substantial. As Thackeray once impatiently said of Macaulay: 'What critic can't point them out?' It was the contention of James Thomson that an overweening concern for formal impeccability is a fatal sign of weakened vitality. Intensity of imagination—and Melville exhibited it prodigally in *Moby-Dick*—is an infinitely rarer and more precious gift than technical sophistication. Shakespeare has survived, despite his 'monstrous irregularities.' But since Shakespeare, as Francis Thompson has observed, there has been a gradual decline from imperfection. Milton, at his most typical, was far too perfect; Pope was ruined by his quest for the quality. No thoughtful person can contemplate without alarm the idolatry bestowed upon this quality by the contemporary mind: an idolatry that threatens to reduce all art to the extinction of unendurable excellence. How insipid would be the mere adventures of a Don Quixote recounted by a Stevenson.

The astonishing variety of contradictory qualities synthesised in *Moby-Dick* exists nowhere else in literature, perhaps, in such paradoxical harmony. These qualities, in differences of combination and emphasis, are discoverable, however, in all of Melville's writings. And he published, besides anonymous contributions to periodicals, ten novels and five volumes of poetry (including the two volumes privately printed at the very close of his life). There survives, too, a bulk of manuscript material: a novel, short stories, and a body of verse. And branded on everything that Melville wrote is the mark of the extraordinary personality that created *Moby-Dick*.

—Raymond Weaver, "Herman Melville,"
Herman Melville, Mariner and Mystic,
New York: Doran, 1921, pp. 15–32

Lincoln Colcord "Notes on *Moby Dick*" (1922)

In the following essay, Lincoln Colcord identifies with the sea, and with "real" sailors, which is understandable given the fact that this Mainer (from Penobscot Bay) was actually born at sea, aboard a bark called *The Charlotte A. Littlefield*. Colcord writes during the revival, and students will notice that he seems radically of two minds when discussing Melville. In turns, he lavishes on the author both exuberant praise ("The Whiteness of the Whale" is a prize example of "the magic of literary power") and harsh condemnation (Melville's portrait of a "toy" ship "beset by a heavy circular storm" fails). But this is an important and representative essay. Modernists and critics during the Melville revival were impressed by the organic and symbolic force of Melville's investigation of psychology and tragedy, but still needed to account for formal oddities in the text. Colcord is a great example of this position. He points out that Melville's narrator does not always remain before the reader. Colcord reads the pace shift toward the end of the book, the plunging ruin of the ship and crew, as too sketchily drawn. He objects to the short chapters. He generally points out that the text is not formally a cohesive whole, and in stating such, he gestures to other writers collected here, such as Duyckinck and Olson, who also consider the structure of *Moby-Dick*.

Perhaps most importantly, he finds a lack of "nautical verisimilitude" in the same author MacMechan declares "bringing to the landsman the very salt of the sea breeze." Colcord, a free sailor, a man of the "quarter-deck," does not fully appreciate Melville's "psychology . . . of the Forecastle." Melville's subjection before the "universal thump" of authority, as Ishmael calls it in *Moby-Dick*, creates for Colcord a "void" in the text. Students should keep Colcord's perspective in mind, and remember as well that Colcord writes after the rise of realism and naturalism, unlike Melville. These distinctions help explain Colcord's impatience with Melville's romantic, Hawthornian, and "transcendentalist" approach to verities. Ultimately, though, Colcord forgives all "irregularity" and deems Melville's struggle with art and life replete with "agonizing greatness."

I

Fresh from a second reading of Melville's *Moby Dick*, I am surprised by the heterodoxy of certain strong impressions. It is a book which leads to violent convictions. I first read it as a boy, on shipboard, somewhere about the world; I was enthralled by the story, but beyond a keen sensation of pleasure I retained no definite recollection of it. Thus, upon a second reading, the book had for me all the delight of a new discovery. Again I was enthralled, this time by more than the story; by all the infernal power and movement of the piece, by that intangible quality which, through suggestion and stimulation, gives off the very essence of genius. I do not mean atmosphere—Conrad creates atmosphere—but something above atmosphere, the aura of sublime and tragic greatness; not light but illumination, the glance of a brooding and unappeasable god.

The art of *Moby Dick* as a masterpiece of fiction lies in the element of purposeful suspense which flows through the tale from beginning to end in a constantly swelling current; and in the accumulating grandeur and terror evoked by the whale-*motif*. This achievement which, like every such feat of genius, defies either description or criticism, is what makes the book superlatively great. Melville performs the most difficult task of literary creation—that of encompassing and fixing the vague form of a tremendous visionary conception.

The high-water mark of inspiration in the book is reached in the dramatic dialogue between Ahab and the carpenter over the making of the wooden leg. This scene is preceded by the finest piece of descriptive characterization in the volume, written in Melville's own style (not aped after Sir Thomas Browne): the sketch of the old ship-carpenter. Starting abruptly from the heights of this description, the dialogue soars straight to the realm of pure literary art. It is the equal of Shakespeare's best dialogue. One longs to hear it given by a couple of capable actors: the scene, the confusion of the 'Pequod's' deck by night on the whaling-grounds; the lurid flame of the smithy in the background, in the foreground the old bewhiskered carpenter planing away at Ahab's ivory leg: before the foot-lights an audience familiar with the book, or, lacking this, any intelligent audience, the want of special knowledge being supplied by a plain prologue. The scene exactly as it stands is magnificently dramatic.

This, however, is a burst of inspiration. The ablest piece of sustained writing in *Moby Dick* unquestionably is the extraordinary chapter on 'The Whiteness of the Whale.' Here we have a *tour de force* without excuse in the narrative, a mere joyous rush of exhilaration and power, a throwing out of the arms with a laugh and a flash of the eye. 'The Whiteness of the Whale,' I said to myself, as I came to this chapter; 'what the devil have we now?' I feared that Melville would exceed his licence, that he might be going to strain the case a little. For it seemed an inconsequential heading for a chapter; and when I ran over the leaves, noting how long the effort was, my heart misgave me. But before a page is finished, the reader catches the idea and perceives the masterliness of the attack. Throughout the chapter, as one watches the author play with his theme, letting it rise and fall naturally (nothing is ever still that comes from Melville's hand—even his calms shimmer and shake with an intensity of heat); as one follows this magically dexterous exercise, all of which, apart from its intrinsic beauty, contributes in some ineffable manner to the charm and mystery of the tale; one is aware of the thrill which comes but seldom in a lifetime of reading.

As a piece of sheer writing, this chapter on the whiteness of the whale is a remarkable achievement. Its creator could do anything with words. I wonder that it has not been more commonly utilized in the higher teaching of English; I know of no effort in the language which affords a better study of what can be accomplished by the magic of literary power.

II

Moby Dick stands as one of the great nautical books of the world's literature. What I have to say of it on this score, therefore, may to Melville's public, which is almost exclusively a shore-public, appear to be malicious heresy. But I am concerned only with establishing what seems to me an interesting verity; I want to find the real Melville, because he is so well worth finding; l would not be engaged in criticism had I not first become engaged in love and admiration.

I am surprised, when all is said and done, to find how little of real nautical substance there is in *Moby Dick*. It would not be overstating the case to say that the book lacks the final touch of nautical verisimilitude. In criticizing the book from this viewpoint, one must, of course, make due allowance for the refining and rarifying influence of the imaginative pitch to which the whole work is cast; an influence which naturally tends to destroy a share of nautical realism, as, indeed, it tends to destroy all realism. Yet, when this allowance is made, there remains in *Moby Dick* a certain void, difficult of estimate or description, where the shadows, at least, of nautical reality should stand.

This void, of course, appears only to the sailor who reads the book; no one else would notice it. It is not that the book lacks the framework of nautical reality; it would be idle for me to attempt to deny what plainly exists. *Moby Dick*, indeed, is in the generic sense of the term a nautical piece; it is a tale of ships, sailing, and the sea. We have a view of the 'Pequod,' of certain seafaring scenes and operations; we have a picture of the business of whaling, the handling of boats, the cutting in of the great fish alongside the ship, the final labours on deck and in the hold; we have a general background of nautical affairs, so that the scenes inevitably stand out against a tracery of sails, clouds, horizon and sea; and all this is correctly written, from the nautical standpoint, save in a few insignificant particulars. Melville's treatment of the whaling-industry, in fact, is classic. No one else has done such work, and no one ever will do it again; it alone serves to rescue from oblivion one of the most extraordinary episodes of human enterprise.

But this fidelity to the business of whaling is not precisely what I mean by nautical verisimilitude. How, then, shall I define the lack of this verisimilitude which I find in *Moby Dick*? Shall I put it that there is not quite enough of sure detail, in any instance where a nautical scene or evolution is described, to convince the sailor-reader that the man who wrote the words understood with full instinctive knowledge what he was writing about? A sailor, a seaman in the real sense of the word, would involuntarily have followed so closely the scene or evolution in hand, that he could not have fallen short of the final touch of realism; he would himself have been apart of the picture, he would quite unconsciously have written from that point of view, and the added colour and particularity, in the case of *Moby Dick*, far from detracting from the strength and purpose of the work, would on the contrary have considerably augmented them.

Melville, quite unconsciously, did not write the book that way. To his eye, indeed, it plainly was not so much a nautical work as it was a study in the boundless realm of human psychology. Yet, having taken the sea for his background, he could not have failed, had he been a sailor, to fill the void I mention. From this one gets a measure of Melville's spiritual relation to seafaring.

Most mysteries submit to a simple explanation; they are no mysteries at all. In the present case, a closer view of seafaring alone is needed. All Melville's seafaring experience lay before the mast. He gives no indication that he was in the least degree interested in this experience as a romantic profession; he speaks, of obeying orders, admitting that those who commanded his activities on the sea had a right to require him to do anything under the sun; but I have never seen a passage in which he celebrated the task of learning to be a good seaman—except as a piece of extraneous description—or one showing the slightest interest in the sea professionally. He was decidedly not looking towards the quarterdeck. When afloat, he seems simply to have been mooning around the vessel, indulging his fancy to the full, chiefly observing human nature; realistically intent on the ship's company, but merely romanticizing over the ship herself, in short, not making any advance towards becoming himself a sailor, towards the acquisition of those instinctive reactions which make man and ship dual parts of the same entity.

I would not be thought so absurd as to blame Melville for not becoming a true sailor; I am merely trying to run the fact to earth. He was divinely inefficient as a seaman; he never learned the lore of a ship, beyond attaining the necessary familiarity with her external parts, with the execution of simple commands and with the broader features of her control and operation. His nautical psychology was that of the forecastle, the psychology of obeying orders. For months on end, at sea, he felt no curiosity to know where the ship was or whither she was going; he never understood exactly why she was made to perform certain evolutions; he helped to execute the order, and watched the result with a mild and romantic perplexity. The psychology of the quarterdeck, the psychology of handling a vessel, was foreign to him.

This is why his nautical atmosphere is made up of relatively unimportant details and insignificant evolutions, such as a green man before the mast would have compassed; while infinitely more important details and more significant evolutions, and the grasp of the whole ship as a reality, all of which would have been in the direct line of the narrative, and would only have intensified the effect he was striving to produce, were passed over in silence because they were beyond his ken. He might have made the ship, as well as the whale, contribute to the mysterious grandeur of the book's main theme; in no single instance does he attempt to do so. The 'Pequod,' to all intents and purposes, is a toy ship; when, indeed, she is not a ship nautically fictitious, a land-lubber's ship, a ship doing the impossible.

If Captain Ahab says 'Brace the yards!' once, he says it a hundred times; whereas there are dozens of commands that he might have shouted with stronger effect, both realistic and literary; whereas, furthermore, the order to 'brace the yards' means nothing in particular, without a qualifying direction, and never would be given in this incomplete form on a ship's deck. This is a minor instance; but the sum of these nautical ineptitudes throughout the book is fairly staggering.

To cite a major instance, the account of the typhoon off the coast of Japan is a sad failure; it might have been written by one of your Parisian arm-chair romanticists, with a knowledge of the sea derived from a bathing-beach experience. The ship is an imaginary piece of mechanism; no coherent sense of the storm itself is created; no realization of the behaviour of a vessel in a typhoon runs behind the pen. Ahab's battered quadrant, thrown to the deck and trampled on the day before, is allowed to come through the storm reposing as it fell, so that his eye may be caught by it there when the weather has cleared. In fact, both as a piece of writing and as an essential of the tale, the scene wholly fails to justify itself. It serves no apparent purpose; it seems to have been lugged in by the ears.

How a man with an experience of some years on the sea, a man who could write the superlative chapter on the whiteness of the whale, should fail so completely to present an adequate or even an understanding picture of a ship beset by a heavy circular storm—here is a mystery not so easy of solution. It would seem to be plainly evident that Melville had never passed through a typhoon, and never, probably, had been on the Japan whaling-grounds. But he must have seen plenty of storms at sea. With all his passionate descriptive power, however, he is strangely handicapped when he comes to imagine a scene beyond the range of his experience; his literary equipment did not readily lend itself to the translation of an imaginative picture in terms of reality.

Certainly Melville had in his blood none of the 'feeling of the sea,' that subtle reaction which is the secret animating spring of the real sailor. Romantic appreciation he had, and imaginative sentiment; but these must never be confounded with seamanship. Yet, in defence of his nautical laxity in the latter half of *Moby Dick*, it should be recognized that, by the time he had reached these chapters, he must have been exhausted with the intensity of the emotional effort; and that, after juggling with forms for two-thirds of the volume, he had now definitely forsaken all attempts at realism. Ahab alone would have worn out an ordinary man in short order.

III

I do not remember having seen in print a discussion of the extraordinary technical development of *Moby Dick*. In terms of the craft of writing, the book is a surpassing feat of legerdemain. Briefly, *Moby Dick* is the only piece of fiction I know of, which at one and the same time is written in the first and the third persons. It opens straightforwardly as first-person narration. 'Call me Ishmael'—'I thought I would sail about a little'—'I stuffed a shirt or two into my carpet bag, tucked it under my arm, and started for Cape Horn and the Pacific.' So it runs throughout the opening scenes in New Bedford and Nantucket; the characters are real persons, seen through Ishmael's eyes; they speak real speech; the scenes are delineated with subjective realism. Melville is telling a story. His (or Ishmael's) meeting with Queequeg, and their first night together in the big feather bed at the Spouter Inn, are intensely human and alive. Even Bildad and Peleg are creations of realism. The first note of fancifulness is introduced with the Ancient Mariner who accosts Ishmael and Queequeg on the pier in Nantucket. The book, however, still holds to the technical channel of first person narration; and it is through Ishmael's eyes that one sees the 'Pequod' sail from Nantucket.

Then, without warning, the narrative in Chapter twenty-nine jumps from the first to the third person; begins to relate conversations which could not possibly have been overheard by Ishmael and to describe scenes which his eye could not possibly have seen; follows Ahab into his cabin and Starbuck into the recesses of his mind, and launches boldly on that sea of mystical soliloquy and fanciful unreality across which it sweeps for the remainder of the tale. As it progresses, Ishmael sinks farther and farther from sight, and the all-seeing eye of the third person comes more and more into play.

Yet, even at this stage, the technical form of first person narration is not entirely abandoned; is kept along, as it were, like an attenuated wraith. As the 'Pequod' sights ship after ship, the narrative momentarily reappears, only to be discarded once more at the first opportunity; so that, of the main body of the book, it may truly be said that it is written in both the first and the third persons. For instance, chapter ninety-one. 'The "Pequod" Meets the "Rosebud"': 'It was a week or two after the last whaling-scene recounted, and when we [not they] were slowly sailing over a sleepy, vapoury, midday sea. . . .' This is a recurrence to first person narration in the midst of pages of third-person soliloquy. But turning to Chapter CXXVIII, 'The "Pequod" Meets the "Rachel"': 'Next day, a large ship, the "Rachel," was descried, bearing directly down upon the "Pequod," all her spars thickly clustering with men'—this might be either first or third person; the context shows it to be the latter. Ishmael has been definitely forsaken, and hereafter remains in abeyance until the end of the book; when, suddenly, he reemerges in the epilogue.

The quarrel between the persons, however, does not by any means comprise the whole technical irregularity of *Moby Dick*. There is the introduction of the form of dramatic dialogue; an innovation singularly successful, and remarkably in keeping both with the mood of the moment when it is introduced and with the general tone of mystical formlessness pervading the whole work. There is the adroit suspending of the narrative by those absorbing chapters of plain exposition, descriptive of whales and whaling: the gradual revealing of the secrets of the whale, while the final nameless secret is withheld, while fancy and terror feed and grow on suspense. There is the totally ideal development of the characterization, as Ahab and Starbuck and Stubbs and all the rest indulge themselves in the most high-flown and recondite reflections and soliloquies. Finally, there is the bizarre method of chaptering—each chapter a little sketch, each incident having its own chapter; some of the chapters only half a page in length, others a page or two; a hundred and thirty-five chapters in all, together with forewords on etymology and extracts, and an epilogue. In short, *Moby Dick* as a technical exercise is utterly fantastic and original. Melville has departed from every known form of composition; or rather, he has jumbled many forms into a new relation, choosing among them as fancy dictated.

It is safe to say that no literary craftsman of the present day would so much as dream of attempting the experiment which *Moby Dick* discloses on its technical side. Such an attempt would be answered by both critics and public with the ostracism which modern Western culture reserves for irregularity. Here we have a striking commentary on the rigidity of our present literary technique; a technique which rules style and matter, and dominates the literary field, as never before. We speak of ourselves as individualists, freely developing new forms; we like to regard the period of 1840 as a time of stilted and circumscribed literary expression. Yet the truth of the matter seems to be quite otherwise. We are slaves to the success of a literary convention, while the writers of 1840 were relatively free. I am not aware that *Moby Dick* was received at the time of its publication with any degree of surprise at its technical form, whatever surprise or opposition may have been called forth by its content. Neither am I aware that Melville himself felt that he was doing an extraordinary thing in adopting a unique but natural technical form for the expression of an original creative effort. His letters to Hawthorne during the composition of *Moby Dick* betray no self-consciousness on this score. In fact, he seems to have retained a perfectly free relation with his technical medium.

IV

The exhaustion in the latter part of *Moby Dick*, of which I have already spoken, seems to me to become startlingly apparent at the crisis of the book, which is reached in the last chapter. Cavilous as the criticism may sound from the viewpoint of a broader appreciation, I sincerely feel that Melville failed to reap in his crisis all that he had sown throughout the body of the tale. The chase of the white whale is splendid; in the daily fight between Ahab and this sinister embodiment of evil Melville is at his best, everything goes magnificently up to the very last; but the final attack of Moby Dick on the ship, and the sinking of the 'Pequod' with all her company, are inadequate to the point of anti-climax.

There should have been a more generous descriptive effort at this pass; Melville could picture a scene superbly, and he should have spared no pains to do it here. He seems instead to have adopted an affectation of simplicity. He will rest on his oars now, let the momentum of the book carry it forward, allow the various lines of suspense and horror to culminate of their own accord; in fine, he will sketch the winding up of the piece, leaving the actual descriptive effort to the reader's imagination.

But in this he made a critical error; while it is a fine thing to utilize the reader's imagination, it is disastrous to tax it too far. The last pages of *Moby Dick* do not give us the ending for which we have been prepared; which, with the keenest anticipation, we have been awaiting. Having created such intense suspense, Melville was under the imperative obligation to provide for its satisfaction a flash of equally intense realism. The imagination, having too readily devoured the feast that he has set forth, and finding its hunger only increased thereby, is suddenly let down and disappointed. In this unhappy, defrauded state, it fastens upon the first thing at hand, which is the catastrophe itself; recognizing at once the fantastic nature of that complete oblivion which so causelessly descends on the 'Pequod' and her company. For, as a matter of sober fact, a ship of her size would not, in sinking, have drawn down into her vortex an agile cat, much less a crew of whalers, used to being pitched out of boats in the open sea, and surrounded with quantities of dunnage for them to ride when the decks had gone from under.

Turning to the last chapter of *Moby Dick*, one may note that it contains but a brief paragraph describing the whale's frantic attack on the vessel. No horror is created, no suspense, no feverish excitement. It is another of art's vanished opportunities. There should have been a close-packed page or two of tumultuous visualization; then, with the gigantic whale dashing head-on toward the devoted 'Pequod,' a pause in the narrative, to let suspense rankle, while a few paragraphs were occupied with a dissertation on the sinking of vessels—not the sinking of vessels by whales, which matter has already been examined, but the sinking of vessels; about how difficult, how unusual, it would be for a ship to carry her whole company beneath the waves; about Starbuck's knowledge of this fact; about their frantic preparations for escape—then, loosing every ounce of reserve literary power, a description of the crash, the catastrophe, the peculiar and malignant combination of circumstances, easily to be imagined, which, in spite of common experience, did actually destroy this whole ship's company. The whale should have dashed among the debris and floating men, after the ship had gone down, to complete the work of destruction. The scene should have been cast in the form of first person narration, and Ishmael should have been near enough to see it all. (He was adrift, it will be remembered, and did not go down with the vessel; but the return to the first person is reserved for the epilogue, while the crisis of the story is told in an especially vague form of the third person.) We should have been given a final view of the white whale, triumphantly leaving the scene and resuming the interrupted course of his destiny. In short, there are dozens of strokes of realism neglected in this chapter which plainly demand to be driven home.

Melville chose to end the book on a note of transcendentalism; he himself does not seem to have visualized the scene at all. The influence of Hawthorne, one suspects, was largely responsible for this grave error. Hawthorne was living just over the hill in the Berkshires that summer. The intense and lonely Melville had fallen under his fascination; he thought that he had at last found a friend. He was captivated, also, by that vague imaginative method of thought and style out of which Hawthorne wove his tales; and, quite naturally, his own work reflected this influence. For Melville was that man of genius known as the passionate hunter; he was the taster of all sensations, the searcher of all experience, the sampler of every form and style. And, as so often happens with such people, it was his tragic fate never entirely to find himself. The secret quarry of life constantly eluded him.

The influence of Hawthorne is painfully evident throughout the last two-thirds of *Moby Dick*; painfully evident, because it is so incongruous with

Melville's natural manner which is that of narrative realism; he must be there in person—he makes the scene alive with amazing vitality where he stands. In the same sense, his natural power of characterization is in the descriptive or analytical field; I am not aware that he has ever put into the mouth of a single character a realistic speech. Wherever, in *Moby Dick*, he gets his best effects, he gets them through the exercise of his natural manner. Certain scenes stand out vividly. Certain pages of analytical characterization are instinct with truth and greatness. The natural impulse keeps bursting through. But the bulk of the characterization is cast in a method artificial to him; he constantly tries to raise the pitch of the tale, to inflate the value of the words. Too much of the descriptive matter likewise is forced through unnatural channels, losing the air of mastery in its adaptation to the less vigorous form of the third person.

Thus the book, in its composition, represents a struggle between realism and mysticism, between a natural and an artificial manner. It begins naturally, it ends artificially. This in a measure explains the strange confusion of the technique, the extravagant use of the two separate persons. Only the most extraordinary creative power could have struck art and achievement from such an alien blend.

What, then, of the allegory?—for we are told that *Moby Dick* is a masterpiece of this form of composition. I must confess that I did not follow the allegory closely, and did not find that it was forced on my attention; and now that I look back on the book, I fail exactly to see wherein it lies. What, for instance, does Ahab represent, and what the white whale? I am not certain that Melville meant the story to be an allegory. In fact, does he not somewhere fiercely disclaim the imputation? But it is the fate of all work done in the manner of transcendentalism to land sooner or later in the rarified atmosphere of allegory, whether it means anything or not, whether or not the allegory seems to point anywhere in particular. Transcendentalism is the stuff of allegory. Melville hated allegory, and would have hated transcendentalism, had he not just then happened to come under the influence of a transcendentalist. This put him in a bad fix, and made him, whether he willed it or not, write a book which looked like allegory. Do we need a better explanation of his turning so fiercely against the imputation?

Not because of its allegorical significance, and not, indeed, because of its mysticism, considered as a thing apart, does this book of the chase of the white whale live among the immortal works of literature; but rather because of its irrepressible triumph of realism over mysticism, because of the inspired and gripping story that builds itself up out of a passionate flow of words. For my part, I like Ahab as Ahab, not as a symbol of something or other; and Ahab lives as Ahab, marvellously enough, in spite of the wild unreality of his constant meditations and ebullitions. Yes, and because of it; the overshadowing demoniac terror of the story lends reality to unreality, charm and substance to mystical formlessness. This is the mark of genius in the creator. Yet even genius may carry things too far, Ahab manages to live as Ahab, but Starbuck—well Starbuck struts and swells a little, betrayed by an overdose of transcendentalism.

V

If I have seemed to wish that *Moby Dick* had been written in the form of unalloyed narrative realism, that Melville had left off altogether his dalliance with transcendentalism, I would correct the impression now. As a piece of pure realism, the book obviously would not have been the inspired achievement that it is in its present form. The creative struggle that Melville was undergoing at the time of its composition was the intensifying medium through which the work rose to superlative heights. The chapters flow easily, as though he did not realize their duality of form and temper, but felt them to be parts of a unified, continuous product; but the grievous battle taking place within him caused him to produce what actually are gigantic fragments, struck from mountains of fire and anguish, which slowly and ponderously arrange themselves into the delineation of a majestic idea.

Moby Dick is not the allegory of Ahab's struggle with destiny; it is rather the story of Melville's struggle with art and life. Without this struggle, there would have been no agonizing greatness; only another *Typee*, a splendid tale, a perfect example of literary realism. But, given the struggle, there had to be from page to page this singular conflict in style and form and matter, the confused, reflected gleams of a hidden conflagration; so that to wish the conflict away would be to wish away the book's divinity.

—Lincoln Colcord, "Notes on *Moby Dick*," *Freeman*, 5, August 1922, pp. 559–62, 585–87

D.H. Lawrence
"Herman Melville's *Moby Dick*" (1923)

While D.H. Lawrence is best known for poetry collected in books such as *Birds, Beast, and Flowers* and for novels such as *Women in Love*, his *Studies in Classical American Literature* has left an indelible mark on the critical landscape. The essay included here (from the 1923 first American edition of *Studies*) starkly reveals the author's idiosyncratic style and trenchant voice.

Notice that Lawrence often writes in fragments, that his language seems conversational or free-associative, his lavish prose challenging the restrained critical conventions of his time. Lawrence's strong opinions also provoke our engagement. Consider his assertion that Melville is overly serious, that he is "sententious," that he "brays" and seems "clownish." This scathing critique of narrative voice in *Moby-Dick* might be useful to students exploring the relationship between Melville's prose and the prose of other authors, or exploring the variation of voice found within the novel. If Melville "preaches and holds forth," what is his relationship to writers, such as Emerson and Douglass, who more often stood behind a podium? What is Melville doing in "The Sermon," a chapter that self-consciously preaches?

In the first chapter of *Studies,* Lawrence writes of his desire to explore the American "spirit of place" in order to "save the tale from the artist who created it." Students interested in reader-response criticism or psychoanalytic interpretations of *Moby-Dick* have here an early example of a critic finding discrepancy between literal, intended meaning and less easily captured or detected sorts of intentionality. In an early foray into Freudian analysis, Lawrence reads the white whale as the "deepest blood-being of the white race" in America. He declares the hunt for the whale Melville's coded expression of a national "truth"—that whites, pressed round by other races, have finally engendered their own "Doom." For Lawrence, Melville displaces meaning into symbols and into allegory. Students using this volume to compare and contrast the work of Hawthorne and Melville may find what Lawrence has to say here of great value.

Students investigating how Melville expresses important ideas about American national identity may want to compare this essay with Archibald MacMechan's extended discussion of "Americanism" in *Moby-Dick,* also included in this section. Students will want to know that Lawrence's fatalistic conclusions concerning race in America were influenced by the fact that he read an edition of the novel containing no epilogue, in which Ishmael dies with his shipmates.

Critics have long noted that *Moby-Dick* seems to establish a tension with itself, and it is in this context that Lawrence may be most useful to student writers. Is *Moby-Dick* a novel or a book about the whale fishery? Lawrence adds new twists to critical conversations of this sort. His distinction between Melville as "man" and "artist," between meaning as literal and symbolic, as well as his preference for national over private contexts for interpretation are all important benchmarks for students wishing to write about the complexity of *Moby-Dick*.

——— ——— ———

Moby Dick, or the White Whale.

A hunt. The last great hunt.

For what?

For Moby Dick, the huge white sperm whale: who is old, hoary, monstrous, and swims alone; who is unspeakably terrible in his wrath, having so often been attacked; and snow-white.

Of course he is a symbol.

Of what?

I doubt if even Melville knew exactly. That's the best of it.

He is warm-blooded, he is lovable. He is lonely Leviathan, not a Hobbes sort. Or is he?

But he is warm-blooded and lovable. The South Sea Islanders, and Polynesians, and Malays, who worship shark, or crocodile, or weave endless frigate-bird distortions, why did they never worship the whale? So big!

Because the whale is not wicked. He doesn't bite. And their gods had to bite.

He's not a dragon. He is Leviathan. He never coils like the Chinese dragon of the sun. He's not a serpent of the waters. He is warm-blooded, a mammal. And hunted, hunted down.

It is a great book.

At first you are put off by the style. It reads like journalism. It seems spurious. You feel Melville is trying to put something over you. It won't do.

And Melville really is a bit sentientious: aware of himself, self-conscious, putting something over even himself. But then it's not easy to get into the swing of a piece of deep mysticism when you just set out with a story.

Nobody can be more clownish, more clumsy and sententiously in bad taste, than Herman Melville, even in a great book like *Moby Dick*. He preaches and holds forth because he's not sure of himself And he holds forth, often, so amateurishly.

The artist was so *much* greater than the man. The man is rather a tiresome New Englander of the ethical mystical-transcendentalist sort: Emerson, Longfellow, Hawthorne, etc. So unrelieved, the solemn ass even in humour. So hopelessly *au grand sérieux*, you feel like saying: Good God, what does it matter! If life is a tragedy, or a farce, or a disaster, or anything else, what do I care! Let life be what it likes. Give me a drink, that's what I want just now.

For my part, life is so many things I don't care what it is. It's not my affair to sum it up. Just now it's a cup of tea. This morning it was wormwood and gall. Hand me the sugar.

One wearies of the *grand sérieux*. There's something false about it. And that's Melville. Oh dear, when the solemn ass brays! brays! brays!

But he was a deep, great artist, even if he was rather a sententious man. He was a real American in that he always felt his audience in front of him. But when he ceases to be American, when he forgets all audience, and gives us his sheer apprehension of the world, then he is wonderful, his book commands a stillness in the soul, an awe.

In his 'human' self, Melville is almost dead. That is, he hardly reacts to human contacts any more; or only ideally: or just for a moment. His human-emotional self is almost played out. He is abstract, self-analytical and abstracted. And he is more spellbound by the strange slidings and collidings of Matter than by the things men do. In this he is like Dana. It is the material elements he really has to do with. His drama is with them. He was a futurist long before futurism found paint. The sheer naked slidings of the elements. And the human soul experiencing it all. So often, it is almost over the border: psychiatry. Almost spurious. Yet so great.

It is the same old thing as in all Americans. They keep their old-fashioned ideal frock-coat on, and an old-fashioned silk hat, while they do the most impossible things. There you are: you see Melville hugged in bed by a huge tattooed South Sea Islander, and solemnly offering burnt offering to this savage's little idol, and his ideal frock-coat just hides his shirt-tails and prevents us from seeing his bare posterior as he salaams, while his ethical silk hat sits correctly over his brow the while. That is so typically American: doing the most impossible things without taking off their spiritual get-up. Their ideals are like armour which has rusted in, and will never more come off. And meanwhile in Melville his bodily knowledge moves naked, a living quick among the stark elements. For with sheer physical vibrational sensitiveness, like a marvellous wireless-station, he registers the effects of the outer world. And he records also, almost beyond pain or pleasure, the extreme transitions of the isolated, far-driven soul, the soul which is now alone, without any real human contact.

The first days in New Bedford introduce the only human being who really enters into the book, namely, Ishmael, the 'I' of the book. And then the moment's hearts-brother, Queequeg, the tattooed, powerful South Sea harpooner, whom Melville loves as Dana loves 'Hope'. The advent of Ishmael's bedmate is amusing and unforgettable. But later the two swear 'marriage', in the language of the savages. For Queequeg has opened again the floodgates of love and human connection in Ishmael.

> As I sat there in that now lonely room, the fire burning low, in that mild stage when, after its first intensity has warmed the air, it then only glows to be looked at; the evening shades and phantoms gathering round the casements, and peering in upon us silent, solitary twain: I began to be sensible of strange feelings. I felt a melting in me. No more my splintered heart and maddened hand were turned against the wolfish world. This soothing savage had redeemed it. There he sat, his very indifference speaking a nature in which there lurked no civilized hypocrisies and bland deceits. Wild he was; a very sight of sights to see; yet I began to feel myself mysteriously drawn towards him.

—So they smoked together, and are clasped in each other's arms. The friendship is finally sealed when Ishmael offers sacrifice to Queequeg's little idol, Gogo.

I was a good Christian, born and bred in the bosom of the infallible Presbyterian Church. How then could I unite with the idolater in worshipping his piece of wood? But what is worship?—to do the will of God—*that* is worship. And what is the will of God?—to do to my fellow man what I would have my fellow man do to me—*that* is the will of God.—Which sounds like Benjamin Franklin, and is hopelessly bad theology. But it is real American logic.

> Now Queequeg is my fellow-man. And what do I wish that this Queequeg would do to me? Why, unite with me in my particular Presbyterian form of worship. Consequently, I must unite with him; ergo I must turn idolater. So I kindled the shavings; helped prop up the innocent little idol; offered him burnt biscuit with Queequeg; salaamed before him twice or thrice; kissed his nose; and that done, we undressed and went to bed, at peace with our own consciences and all the world. But we did not go to sleep without some little chat. How it is I know not; but there is no place like bed for confidential disclosures between friends. Man and wife, they say, open the very bottom of their souls to each other; and some old couples often lie and chat over old times till nearly morning. Thus, then, lay I and Queequeg—a cosy, loving pair—

You would think this relation with Queequeg meant something to Ishmael. But no. Queequeg is forgotten like yesterday's newspaper. Human things are only momentary excitements or amusements to the American Ishmael. Ishmael, the hunted. But much more Ishmael the hunter. What's a Queequeg? What's a wife? The white whale must be hunted down. Queequeg must be just 'KNOWN', then dropped into oblivion.

And what in the name of fortune is the white whale?

Elsewhere Ishmael says he loved Queequeg's eyes: 'large, deep eyes, fiery black and bold'. No doubt like Poe, he wanted to get the 'clue' to them. That was all.

The two men go over from New Bedford to Nantucket, and there sign on to the Quaker whaling ship, the *Pequod*. It is all strangely fantastic, phantasmagoric. The voyage of the soul. Yet curiously a real whaling voyage, too. We pass on into the midst of the sea with this strange ship and its incredible crew. The Argonauts were mild lambs in comparison. And Ulysses went *defeating* the Circes and overcoming the wicked hussies of the isles. But the *Pequod*'s crew is a collection of maniacs fanatically hunting down a lonely, harmless white whale.

As a soul history, it makes one angry. As a sea yarn, it is marvellous: there is always something a bit over the mark, in sea yarns. Should be. Then again the masking up of actual seaman's experience with sonorous mysticism sometimes gets on one's nerves. And again, as a revelation of destiny the book is too deep even for sorrow. Profound beyond feeling. You are some time before you are allowed to see the captain, Ahab: the mysterious Quaker. Oh, it is a God-fearing Quaker ship. Ahab, the captain. The captain of the soul.

I am the master of my fate,
I am the captain of my soul!

Ahab!
'Oh, captain, my captain, our fearful trip is done.'

The gaunt Ahab, Quaker, mysterious person, only shows himself after some days at sea. There's a secret about him! What?

Oh, he's a portentous person. He stumps about on an ivory stump, made from sea-ivory. Moby Dick, the great white whale, tore off Ahab's leg at the knee, when Ahab was attacking him.

Quite right, too. Should have torn off both his legs, and a bit more besides.

But Ahab doesn't think so. Ahab is now a monomaniac. Moby Dick is his monomania. Moby Dick must *DIE*, or Ahab can't live any longer. Ahab is atheist by this.

All right.

This *Pequod*, ship of the American soul, has three mates.

1. Starbuck: Quaker, Nantucketer, a good responsible man of reason, forethought, intrepidity, what is called a dependable man. At the bottom, *afraid*.

2. Stubbs: "Fearless as fire, and as mechanical." Insists on being reckless and jolly on every occasion. Must be afraid too, really.

3. Flask: Stubborn, obstinate, without imagination. To him 'the wondrous whale was but a species of magnified mouse or water rat—'

There you have them: a maniac captain and his three mates, three splendid seamen, admirable whalemen, first-class men at their job. America!

It is rather like Mr Wilson and his admirable, 'efficient' crew, at the Peace Conference. Except that none of the Pequodders took their wives along.

A maniac captain of the soul, and three eminently practical mates. America!

Then such a crew. Renegades, castaways, cannibals: Ishmael, Quakers. America!

Three giant harpooners to spear the great white whale.

1. Queequeg, the South Sea Islander, all tattooed, big and powerful.

2. Tashtego, the Red Indian of the sea-coast, where the Indian meets the sea.

3. Daggoo, the huge black negro.

There you have them, three savage races, under the American flag, the maniac captain, with their great keen harpoons, ready to spear the white whale.

And only after many days at sea does Ahab's own boat-crew appear on deck. Strange, silent, secret, black-garbed Malays, fire worshipping Parsees. These are to man Ahab's boat, when it leaps in pursuit of that whale.

What do you think of the ship *Pequod*, the ship of the soul of an American?

Many races, many peoples, many nations, under the Stars and Stripes. Beaten with many stripes.

Seeing stars sometimes.

And in a mad ship, under a mad captain, in a mad, fanatic's hunt.

For what?

For Moby Dick, the great white whale.

But splendidly handled. Three splendid mates. The whole thing practical, eminently practical in its working. American industry!

And all this practicality in the service of a mad, mad chase.

Melville manages to keep it a real whaling ship, on a real cruise, in spite of all fanatics. A wonderful, wonderful voyage. And a beauty that is so surpassing only because of the author's awful flounderings in mystical waters. He wanted to get metaphysically deep. And he got deeper than metaphysics. It is a surpassingly beautiful book, with an awful meaning, and bad jolts.

It is interesting to compare Melville with Dana, about the albatross—Melville a bit sententious.

> I remember the first albatross I ever saw. It was during a prolonged gale in waters hard upon the Antarctic seas. From my forenoon watch below I ascended to the overcrowded deck, and there, lashed upon the main hatches, I saw a regal feathered thing of unspotted whiteness, and with a hooked Roman bill sublime. At intervals it arched forth its vast, archangel wings—wondrous throbbings and flutterings shook it. Though bodily unharmed, it uttered cries, as some King's ghost in supernatural distress. Through its inexpressible strange eyes methought I peeped to secrets not below the heavens—the white thing was so white, its wings so wide, and in those for ever exiled waters, I had lost the miserable warping memories of traditions and of towns. I assert then, that in the wondrous bodily whiteness of the bird chiefly lurks the secret of the spell—

Melville's albatross is a prisoner, caught by a bait on a hook.

Well, I have seen an albatross, too: following us in waters hard upon the Antarctic, too, south of Australia. And in the Southern winter. And the ship, a P. and O. boat, nearly empty. And the lascar crew shivering.

The bird with its long, long wings following, then leaving us. No one knows till they have tried, how lost, how lonely those Southern waters are. And glimpses of the Australian coast.

It makes one feel that our day is only a day. That in the dark of the night ahead other days stir fecund, when we have lapsed from existence.

Who knows how utterly we shall lapse.

But Melville keeps up his disquisition about 'whiteness'. The great abstract fascinated him. The abstract where we end, and cease to be. White or black. Our white, abstract end!

Then again it is lovely to be at sea on the *Pequod*, with never a grain of earth to us.

It was a cloudy, sultry afternoon; the seamen were lazily lounging about the decks, or vacantly gazing over into the lead-coloured waters. Queequeg and I were mildly employed weaving what is called a swordmat, for an additional lashing to our boat. So still and subdued, and yet somehow preluding was all the scene, and such an incantation of reverie lurked in the air that each silent sailor seemed resolved into his own invisible self—

In the midst of this preluding silence came the first cry: 'There she blows! there! there! there! She blows!' And then comes the first chase, a marvellous piece of true sea-writing, the sea, and sheer sea-beings on the chase, sea-creatures chased. There is scarcely a taint of earth—pure sea-motion.

'Give way, men,' whispered Starbuck, drawing still further aft the sheet of his sail; 'there is time to kill a fish yet before the squall comes. There's white water again!—Close to!—Spring!' Soon after, two cries in quick succession on each side of us denoted that the other boats had got fast; but hardly were they overheard, when with a lightning-like hurtling whisper Starbuck said: 'Stand up!' and Queequeg, harpoon in hand, sprang to his feet.—Though not one of the oarsmen was then facing the life and death peril so close to them ahead, yet, their eyes on the intense countenance of the mate in the stern of the boat, they knew that the imminent instant had come; they heard, too, an enormous wallowing sound, as of fifty elephants stirring in their litter. Meanwhile the boat was still booming through the mist, the waves curbing and hissing around us like the erected crests of enraged serpents.

'That's his hump. *There! There*, give it to him!' whispered Starbuck.—A short rushing sound leapt out of the boat; it was the darted iron of Queequeg. Then all in one welded motion came a push from astern, while forward the boat seemed striking on a ledge; the sail collapsed and exploded; a gush of scalding vapour shot up near by; something rolled and tumbled like an earthquake beneath us. The whole crew were half suffocated as they were tossed helter-skelter into the white curling cream of the squall. Squall, whale, and harpoon had all blended together; and the whale, merely grazed by the iron, escaped—

Melville is a master of violent, chaotic physical motion; he can keep up a whole wild chase without a flaw. He is as perfect at creating stillness. The ship is cruising on the Carrol Ground, south of St Helena.—'It was while gliding through these latter waters that one serene and moonlight night, when all the waves rolled by like scrolls of silver; and by their soft, suffusing seethings, made what seemed a silvery silence, not a solitude; on such a silent night a silvery jet was seen far in advance of the white bubbles at the bow—'

Then there is the description of brit.

> Steering north-eastward from the Crozetts we fell in with vast meadows of brit, the minute, yellow substance upon which the Right Whale largely feeds. For leagues and leagues it undulated round us, so that we seemed to be sailing through boundless fields of ripe and golden wheat. On the second day, numbers of Right Whales were seen, who, secure from the attack of a Sperm Whaler like the *Pequod*, with open jaws sluggishly swam through the brit, which, adhering to the fringing fibres of that wondrous Venetian blind in their mouths, was in that manner separated from the water that escaped at the lip. As moving mowers who, side by side, slowly and seethingly advance their scythes through the long wet grass of the marshy meads; even so these monsters swam, making a strange grassy, cutting sound; and leaving behind them endless swaths of blue on the yellow sea. But it was only the sound they made as they parted the brit which at all reminded one of mowers. Seen from the mastheads, especially when they paused and were stationary for a while, their vast black forms looked more like lifeless masses of rock than anything else—

This beautiful passage brings us to the apparition of the squid.

> Slowly wading through the meadows of brit, the *Pequod* still held her way northeastward towards the island of Java; a gentle air impelling her keel, so that in the surrounding serenity her three tall, tapering masts mildly waved to that languid breeze, as three mild palms on a plain. And still, at wide intervals, in the silvery night, that lonely alluring jet would be seen.
>
> But one transparent-blue morning, when a stillness almost preternatural spread over the sea, however unattended with any stagnant calm; when the long burnished sunglade on the waters seemed a golden finger laid across them, enjoining secrecy; when all the slippered waves whispered together as they softly ran on; in this profound hush of the visible sphere a strange spectre was seen by Daggoo from the main-mast head.

> In the distance, a great white mass lazily rose, and rising higher and higher, and disentangling itself from the azure, at last gleamed before our prow like a snow-slide, new slid from the hills. Thus glistening for a moment, as slowly it subsided, and sank. Then once more arose, and silently gleamed. It seemed not a whale; and yet, is this Moby Dick? thought Daggoo—

The boats were lowered and pulled to the scene.

> In the same spot where it sank, once more it slowly rose. Almost forgetting for the moment all thoughts of Moby Dick, we now gazed at the most wondrous phenomenon which the secret seas have hitherto revealed to mankind. A vast pulpy mass, furlongs in length and breadth, of a glancing cream-colour, lay floating on the water, innumerable long arms radiating from its centre, and curling and twisting like a nest of anacondas, as if blindly to clutch at any hapless object within reach. No perceptible face or front did it have; no conceivable token of either sensation or instinct; but undulated there on the billows, an unearthly, formless, chance-like apparition of life. And with a low sucking it slowly disappeared again.

The following chapters, with their account of whale hunts, the killing, the stripping, the cutting up, are magnificent records of actual happening. Then comes the queer tale of the meeting of the *Jeroboam*, a whaler met at sea, all of whose men were under the domination of a religious maniac, one of the ship's hands. There are detailed descriptions of the actual taking of the sperm oil from a whale's head. Dilating on the smallness of the brain of a sperm whale, Melville significantly remarks—'for I believe that much of man's character will be found betokened in his backbone. I would rather feel your spine than your skull, whoever you are—' And of the whale, he adds:

> 'For, viewed in this light, the wonderful comparative smallness of his brain proper is more than compensated by the wonderful comparative magnitude of his spinal cord.'

In among the rush of terrible awful hunts, come touches of pure beauty.

> As the three boats lay there on that gently rolling sea, gazing down into its eternal blue noon; and as not a single groan or cry of any sort, nay not so much as a ripple or a thought, came up from its depths; what landsman would have thought that beneath all that

silence and placidity the utmost monster of the seas was writhing and wrenching in agony!

Perhaps the most stupendous chapter is the one called 'The Grand Armada', at the beginning of Volume III. The *Pequod* was drawing through the Sunda Straits towards Java when she came upon a vast host of sperm whales. Broad on both bows, at a distance of two or three miles, and forming a great semicircle embracing one-half of the level horizon, a continuous chain of whale-jets were up-playing and sparkling in the noonday air. Chasing this great herd, past the Straits of Sunda, themselves chased by Javan pirates, the whalers race on. Then the boats are lowered. At last that curious state of inert irresolution came over the whales, when they were, as the seamen say, gallied. Instead of forging ahead in huge martial array they swam violently hither and thither, a surging sea of whales, no longer moving on. Starbuck's boat, made fast to a whale, is towed in amongst this howling Leviathan chaos. In mad career it cockles through the boiling surge of monsters, till it is brought into a clear lagoon in the very centre of the vast, mad, terrified herd. There a sleek, pure calm reigns. There the females swam in peace, and the young whales came snuffing tamely at the boat, like dogs. And there the astonished seamen watched the love-making of these amazing monsters, mammals, now in rut far down in the sea—

> But far beneath this wondrous world upon the surface, another and still stranger world met our eyes, as we gazed over the side. For, suspended in these watery vaults, floated the forms of the nursing mothers of the whales, and those that by their enormous girth seemed shortly to become mothers. The lake, as I have hinted, was to a considerable depth exceedingly transparent; and as human infants while sucking will calmly and fixedly gaze away from the breast, as if leading two different lives at a time; and while yet drawing moral nourishment, be still spiritually feasting upon some unearthly reminiscence, even so did the young of these whales seem looking up towards us, but not at us, as if we were but a bit of gulf-weed in their newborn sight. Floating on their sides, the mothers also seemed quietly eyeing us.—Some of the subtlest secrets of the seas seemed divulged to us in this enchanted pond. We saw young Leviathan amours in the deep. And thus, though surrounded by circle upon circle of consternation and affrights, did these inscrutable creatures at the centre freely and fearlessly

indulge in all peaceful concernments; yea, serenely revelled in dalliance and delight—

There is something really overwhelming in these whale-hunts, almost superhuman or inhuman, bigger than life, more terrific than human activity. The same with the chapter on ambergris: it is so curious, so real, yet so unearthly. And again in the chapter called 'The Cassoc'—surely the oldest piece of phallicism in all the world's literature.

After this comes the amazing account of the Try-works, when the ship is turned into the sooty, oily factory in mid-ocean, and the oil is extracted from the blubber. In the night of the red furnace burning on deck, at sea, Melville has his startling experience of reversion. He is at the helm, but has turned to watch the fire: when suddenly he feels the ship rushing backward from him, in mystic reversion—

> Uppermost was the impression, that whatever swift, rushing thing I stood on was not so much bound to any haven ahead, as rushing from all havens astern. A stark bewildering feeling, as of death, came over me. Convulsively my hands grasped the tiller, but with the crazy conceit that the tiller was, somehow, in some enchanted way, inverted. My God! What is the matter with me, I thought!

This dream-experience is a real soul-experience. He ends with an injunction to all men, not to gaze on the red fire when its redness makes all things look ghastly. It seems to him that his gazing on fire has evoked this horror of reversion, undoing.

Perhaps it had. He was water-born.

After some unhealthy work on the ship, Queequeg caught a fever and was like to die.

> How he wasted and wasted in those few, long-lingering days, till there seemed but little left of him but his frame and tattooing. But as all else in him thinned, and his cheek-bones grew sharper, his eyes, nevertheless, seemed growing fuller and fuller; they took on a strangeness of lustre; and mildly but deeply looked out at you there from his sickness, a wondrous testimony to that immortal health in him which could not die, or be weakened. And like circles on the water, which as they grow fainter, expand; so his eyes seemed rounding and rounding, like the circles of Eternity. An awe that cannot be named would steal over you as you sat by the side of this waning savage—

But Queequeg did not die—and the *Pequod* emerges from the Eastern Straits, into the full Pacific. 'To any meditative Magian rover, this serene Pacific once beheld, must ever after be the sea of his adoption. It rolls the midmost waters of the world—'

In this Pacific the fights go on:

> It was far down the afternoon, and when all the spearings of the crimson fight were done, and floating in the lovely sunset sea and sky, sun and whale both stilly died together; then such a sweetness and such a plaintiveness, such inwreathing orisons curled up in that rosy air, that it almost seemed as if far over from the deep green convent valleys of the Manila isles, the Spanish land-breeze had gone to sea, freighted with these vesper hymns. Soothed again, but only soothed to deeper gloom, Ahab, who had sterned off from the whale, sat intently watching his final wanings from the now tranquil boat. For that strange spectacle, observable in all sperm whales dying—the turning of the head sunwards, and so expiring—that strange spectacle, beheld of such a placid evening, somehow to Ahab conveyed wondrousness unknown before. 'He turns and turns him to it; how slowly, but how steadfastly, his homage-rendering and invoking brow, with his last dying motions. He too worships fire . . .'

So Ahab soliloquizes: and so the warm-blooded whale turns for the last time to the sun, which begot him in the waters.

But as we see in the next chapter, it is the Thunder-fire which Ahab really worships: that living sundering fire of which he bears the brand, from head to foot; it is storm, the electric storm of the *Pequod*, when the corposants burn in high, tapering flames of supernatural pallor upon the masthead, and when the compass is reversed. After this all is fatality. Life itself seems mystically reversed. In these hunters of Moby Dick there is nothing but madness and possession. The captain, Ahab, moves hand in hand with the poor imbecile negro boy, Pip, who has been so cruelly demented, left swimming alone in the vast sea. It is the imbecile child of the sun hand in hand with the northern monomaniac, captain and master.

The voyage surges on. They meet one ship, then another. It is all ordinary day-routine, and yet all is a tension of pure madness and horror, the approaching horror of the last fight. 'Hither and thither, on high, glided the snow-white wings of small unspecked birds; these were the gentle thoughts of the feminine air; but to and fro in the deeps, far down in the bottomless blue, rushed mighty leviathans, sword-fish and sharks; and these were the strong, troubled, murderous thinkings of the masculine sea—' On this day Ahab confesses his weariness, the weariness of his burden. 'But do I look very old, so very, very old, Starbuck? I feel deadly faint, and bowed, and humped, as though I were Adam staggering beneath the piled centuries since Paradise—' It is the Gethsemane of Ahab, before the last fight: the Gethsemane of the human soul seeking the last self-conquest, the last attainment of extended consciousness—infinite consciousness.

At last they sight the whale. Ahab sees him from his hoisted perch at the masthead—'From this height the whale was now seen some mile or so ahead, at every roll of the sea revealing his high, sparkling hump, and regularly jetting his silent spout into the air.'

The boats are lowered, to draw near the white whale.

> At length the breathless hunter came so nigh his seemingly unsuspectful prey that his entire dazzling hump was distinctly visible, sliding along the sea as if an isolated thing, and continually set in a revolving ring of finest, fleecy, greenish foam. He saw the vast involved wrinkles of the slightly projecting head, beyond. Before it, far out on the soft, Turkish rugged waters, went the glistening white shadow from his broad milky forehead, a musical rippling playfully accompanying the shade; and behind, the blue waters interchangeably flowed over the moving valley of his steady wake; and on either side bright bubbles arose and danced by his side. But these were broken again by the light toes of hundreds of gay fowl softly feathering the sea, alternate with their fitful flight; and like to some flagstaff rising from the pointed hull of an argosy, the tall but shattered pole of a recent lance projected from the white whale's back; and at intervals one of the clouds of soft-toed fowls hovering, and to and fro shimmering like a canopy over the fish, silently perched and rocked on this pole, the long tail-feathers streaming like pennons.
>
> A gentle joyousness—a mighty mildness of repose in swiftness, invested the gliding whale—

The fight with the whale is too wonderful and too awful, to be quoted apart from the book. It lasted three days. The fearful sight, on the third day, of the torn body of the Parsee harpooner, lost on the previous day, now seen lashed on to the flanks of the white whale by the tangle of harpoon lines, has a mystic dream-horror. The awful and infuriated whale turns upon the ship, symbol of this civilized world of ours. He smites her with a fearful shock. And a few minutes later, from the last of the fighting whale-boats comes the cry:

> 'The ship! Great God, where is the ship?' Soon they, through dim bewildering mediums, saw her sidelong fading phantom, as in the gaseous *Fata Morgana*; only the uppermost masts out of the water; while fixed by infatuation, or fidelity, or fate, to their once lofty perches, the pagan harpooners still maintained their sinking lookouts on the sea. And now concentric circles seized the lone boat itself, and all its crew, and each floating oar, and every lance-pole, and spinning, animate and inanimate, all round and round in one vortex, carried the smallest chip of the *Pequod* out of sight—

The bird of heaven, the eagle, St John's bird, the Red Indian bird, the American, goes down with the ship, nailed by Tashtego's hammer, the hammer of the American Indian. The eagle of the spirit. Sunk!

> Now small fowls flew screaming over the yet yawning gulf; a sullen white surf beat against its steep sides; then all collapsed; and the great shroud of the sea rolled on as it rolled five thousand years ago.

So ends one of the strangest and most wonderful books in the world, closing up its mystery and its tortured symbolism. It is an epic of the sea such as no man has equalled; and it is a book of esoteric symbolism of profound significance, and of considerable tiresomeness.

But it is a great book, a very great book, the greatest book of the sea ever written. It moves awe in the soul.

The terrible fatality.

Fatality.

Doom.

Doom! Doom! Doom! Something seems to whisper it in the very dark trees of America. Doom!

Doom of what?

Doom of our white day. We are doomed, doomed. And the doom is in America. The doom of our white day.

Ah, well, if my day is doomed, and I am doomed with my day, it is something greater than I which dooms me, so I accept my doom as a sign of the greatness which is more than I am.

Melville knew. He knew his race was doomed. His white soul, doomed. His great white epoch, doomed. Himself, doomed. The idealist, doomed. The spirit, doomed.

The reversion. 'Not so much bound to any haven ahead, as rushing from all havens astern.'

That great horror of ours! It is our civilization rushing from all havens astern.

The last ghastly hunt. The White Whale.

What then is Moby Dick? He is the deepest blood-being of the white race; he is our deepest blood-nature.

And he is hunted, hunted, hunted by the maniacal fanaticism of our white mental consciousness. We want to hunt him down. To subject him to our will. And in this maniacal conscious hunt of ourselves we get dark races and pale to help us, red, yellow, and black, east and west, Quaker and fire-worshipper, we get them all to help us in this ghastly maniacal hunt which is our doom and our suicide.

The last phallic being of the white man. Hunted into the death of upper consciousness and the ideal will. Our blood-self subjected to our will. Our blood-consciousness sapped by a parasitic mental or ideal consciousness.

Hot-blooded sea-born Moby Dick. Hunted by monomaniacs of the idea.

Oh God, oh God, what next, when the Pequod has sunk?

She sank in the war, and we are all flotsam.

Now what next?

Who knows? *Quien sabe? Quien sabe, señor?*

Neither Spanish nor Saxon America has any answer.

The *Pequod* went down. And the *Pequod* was the ship of the white American soul. She sank, taking with her negro and Indian and Polynesian, Asiatic and Quaker and good, businesslike Yankees and Ishmael: she sank all the lot of them.

Boom! as Vachel Lindsay would say.

To use the words of Jesus, *IT IS FINISHED.*

Consummatum est!

But *Moby Dick* was first published in 1851. If the Great White Whale sank the ship of the Great White Soul in 1851, what's been happening ever since?

Post-mortem effects, presumably.

Because, in the first centuries, Jesus was Cetus, the Whale. And the Christians were the little fishes. Jesus, the Redeemer, was Cetus, Leviathan. And all the Christians all his little fishes.

—D.H. Lawrence, "Herman Melville's *Moby Dick*,"
Studies in Classic American Literature,
New York: Thomas Seltzer, 1923, pp. 376–92

Carl Van Doren
"Mr. Melville's *Moby Dick*" (1924)

This astounding romance is neither so sane as *Typee* and *Omoo* nor so mad as *Mardi*, but occupies a fruitful ground between those two extremes of Herman Melville's art. It bears, indeed, the marks of a hand which moves as if it had learned its tricks during the early nineteenth century. Echoes of Carlyle roar through its rhythms; the wings of transcendentalism wheel over it, shutting out at times the secular sun. The narrative marches under a load of erudition, concerning whales and whalers, which recalls those simpler days when fiction and history had not agreed upon the division of labor with which each is now satisfied. Mr Melville obviously lacks the realist's conviction that the bare facts of human life are in themselves eloquent, and so permits himself to lean a great deal upon certain misty symbols to give his meaning its rich colors and ominous shadows. For any but those among its readers who have an expert's interest in the technique of whale hunting or who take a connoisseur's delight in the manipulation of witty and poetical prose, the book is sure to seem too long, perhaps by a third. There must be plain men who would find the voyage of the story shorter than the volume. And yet, touched by certain conventions of its generation as it is, *Moby Dick* presents a face which is almost as timeless as an ocean or a heath. If there is a greater sea tale in modern literature, that tale has not yet been published.

Even to mention the word 'tale' in connection with this history is to call to mind the hollow distance between it and the ordinary novel of the sea. Mr Melville is never merely brisk nor jaunty, never merely racy nor knowing, never merely hilarious nor sentimental. From the first sentence he writes always in something of the grand style. 'Call me Ishmael,' says his narrator in the first sentence, thus cutting himself off from the world of the customary. Bored with the dry land, he goes to New Bedford, takes up with a cannibal harpooner, ships with him upon the Quaker owned 'Pequod' for three years in the South Seas, learns first that Captain Ahab has lost his leg in the jaws of a whale, then that he is set upon avenging himself for his loss, and finally that he is a madman, sworn to destroy the great white Moby Dick, though in so doing he has to sink his ship with all its motley population, so vast and fixed has his will to vengeance become. By the time Ishmael has begun to comprehend the situation they are deep in the magical Pacific, where Ahab gradually compels his crew to share some of his frenzy. They harry the sea for the whale, but Moby Dick has an essence of immortality in him, the terrible immortality of a fiend, and in the end he demolishes the ship. Only

Ishmael survives to bring back the epic log of the voyage. And if the theme is thus larger than the theme of the ordinary nautical romance, it becomes still larger in the handling. This last cruise of the 'Pequod' is more than a routine expedition for the profits to be got by murdering whales. It is a cosmic issue. With so much madness at the helm, the hunt is bound to end in catastrophe. Tragedy broods over the ship and Ahab from the hour they sail. But with what mighty deliberateness it closes its fist upon them, these storm pitched hunters of the deep! How cannily it waits till it has the mother of all the oceans for its stage! With what a swift stroke it finally closes the account of the venturers who have dared to challenge the insolent supremacy of the devils and the gods!

Mr Melville is perhaps partly intent on mystifying when he says he fears that ignorant landsmen may scout at the story 'as monstrous fable, or still worse and more detestable, a hideous and intolerable allegory.' It is true that gossip along the seaboard reports an actual white whale, called Mocha Dick according to Mr J. N. Reynolds, which long laughed at all its pursuers and became the object of many hatreds before it was finally captured off the coast of Chile. But much has happened to this theme in passing through Mr Melville's imagination. Suppose, it has occurred to that imagination, there were some victim of the monster who had vowed to have revenge. He would realize that his chances for meeting Moby Dick on the broad Pacific must be very few, and if the meeting were long delayed he might well brood upon his purpose till it had acquired a stupendous significance for him. So with the captain of the 'Pequod': 'All that most maddens and torments; all that stirs up the lees of things; all truth with malice in it; all that cracks the sinews and cakes the brain; all the subtle demonisms of life and thought; all evil, to crazy Ahab, were visibly personified and made practically assailable in Moby Dick.' The man is in the grip of a passion so single and inveterate that his mind cannot admit the possibility of giving up or turning aside. Absolute master of his crew, out of sight of all civil restraints, opposed by nothing except the magnitude of his task and the craft of his antagonist, Ahab becomes more truly a monster than Moby Dick. He is vengeance in the flesh, a seeker without bounds to his desire. Whatever Mr Melville may say about his mad hero, Ahab has a hundred symbolical or allegorical implications.

Having a hundred of them, Ahab is likely, of course, to find interpreters who will each insist that he has the one true key. This authority on the riddle will maintain that the romance is an allegory of the proud soul riding to its doom; this, that it is an allegory of the speculative soul following the problem of evil to its fatal lair; this, that it is an allegory of the violated soul going to the end of the earth for justice; this, that it is an allegory of the perverse soul leaving its natural companions to catch a glimpse of some satanic grail; this, that it is an allegory of the infatuated soul skirting continents and crossing oceans for the sake of union with an object which it equally loves and hates. Since so many interpretations seem each of them applicable, probably no one of them deserves to be finally accepted. The matter is too immense to be summed up in any simple formula. Different dispositions will find themselves reflected in the many facets of the drama. Its variety is one measure of its greatness, as is also that profound vitality which will make it long capable of being wrangled over by rival critics who can no more come to agreement than they can about the meaning of experience itself.

This much, however, is clear and unmistakable: Ahab is at once a kind of Faust and a kind of Lucifer, brought up in Nantucket and fed from his youth on Calvinistic theology. Accustomed to the dangers of his occupation, he might naturally have been expected to regard the loss of his leg as a mere accident for which nothing could be blamed. Accustomed to the doctrine of predestination, he might as naturally have been expected to regard his loss as the will of God, working mysteriously yet righteously. But Ahab cannot be reconciled by either of the orthodoxies in which he has been bred. He must know the cause of his misfortune and must pay back blow for blow. He is in rebellion against whatever god or whatever godless chaos has wrought this havoc upon him, against whatever it is that Moby Dick is or represents. 'That inscrutable thing is chiefly what I hate; and be the white whale principal, I will wreak that hate upon him. Talk not to me of blasphemy, man; I'd strike the sun if it insulted me.' 'The prophecy was that I should be dismembered; and— Aye! I lost this leg. I now prophesy that I will dismember my dismemberer. Now, then, be the prophet and the fulfiller one. That's more than ye, ye great gods, ever were.' No wonder that, with so blazing a titan for its hero, the story grows sulphurous toward the close, hinting that the gods, disturbed upon both their upper and their nether thrones, invoked thunder, ocean, and the hugest of the beasts of creation to put down this impious man who had dared to crowd so close upon their secrets. No wonder that almost a race seems to have perished when the 'Pequod' goes down, a skyhawk nailed to her mast, into the level waters, and Moby Dick, unharmed and unperturbed, glides away to other business. Only such a fate could be worthy of such a hero.

Mr Melville's romance, however, is by no means entirely theological. It is packed with history. Better than any other novel it reproduces the works and days of the whalers in that time, now so incredibly forgotten, when they went out from Nantucket in fleets to the most distant and most enormous of the American frontiers. New Bedford and the hard little island are here described with as lively a pen as Mr Melville employed in his account of the cannibals of *Typee*: the inns, the docks, the ships, the people of all degrees. He is even more detailed when Ishmael has got to sea, in the whaler's true element. The whole literature of whaling, no less than all its devices, seems to be at his finger's ends. He classifies whales like a cetologist; he stands by with anatomical explanations while they are being cut up and turned to human use; he abounds in anecdotes of old adventure. Obviously with a set purpose, Mr Melville has brought together in the 'Pequod' the various tribes of men who went whaling: not only Yankees, but an Indian, a Negro, a cannibal from the South Seas, a Dutchman, a Frenchman, an Icelander, a Maltese, a Sicilian, a Chinese, a Manxman, a Lascar, a Tahitian, a Portuguese, a Dane, an Englishman, a Spaniard, an Irishman, a mysterious boat crew of Asiatics; and each tribe or type is accurately distinguished. Nor is the 'Pequod,' for all its errand is so lonely, lost in the Pacific. Its path crosses that of many another vessel, and they hail one another and exchange the news of the ocean till there has been woven of their crossings and exchanges a solid fabric of knowledge concerning all that goes on there. The pageant is immense, but it is not dim.

The excessive length of *Moby Dick* is due to the abundance of its erudition. A more artful writer could have produced the same air of threatening postponement in the catastrophe without ransacking so many encyclopaedias. A more artful writer, too, would have known better than to fall so often into blank verse in his elevated passages. Nevertheless, there is evidence of a powerful control of the materials of the book in the fact that it is as well constructed as it is. And the language, spirited, flexible, pungent, sardonic, exuberant, is superb.

> The Nantucketer, he alone resides and riots on the sea; he alone, in Bible language, goes down to it in ships; to and fro ploughing it as his own special plantation. There is his home; *there* lies his business, which a Noah's flood would not interrupt, though it overwhelmed all the millions in China. He lives on the sea, as prairie cocks in the prairie; he hides among the waves, he climbs them as chamois hunters climb the Alps. For years he knows not the land; so that when he comes to it at last, it smells like another world, more strangely than the moon would to an Earthsman. With the landless gull, that at sunset folds her wings and is rocked to sleep between billows; so at nightfall, the Nantucketer, out of sight

of land, furls his sails, and lays him to rest, while under his very pillow rush herds of walruses and whales.

Mr Melville can be intense or insinuating, archaic or vernacular, downright or poetical; he is never commonplace. No one of his senses seems ever to grow dull. He writes with the energy of a man who is tirelessly alert, even in his most learned chapters nipping the heels of his exposition so that it caracoles like a thoroughbred. Even his mannerisms, except possibly his irritating blank verse, have something about them which is obstinately distinctive. Though he may have limited his audience for *Moby Dick* by his mannerisms, he almost certainly has written a book which, despite them and partly by reason of them, will awaken half frantic enthusiasms in numerous bosoms for many years to come.

—Carl Van Doren, "Mr. Melville's *Moby Dick*,"
New York *Bookman*, 59, April 1924, pp. 154–57

Charles Olson (1947)

Charles Olson was a second-generation modernist poet, an idiosyncratic and much admired Melville scholar who was eventually associated with both the Black Mountain Poets and the Beats. But when he wrote *Call Me Ishmael,* he was making the transition into poetry from his long, academic, near obsession with Melville. For this reason his writing may seem structurally and stylistically odd to students encountering it for the first time, at times more a prose poem than a typical critical study. Students might notice that the voice and tone of D.H. Lawrence's critical assessments of Melville, also included in this volume, clearly influenced Olson. Students might find it useful to consider how the subject of Olson's text—Melville and his main prose inspirations—might have helped license his own flights of poetic invention.

Olson opens his discussion by pointing to the problem of why *Moby-Dick* moves rather jarringly from its comedic opening chapters, through the cetology (the study of whales) chapters, and then lapses into the dark, tragic vision that holds sway for the majority of the latter part of the book. This problem was first alluded to in an early Duyckinck review also included in this volume, subsequently raised directly as an issue by Leon Howard in 1939, then, after Olson, taken up in an essay by George R. Stewart titled "The Two Moby-Dicks." Scholars today still debate the issue, though most feel that James Barbour settled it in his 1975 essay titled "The Composition of Moby-Dick." If the theory is complex and fascinating, its history and development long, its lineaments are well sketched by Olson. Melville had almost finished his whaling book when he encountered Hawthorne and a large-print set of Shakespeare volumes—a set fit for his weak eyes. This coming together of man and material changed everything. Students exploring the composition of *Moby-Dick*, or the influence of Hawthorne, or of Shakespeare, or of tragic vision in general on Melville, should find in Olson a good place to begin their inquiries.

Olson is also important as a practitioner of myth criticism. In Melville he found an inspirational myth of American "genius"—of American industry, space, and consciousness. In this respect, students might take note of Olson's closing poetic assertion. Out of the confluence (turned tragic conflagration) of Melville's greatest sources emerged the "bronze" of *Moby-Dick*—a metal symbolic of the origins of classical spirit, narrative, tragedy, and national mythology. Olson's text is a strong place to start for students considering how Melville's best-known book engages the issue of nationalism and empire.

I take SPACE to be the central fact to man born in America, from Folsom cave to now. I spell it large because it comes large here. Large, and without mercy.

It is geography at bottom, a hell of wide land from the beginning. That made the first American story (Parkman's): exploration.

Something else than a stretch of earth—seas on both sides, no barriers to contain as restless a thing as Western man was becoming in Columbus' day. That made Melville's story (part of it).

Plus a harshness we still perpetuate, a sun like a tomahawk, small earthquakes but big tornadoes and hurrikans, a river north and south in the middle of the land running out the blood.

The fulcrum of America is the Plains, half sea half land, a high sun as metal and obdurate as the iron horizon, and a man's job to square the circle.

Some men ride on such space, others have to fasten themselves like a tent stake to survive. As I see it Poe dug in and Melville mounted. They are the alternatives.

Americans still fancy themselves such democrats. But their triumphs are of the machine. It is the only master of space the average person ever knows, oxwheel to piston, muscle to jet. It gives trajectory.

To Melville it was not the will to be free but the will to overwhelm nature that lies at the bottom of us as individuals and a people. Ahab is no democrat. *Moby-Dick*, antagonist, is only king of natural force, resource.

I am interested in a Melville who decided sometime in 1850 to write a book about the whaling industry and what happened to a man in command of one of the most successful machines Americans had perfected up to that time—the whaleship.

This captain, Ahab by name, knew space. He rode it across seven seas. He was an able skipper, what the fishing people I was raised with call a highliner. Big catches: he brought back holds barrel full of the oil of the sperm, the light of American and European communities up to the middle of the 19th century.

This Ahab had gone wild. The object of his attention was something unconscionably big and white. He had become a specialist: he had all space concentrated into the form of a whale called *Moby-Dick*. And he assailed it as Columbus an ocean, LaSalle a continent, the Donner Party their winter Pass.

I am interested in a Melville who was long-eyed enough to understand the Pacific as part of our geography, another West, prefigured in the Plains, antithetical.

The beginning of man was salt sea, and the perpetual reverberation of that great ancient fact, constantly renewed in the unfolding of life in every human individual, is the important single fact about Melville. Pelagic.

He had the tradition in him, deep, in his brain, his words, the salt beat of his blood. He had the sea of himself in a vigorous, stricken way, as Poe the street. It enabled him to draw up from Shakespeare. It made Noah, and Moses, contemporary to him. History was ritual and repetition when Melville's imagination was at its own proper beat.

It was an older sense than the European man's, more to do with magic than culture. Magic which, in contrast to worship, is all black. For magic has one purpose: compel men or non-human forces to do one's will. Like Ahab, American, one aim: lordship over nature.

I am willing to ride Melville's image of man, whale and ocean to find in him prophecies, lessons he himself would not have spelled out. A hundred years gives us an advantage. For Melville was as much larger than himself as Ahab's hate. He was a plunger. He knew how to take a chance.

The man made a mess of things. He got all balled up with Christ. He made a white marriage. He had one son die of tuberculosis, the other shoot himself. He only rode his own space once—*Moby-Dick*. He had to be wild or he was nothing in particular. He had to go fast, like an American, or he was all torpor. Half horse half alligator.

Melville took an awful licking. He was bound to. He was an original, aboriginal. A beginner. It happens that way to the dreaming men it takes to discover America: Columbus and LaSalle won, and then lost her to the competent. Daniel Boone loved her earth. Harrod tells the story of coming upon Boone one day far to the west in Kentucky of where Harrod thought any white man had ever been. He heard sound he couldn't place, crept forward to a boulder and there in a blue grass clearing was Boone alone singing to himself. Boone died west of the Mississippi, in his own country criminal—"wanted," a bankrupt of spirit and land.

Beginner—and interested in beginnings. Melville had a way of reaching back through time until he got history pushed back so far he turned time into space. He was like a migrant backtrailing to Asia, some Inca trying to find a lost home.

We are the last "first" people. We forget that. We act big, misuse our land, ourselves. We lose our own primary.

Melville went back, to discover us, to come forward. He got as far as *Moby-Dick*.

Ortega y Gasset puts it that the man of antiquity, before he did anything, took a step like the bullfighter who leaps back in order to deliver the mortal thrust.

Whitman appears, because of his notation of the features of American life and his conscious identification of himself with the people, to be the more poet. But Melville had the will. He was homeless in his land, his society, his self.

Logic and classification had led civilization toward man, away from space. Melville went to space to probe and find man. Early men did the same: poetry, language and the care of myth, as Fenollosa says, grew up together. Among the Egyptians Horus was the god of writing and the god of the moon, one figure for both, a WHITE MONKEY.

In place of Zeus, Odysseus, Olympus we have had Caesar, Faust, the City. The shift was from man as a group to individual man. Now, in spite of the corruption of myth by fascism, the swing is out and back. Melville is one who began it.

He had a pull to the origin of things, the first day, the first man, the unknown sea, Betelgeuse, the buried continent. From passive places his imagination sprang a harpoon.

He sought prime. He had the coldness we have, but he warmed himself by first fires after Flood. It gave him the power to find the lost past of America, the unfound present, and make a myth, *Moby-Dick*, for a people of Ishmaels.

The thing got away from him. It does, from us. We make AHAB, the WHITE WHALE, and lose them. We let John Henry go, Negro, worker, hammering man:

He lied down his hammer an' he died.

Whitman we have called our greatest voice because he gave us hope. Melville is the truer man. He lived intensely his people's wrong, their guilt. But he remembered the first dream. The *White Whale* is more accurate than *Leaves of Grass*. Because it is America, all of her space, the malice, the root.

—Charles Olson, *Call Me Ishmael*, New York: Reynal & Hitchcock, 1947, pp. 11–15

PIERRE

Anonymous
"Pierre; or, The Ambiguities" (1852)

Like the short *Athenaeum* review of *Pierre*, this piece levels the charge that the novel suffers from too much "transcendentalism." What does this repeated assessment mean? Students exploring the extent to which Melville dove into such Emersonian matters might examine how Pierre's self-reliant behaviors, or his sympathies with other characters, might have called forth such venom from critics. What, after all, is "transcendental" about *Pierre*? How does that stock critical insult work? This review also directly charges Melville with "supersensuousness," with attacking "the family" by "hint[ing]" at "incestuous relation[s]". The theme of family is an important one to the book, and later criticism will trace plot elements in *Pierre* to certain events and genealogical concerns that marked Melville's actual life. Some critics thus have found more than a little Melville in *Pierre*, and in Pierre the character, as both family man and writer. Finally, students concerned with Melville's use of language will find this essay of import, for it takes up and disparages the author's predilection for coining words. Students might compare such an attack on Melville's language usage with commentary embedded in other essays collected here, especially appreciations of *Moby-Dick*. How do the judgments differ?

The purpose of Mr. Melville's story, though vaguely hinted, rather than directly stated, seems to be to illustrate the possible antagonism of a sense of duty, conceived in the heat and impetuosity of youth, to all the recognised laws of social morality; and to exhibit a conflict between the virtues. The hero of the tale is Pierre, a fiery youth full of love and ardor. He is the last of the Glendennings, a family that can boldly face the memory of at least two generations back without blushing, which is a pretty fair title to an American nobility. He is an only son, the pride of his mother and his house, and the expectant heir of its wide domains. A warm affection unites Mrs. Glendenning, an aristocratic dame, and Pierre, and the heart of the proud woman is all content in the responsive love of her son. A certain Lucy Tartan, with all the requisite claims for a novelist's beauty, wins the affection of and in due course of time is betrothed to Pierre. All appears smooth and prosperous to a future of happiness, when a mysterious darkeyed, dark-haired damsel, Isabel, proves herself to the satisfaction of Pierre, though on testimony that would not pass current in any court of law, to be his sister, the natural child of his father. Here is a sad blot upon the memory of a Glendenning, a living testimony of the sin of one who had been embalmed in the heart of Pierre, as pure and without reproach. Pierre, tortured with this damning fact that pollutes his filial ideal of a virtuous parent, conceives and rightly, that he has two duties to perform: to screen his dead father's memory and give to a living sister her due, a brother's affection. Pierre impetuously decides that the only way of reconciling these two duties is by the expedient of a pretended marriage with Isabel, and thus shield the memory of his father while he protects and unites himself in brotherly affection with his sister.

Mark the tragical result. The proud mother's proudest hopes are blasted by this supposed marriage; she drives Pierre from her house, disinherits him and dies a maniac. Pierre, an outcast, seeks in the company of his sister, his pretended wife, a refuge with his cousin, a rich denizen of the city, is totally ignored by him and repelled from his door. He is compelled to seek his livelihood with his pen. While he is thus engaged, struggling with poverty and misery, Lucy Tartan, who has survived the first shock from the agony of

Pierre's abandonment and supposed marriage, unable to live without Pierre and instinctively justifying his infidelity on a principle, by no means clear to the reader, of abstract faith to her former lover, resolves to live with him, and joins the household of Pierre and Isabel. Lucy is followed to Pierre's dwelling by her brother and Pierre's cousin, who has succeeded Pierre as a suitor of Lucy. They attempt to force Lucy away, but she is rescued by Pierre with the aid of his fellow lodgers. Vengeance is sworn by the brother and cousin. An insulting letter is written to Pierre, denouncing him as a seducer and liar. To add to the agony of Pierre he receives at the same time a letter from his publishers, rejecting his novel. Pierre is outrageous, and arming himself with two pistols, seeks out his cousin, finds him, is struck by him, and in return shoots his cousin doubly dead with the two pistols. He is thrown into prison. He is sought out there by Isabel and Lucy. Lucy learning for the first time, from an agonizing cry of "brother" from Isabel, that she was Pierre's sister and not his wife, swoons away and dies. While Isabel and Pierre, conjointly help themselves in a fraternal way, to a draught of poison that Isabel has concealed upon her person, and they also die—*felo de se.* Nor is this the end of the casualty, the full list of the dead and wounded, for the surviving Tartan family must be necessarily plunged in irretrievable agony, leading to the probable result of some broken and various wounded hearts, on account of the death and supposed dishonor of Lucy.

Mr. Melville may have constructed his story upon some new theory of art to a knowledge of which we have not yet transcended; he evidently has not constructed it according to the established principles of the only theory accepted by us until assured of a better, of one more true and natural than truth and nature themselves, which are the germinal principles of all true art.

The pivot of the story is the pretended marriage of Pierre with his sister, in order to conceal her illegitimacy and protect his father's memory. Pierre, to carry out his purpose, abandons mother, home, his betrothed, all the advantages of his high social position, wealth and its appointments of ease and luxury and respect, and invites poverty, misery, infamy, and death. Apart from the very obvious way of gaining the same object at an infinitely smaller cost, is it natural that a loving youth should cast away the affection of his mother and his betrothed and the attachment of home to hide a dim stain upon his father's memory and to enjoy the love of an equivocal sister? Pierre not only acts thus absurdly, but pretends to act from a sense of duty. He is battling for Truth and Right, and the first thing he does in behalf of Truth is to proclaim to the whole world a falsehood, and the next thing he does is to commit in behalf of Right, a half a dozen most foul wrongs.

The combined power of New England transcendentalism and Spanish Jesuitical casuistry could not have more completely befogged nature and truth, than this confounded Pierre has done. It is needless to test minutely the truth and nature of each character. In a word, Pierre is a psychological curiosity, a moral and intellectual phenomenon; Isabel, a lusus naturae; Lucy, an incomprehensible woman; and the rest not of the earth nor, we may venture to state, of heaven. The object of the author, perhaps, has been, not to delineate life and character as they are or may possibly be, but as they are not and cannot be. We must receive the book, then, as an eccentricity of the imagination.

The most immoral *moral* of the story, if it has any moral at all, seems to be the impracticability of virtue; a leering demoniacal spectre of an idea seems to be speering at us through the dim obscure of this dark book, and mocking us with this dismal falsehood. Mr. Melville's chapter on "Chronometricals and Horologicals," if it has any meaning at all, simply means that virtue and religion are only for gods and not to be attempted by man. But ordinary novel readers will never unkennel this loathsome suggestion. The stagnant pool at the bottom of which it lies, is not too deep for their penetration, but too muddy, foul, and corrupt. If truth is hid in a well, falsehood lies in a quagmire.

We cannot pass without remark, the supersensuousness with which the holy relations of the family are described. Mother and son, brother and sister are sacred facts not to be disturbed by any sacrilegious speculations. Mrs. Glendenning and Pierre, mother and son, call each other brother and sister, and are described with all the coquetry of a lover and mistress. And again, in what we have termed the supersensuousness of description, the horrors of an incestuous relation between Pierre and Isabel seem to be vaguely hinted at.

In commenting upon the vagueness of the book, the uncertainty of its aim, the indefiniteness of its characters, and want of distinctness in its pictures, we are perhaps only proclaiming ourselves as the discoverers of a literary mare's nest; this vagueness, as the title of the *Ambiguities* seems to indicate, having been possibly intended by the author, and the work meant as a problem of impossible solution, to set critics and readers a woolgathering. It is alone intelligible as an unintelligibility. . . .

All the male characters of the book have a certain robust, animal force and untamed energy, which carry them through their melodramatic parts—no slight duty—with an effect sure to bring down the applause of the excitable and impulsive. Mr. Melville can think clearly, and write with distinctness and force—in a style of simplicity and purity. Why, then, does he allow his mind to run riot amid remote analogies, where the chain of association is invisible to mortal minds? Why does he give us incoherencies of thought, in infelicities of language? Such incoherency as this:—"Love is both Creator's and Saviour's gospel to mankind; a volume bound in rose-leaves, clasped with violets, and by the beaks of humming birds, printed with peach-juice on the leaves of lilies. Endless is the account of love. Time and space cannot contain Love's story. All things that are sweet to see, or taste, or feel, or hear, all these things were made by Love, and none other things were made by Love. Love made not the Arctic zones, but Love is ever reclaiming them. Say, are not the fierce things of this earth daily, hourly going out? Where are now your wolves of Britain? Where in Virginia now find you the panther and the pard? Oh, Love is busy everywhere. Everywhere Love hath Moravian missionaries. No propagandist like to Love. The south wind wooes the barbarous north; on many a distant shore the gentler west wind persuades the arid east. All this earth is Love's affianced; vainly the demon Principle howls to stay the banns." Such infelicities of expression, such unknown words as these, to wit: "humanness," "heroicness," "patriarchalness," "descendedness," "flushfulness," "amaranthiness," "instantaneousness," "leapingly acknowledging," "fateful frame of mind," "protectingness," "youngness," "infantileness," "visibleness," *et id genus omne!*

The author of *Pierre; or, the Ambiguities;* the writer of a mystic romance, in which are conjured up unreal nightmare-conceptions, a confused phantasmagoria of distorted fancies and conceits, ghostly abstractions and fitful shadows, is certainly but a spectre of the substantial author of *Omoo* and *Typee*, the jovial and hearty narrator of the traveller's tale of incident and adventure. By what *diablerie,* hocus-pocus, or thimble-rigging, "now you see him and now you don't" process, the transformation has been effected, we are not skilled in necromancy to detect. Nor, if it be a true psychological development, are we sufficiently advanced in transcendentalism to lift ourselves skywards and see clearly the coming light with our heads above the clouds. If this novel indicates a chaotic state of authorship,—and we can distinguish fragmentary elements of beauty—out of which is to rise a future temple of order, grace, and proportion, in which the genius of Mr. Melville is to enshrine itself, we will be happy to worship there; but let its foundation be firmly based on *terra firma,* or, if in the heavens, let us not trust our common sense to the flight of any waxen pinion. We would rejoice to meet Mr. Melville again in the hale company of sturdy sailors, men of flesh and blood, and, strengthened by the wholesome air of the outside world, whether it be land-breeze or sea-breeze, listen to his narrative of a traveller's tale, in which he has few equals in power and felicity.

—Unsigned, "Pierre; or, The Ambiguities"
Literary World, August 21, 1852, pp. 118–20

Anonymous "Review of New Books" (1852)

While this reviewer admits that Melville hits new heights of "subtlety of thinking and unity of purpose," the subject swiftly turns to insinuating notice that the book is somehow "unhealthy." A string of vague modifiers seems to point to Melville's unsubtle suggestions of incestuous love between Pierre, "sister Mary," as he calls his mother, and Isabel. Is this what the reviewer cannot stand, what is "as disgusting . . . as physical disease"?

This work is generally considered a failure. The cause of its ill-success is certainly not to be sought in its lack of power. None of Melville's novels equals the present in force and subtlety of thinking and unity of purpose. Many of the scenes are wrought out with great splendor and vigor, and a capacity is evinced of holding with a firm grasp, and describing with a masterly distinctness, some of the most evanescent phenomena of morbid emotions. But the spirit pervading the whole book is intolerably unhealthy, and the most friendly reader is obliged at the end to protest against such a provoking perversion of talent and waste of power. The author has attempted seemingly to combine in it the peculiarities of Poe and Hawthorne, and has succeeded in producing nothing but a powerfully unpleasant caricature of morbid thought and passion. Pierre, we take it, is crazy, and the merit of the book is in clearly presenting the psychology of his madness; but the details of such a mental malady as that which afflicts Pierre are almost as disgusting as those of physical disease itself.

—Unsigned, "Review of New Books,"
Graham's Magazine, October 1852, p. 445

Anonymous "Pierre, or The Ambiguities" (1852)

While ample plot summary indicates that the anonymous author collected here has closely read *Pierre,* the writer clearly does not like the book.

This review, read alongside the harsh sentiments expressed in *Literary World,* reflect how brutal the practice of reviewing could be in the nineteenth century. Students might explore how these reviews do and do not actually critique Melville's writing. Also, if both reviews dismiss the book, they do so by taking Melville at his word. Neither explores in any depth how Melville might be engaged in a critique of contemporary literary form, such as the sentimental novel, or whether he might be practicing irony, or attempting to construct some sort of radically inventive parody. Students considering how literary, social, or market sensibilities manufactured or reinforced reader expectations or authorial behavior will find these two remarkably brutal reviews of note. Students might consider whether the magazine reviews of Melville's work collected in this volume seem to have had any effect on what he produced? Did he listen and react in one way or another to his critics?

A bad book! Affected in dialect, unnatural in conception, repulsive in plot, and inartistic in construction. Such is Mr. Melville's worst and latest work.

   Some reputations seem to be born of accident. There are common-place men who on some fine day light, unknown to themselves, upon a popular idea, and suddenly rise on the strength of it into public favor. They stride the bubble for a little while, but at last its prismatic hues begin to fade; men see that the object of their applause has after all but an unsubstantial basis, and when at length the frail foundation bursts, they fall back into their original obscurity, unheeded and unlamented. Mr. Melville has experienced some such success. A few years back, he gave to the world a story of romantic adventure; this was untrue in its painting, coarse in its coloring, and often tedious and prolix in its descriptive passages. But there was a certain air of rude romance about it, that captivated the general public. It depicted scenes in a strange land, and dealt with all the interests that circle around men whose lives are passed in peril. Nor were appeals to the grosser instincts of humanity wanting. Naked women were scattered profusely through the pages, and the author seemed to feel that in a city where the ballet was admired, *Typee* would be successful.[1] Mr. Melville thought he had hit the key-note to fame. His book was reprinted in all directions, and people talked about it, as much from the singularity of its title as from any intrinsic merit it possessed.

   This was encouraging, and Mr. Melville evidently thought so, for he immediately issued a series of books in the same strain. Omoo, *Mardi, White-Jacket, Redburn,* followed one another in quick succession; and the foolish critics, too blind to perceive that the books derived their chief interest from the fact of the scenes being laid in countries little known, and that the author had no other stock in trade beyond tropical scenery and eccentric sailors, applauded to the very echo. This indiscriminating praise produced its usual effect. Mr. Melville fancied himself a genius, and the result of this sad mistake has been—*Pierre.*

As a general rule, sea-stories are very effective, and to those versed in nautical lore, very easy writing. The majority of the reading public are landsmen, and the events of an ocean-life come to them recommended by the charm of novelty. They cannot detect the blunders, and incongruity passes with them for originality. The author can make his vessel and his characters perform the most impossible feats, and who, except the favored few that themselves traverse the sea professionally, will be one bit the wiser? The scope for events is also limited, and this very limitation renders the task of writing a sea-tale more simple. A storm, a wreck, a chase and a battle, a mutiny, desertions, and going into and leaving port, with perhaps a fire at sea, form the principal "properties" of a salt-water artist. Considerable descriptive powers are, we admit, necessary to the management of these materials. The storm must be wild, the battle fierce, and the fire terrible; but these, after all, are broad outlines, and require little delicacy of handling to fill them in. Sometimes, as in the *Pilot,* one finds a veil of pathetic tenderness and grace flung over the characters, but as a general rule in nautical fictions, the wit is coarse, the pathos clumsy, and the most striking characters are invariably unnatural.

It is when a writer comes to deal with the varied interests of a more extended life; when his hand must touch in harmonious succession the numberless chords of domestic sorrows, duties and affections, and draw from each the proper vibration; when he has to range among the ever-changing relations of every-day humanity, and set each phase of being down in its correct lineaments; it is then he discovers that something more is necessary for the task than a mere arrangement of strong words in certain forms,—or the trick of painting nature, until, like a ranting actress, she pleases certain tastes according as she deviates from truth.

Mr. Melville's previous stories, all seaborn as they were, went down the public throat because they were prettily gilt with novelty. There are crowds of people who will run after a new pill, and swallow it with avidity, because it is new, and has a long Greek name. It may be made of bread, or it may be made of poison; the novelty of the affair renders all considerations of its composition quite immaterial. They learn the name, eat the bolus, and pay the doctor. We have a shrewd suspicion that the uncouth and mysterious syllables with which Mr. Melville baptized his books had much to do with their success. Like Doctor Dulcamara, he gave his wares an exciting title, and trusted to Providence for the rest. The enchantment worked. The mystic cabala of *"Omoo,* by the author of *Typee,"* was enough in itself to turn any common novel-reader's brain, and the boob went off as well as a collection of magic rings would in Germany, or the latest batch of *Agnus Deis* in an Italian village. People had little opportunity of judging of their truth. Remote scenes and savage actors gave a fine opportunity for high coloring and exaggerated outline, of which Mr. Melville was not slow to avail himself, and hence Fayaway is as unreal as the scenery with which she is surrounded.

We do not blame Mr. Melville for these deviations from truth. It is not much matter if South Sea savages are painted like the heroes of a penny theatre, and disport themselves amid pasteboard groves, and lakes of canvas. We can afford Mr. Melville full license to do what he likes with "Omoo" and its inhabitants; it is only when he presumes to thrust his tragic *Fantoccini* upon us, as representatives of our own race, that we feel compelled to turn our critical Ægis upon him, and freeze him into silence.

Pierre aims at something beyond the mere records of adventure contained in *Mardi* and *Omoo.* The author, doubtless puffed up by the very false applause which some critics chose to bestow upon him, took for granted that he was a genius, and made up his mind to write a fine book; and he has succeeded in writing a fine book with a vengeance. Our experience of literature is necessarily large, but we unhesitatingly state, that from the period when the Minerva press was in fashion, up to the present time, we never met with so turgid, pretentious, and useless a book as *Pierre.* It is always an unpleasant and apparently invidious statement for a critic to make, that he can find nothing worthy of praise in a work under consideration; but in the case of *Pierre* we feel bound to add to the assertion the sweeping conclusion, that there we find every thing to condemn. If a repulsive, unnatural and indecent plot, a style disfigured by every paltry affectation of the worst German school, and ideas perfectly unparalleled for earnest absurdity, are deserving of condemnation, we think that our already expressed sentence upon *Pierre* will meet with the approval of every body who has sufficient strength of mind to read it through.

Mr. Pierre Glendinning, the hero of the book, and intended by the author to be an object of our mournful admiration, supports in the course of the story the arduous characters of a disobedient son, a dishonest lover, an incestuous brother, a cold-blooded murderer, and an unrepentant suicide.

This *repertoire* is agreeably relieved by his playing the part of a madman whenever he is not engaged in doing any thing worse.

This agreeable young gentleman is the only son of a widow lady of large fortune, who coquets in her old age with suitors about the same age as Pierre. And to render the matter still more interesting, Pierre by mutual consent sinks the son, and deports himself by word and look towards his mother as a lover; while she, charming coquette of fifty that she is, readily imitates this delightful *abandon*. The early character of Mr. P. Glendinning, as traced by our author, is exceedingly fine; we will, however, spare it to our readers, merely stating on Mr. Melville's authority, that in him might be observed "the polished steel of the gentleman, girded with Religion's silken sash;" which sash, his great-grandfather had somehow or other taught him, "should, in the last bitter trial, furnish its wearer with glory's shroud." Setting aside the little incompatibility of religion having any thing to do, even in sashes, with martial glory, we cannot help thinking that the mere mention of making a shroud out of so scanty an article as a sash, is quite sufficient to scandalize any respectable undertaker.

Well, this be-sashed young gentleman, who lives alone with his mother at the family place of Saddle Meadows, is engaged formally to a very flighty young lady named Lucy Tartan. If there is any thing to which we object particularly in this young couple, it is the painful habit they have contracted of *tutoyer*-ing each other through whole pages of insane rhapsody. We cannot believe that the indiscriminate use of "thee" and "thou" makes the nonsense with which it is generally connected one atom more readable. On the contrary, it has a most unpleasant effect, for it deprives the mad passages in which it occurs of the only recommendation that can palliate insanity, that is, simplicity.

Notwithstanding Mr. P. Glendinning's being already supplied with a mother and a mistress, he is pursued by indefinite longings for a sister. His reason for this imperious craving is rather a pugnacious one, and almost inclines us to believe that the young gentleman must have had some Celtic blood in his veins. If he had but a sister, he alleges he would be happy, because "it must be a glorious thing to engage in a mortal quarrel on a sweet sister's behalf!" This, it must be confessed, is a strange fancy, but we suppose it is to be accounted for by the fact of Saddle Meadows being rather a dull place, and Mr. Pierre believing that a little fighting was the best thing in the world for the blues.

By a chain of the most natural circumstances in the world—we mean in Mr. Melville's books—this sister is most unexpectedly supplied. In fact, though the author says nothing about it, we are inclined to think that he imported her direct from a lunatic asylum for the occasion. She proves to be an illegitimate daughter of Pierre's father, and judging from her own story, as well as we could understand it, appears to have been dry-nursed by an old family guitar; an allegory almost as fine as that of Romulus and Remus. If we suppose this paternal instrument to have been out of tune at the time that it assumed the responsibility of the little Isabel, that young lady's singular turn of mind is at once accounted for; but if we go a little farther, and suppose the worthy instrument to have been cracked, we explain still more satisfactorily the origin of her very erratic conduct.

"Sister Isabel," being an illegitimate Glendinning, is of course inadmissible to the refined atmosphere breathed by the aristocratic Mrs. Glendinning, who has rather strong ideas upon such subjects. Accordingly, Pierre, who is afraid to mention to his mother the discovery he has made, and moved to compassion by the forlorn state of the young lady, who lives with her faithful guitar in a charming cottage on the edge of a beautiful lake, takes compassion on her desolate condition, and determines to devote his life to her. He therefore conceives the sublime idea of obviating all difficulties—for difficulties there must have been, or Mr. Melville would not say so, though we confess that we have not been so fortunate as to discover them—by presenting her to the world as his wife! The reasons alleged by this virtuous hero are detailed at some length by Mr. Melville, as if he knew that he could not apologize too much for presenting such a picture to the world. Firstly, Pierre wishes to conceal the fact of Isabel's being the offspring of his father's sin, and thereby protect his parent's reputation. Secondly, he is actuated by a desire not to disturb his mother's mind by any disclosure which would destroy the sacredness of her deceased husband's memory; and lastly, he entertains towards this weird sister feelings which Mr. Melville endeavors to gloss over with a veil of purity, but which even in their best phase can never be any thing but repulsive to a well constituted mind.

Now, in this matter Mr. Melville has done a very serious thing, a thing which not even unsoundness of intellect could excuse. He might have been mad to the very pinnacle of insanity; he might have torn our poor language into tatters, and made from the shreds a harlequin suit in which to play his tricks; he might have piled up word upon word, and adjective upon adjective, until he had built a pyramid of nonsense, which should last to the admiration of all men; he might have done all this and a great deal more, and we should not have complained. But when he dares to outrage every principle of virtue; when he strikes with an impious, though, happily, weak hand, at the very foundations of society, we feel it our duty to tear off the veil with which he has thought to soften the hideous features of the idea, and warn the public against the reception of such atrocious doctrines. If Mr. Melville had reflected at all—and certainly we find in him but few traces of reflection—when he was writing this book, his better sense would perhaps have informed him that there are certain ideas so repulsive to the general mind that they themselves are not alone kept out of sight, but, by a fit ordination of society, every thing that might be supposed to even collaterally suggest them is carefully shrouded in a decorous darkness. Nor has any man the right, in his morbid craving after originality, to strip these horrors of their decent mystery. But the subject which Mr. Melville has taken upon himself to handle is one of no ordinary depravity; and however he may endeavor to gloss the idea over with a platonic polish, no matter how energetically he strives to wrap the mystery in a cloud of high-sounding but meaningless words, the main conception remains still unaltered in all its moral deformity. We trust that we have said enough on this topic. It is a subject that we would gladly not have been obliged to approach, and which we are exceedingly grieved that any gentleman pretending to the rank of a man of letters should have chosen to embody in a book. Nor can we avoid a feeling of surprise, that professedly moral and apparently respectable publishers like the Messrs. Harper should have ever consented to issue from their establishment any book containing such glaring abominations as *Pierre*.

But to return to the development of this chaotic volume. Mr. P. Glendinning, actuated by this virtuous love for his sister, informs his proud mother that he is married. She, knowing not the true relationship that binds them together, spurns her unworthy son from her house for having degraded the family name so far by making a *mésalliance;* and the worthy young gentleman, after having nearly killed Miss Lucy Tartan, his betrothed, with the same intelligence, and left his mother in a fit of indignation which has every chance of becoming a fit of apoplexy, sets out with—we really do not know what to call her, for Mr. Melville has so intertwined and confused the wife with the sister, and the sister with the wife, that we positively cannot tell one from the other; so we may as well compromise the matter by calling her simply Isabel. He sets out then with Isabel, in a perfect enthusiasm of virtue, for the city, having first apprised a fashionable cousin of his, one Mr. Glendinning Stanly, that he was on his way, and requesting him to prepare his house for his reception. This fashionable cousin, however, takes very little trouble about the matter; and accordingly, when Pierre and Isabel arrive accompanied by a young lady of loose morals named Delly, they find no house or welcome. A series of incidents here follow, which are hardly worth reciting. They consist of Pierre's quarrel with Stanly, a scene in a police station, a row with a cabman, and ending by Pierre's taking rooms in some out-of-the way place, inhabited by a colony of poor authors, who bear the general denomination of Apostles, just in this part of the book it comes out suddenly that Pierre is an author, a fact not even once hinted at in the preceding pages. Now the reader is informed, with very little circumlocution, and as if he ought to have known all about it long ago, that Mr. P. Glendinning is the author of a sonnet called the "Tropical Summer," which it seems has called forth the encomiums of the literati, and induced certain proprietors of certain papers to persecute him for his portrait. All this is told in a manner that proves it very clearly to be nothing more than an afterthought of Mr. Melville's, and not contemplated in the original plan of the book, that is, if it ever had a plan. It is dragged in merely for the purpose of making Pierre a literary man, when the author had just brought him to such a stage that he did not know what else to do with him.

Of course, under such circumstances, Mr. P. Glendinning, having the responsibility upon his back of Mrs.—Miss Isabel, his wife-sister, (as Mr. Melville himself would express it,) and the young lady of loose morals, and having no money wherewith to support them, can do nothing better than make his living by writing. Accordingly he writes away in his garret; and we cannot help thinking here, that if he wrote at all in the same style that he speaks, his MSS. must have been excessively original and amusing. Here in this poor place he starves his time away in company with Isabel and the young lady of loose morals. Meanwhile he hears of his mother's death, her bequest of all the property to his cousin Stanly, and the betrothal of that gentleman to his late mistress, Lucy Tartan. This intelligence, however, is soon followed by a remarkable event. Miss Lucy Tartan, true to her old habits of flightiness, conceives the resolution of coming to live with Pierre and Isabel, whom she believes to be his wife. Accordingly, she arrives at the haunt of the Apostles, and takes up her abode with her old lover, very much to the disgust of Madam Isabel, who acts much more like a jealous wife than a sister. In this comfortable state they all live together until Mr. Glendinning Stanly and Miss Lucy Tartan's brother arrive at Pierre's domicile to reclaim the fugitive. She refuses to go, however, and Mr. Pierre thrusts them out of the house. Immediately after he receives two notes: one from a bookseller, for whom he was writing a work, informing him that he is a swindler; the other from Messrs. Stanly and Tartan, putting him in possession of the fact that he is a liar and a scoundrel—all of which conclusions the reader arrives at long before this epoch.

Mr. P. Glendinning on reading these notes immediately proceeds to stand on them. This operation is minutely described by our author, and is evidently considered by him as a very effective piece of business. Putting a note under each heel of his boots, appears to be with Mr. P. Glendinning the very climax of vengeance. Having stood for a sufficiently long time upon the epistles, he proceeds to enter an Apostle's room, and burglariously abstract from thence a pair of pistols, which he loads with the unpleasant letters. Then marching into the street, he meets with, and is cowhided by, Mr. Stanly, and in consequence thereof shoots that individual with two distinct pistols. One would have been meagre, but two bullet-holes make the thing dramatic.

Mr. P. Glendinning now makes his appearance in prison; a place that, if fitness were any recommendation, he ought to have been in long ago. Here he raves about as usual in compound words and uncompounded ideas, until Lucy and Isabel enter, when there is a terrific amount of dying, and the usual vial of poison makes its appearance. How many persons give up the ghost in the last chapter of this exciting work, we are really unable to decide. But we have a dim consciousness that every body dies, save and except the young lady of loose morals.

Previous to entering more closely upon the singular merits of this book, we have endeavored, we fear but feebly, to give the reader some idea of the ground-work on which Mr. Melville has strung his farrago of words. If we have succeeded, so much the better, for our readers will perhaps appreciate more fully our approaching remarks. If we have not, it matters but little, for the reader will have lost nothing that is worth a regret.

We have already dismissed the immorality of Mr. Melville's book, which is as horrible in its tendency as Shelley's *Cenci,* without a ray of the eloquent genius that lights up the deformity of that terrible play; but we have yet another and less repulsive treat in store for the reader. Mr. Melville's style of writing in this book is probably the most extraordinary thing that an American press ever beheld. It is precisely what a raving lunatic who had read Jean Paul Richter *in a translation* might be supposed to spout under the influence of a particularly moonlight night. Word piled upon word, and syllable heaped upon syllable, until the tongue grows as bewildered as the mind, and both refuse to perform their offices from sheer inability to grasp the magnitude of the absurdities. Who would have believed that in the present day a man would write the following, and another be found to publish it?

> Now Pierre began to see mysteries interpierced with mysteries, and mysteries eluding mysteries; and began to seem to see the mere imaginariness of the so supposed solidest principle of human association. Fate had done this for them. Fate had separated brother and sister, till to each other they somehow seemed so not at all.—Page 193.

There, public! there's a style for you! There, Mr. Hawthorne, you who rely so much upon the quiet force of your language, read that and profit by it! And you, Mr. Longfellow, who love the Germans, and who in *Hyperion* have given us a sample of an ornate and poetical style, pray read it too, and tell us if it is a wise thing to bind 495 pages of such stuff together, and palm it off upon the public as a book! But here is a string of assertions that we think are not to be surpassed; it is positively refreshing to read them:

> Of old Greek times, before man's brain went into doting bondage, and bleached and beaten in Baconian fulling mills, his four limbs lost their barbaric tan and beauty; when the round world was fresh, and rosy, and spicy as a new-plucked apple; all's wilted now! In those bold times, the great dead were not, turkey-like, dished in trenchers, and set down all garnished in the ground to glut the damned Cyclop like a cannibal; but nobly envious Life cheated the glutton worm, and gloriously burned the corpse; so that the spirit uppointed, and visibly forked to heaven!—Page 269.

We pause here. And when our readers have sufficiently recovered their senses to listen, we will remark that until now we were quite unaware that it was the modern practice to bury people in cover dishes or soup tureens, after having garnished them with parsley. Mr. Melville however asserts it, so it *must* be correct. Neither do we see what the Cyclop has to do with the funereal ceremonies alluded to. A church-yard is the last place in which we should think of looking for Polyphemus.

It is rather a curious study, that of analyzing a man's style. By a little careful examination and comparison, we are always able to hunt out the lurking secret of a writer's diction. We can discover Bulwer's trick of culminating periods, and Dickens's dodge of impossible similes and startling adjectives. A perfectly plain and pure style is the only one which we cannot properly analyze. Its elements are so equally combined that no one preponderates over the other, and we are not able to discover the exact boundary line that separates the art of the author from the nature of the man. But who writes such a style now-a-days? We feel convinced that echo will *not* answer, "Mr. Melville."

The author of *Omoo* has his own peculiarities. The English language he seems to think is capable of improvement, but his scheme for accomplishing this end is rather a singular one. Carlyle's compound words and Milton's latinic ones sink into insignificance before Mr. Melville's extraordinary concoctions. The gentleman, however, appears to be governed by a very distinct principle in his eccentricities of composition, and errs systematically. The essence of this great eureka, this philological reform, consists in "est" and "ness," added to every word to which they have no earthly right to belong. Feeling it to be our duty to give currency to every new discovery at all likely to benefit the world or literature, we present a few of Mr. Melville's word-combinations, in the hope that our rising authors will profit by the lesson, and thereby increase the richness and intelligibility of their style:

Flushfulness,	page	7	Solidest,	page	193
Patriarchalness,	page	12	Uncapitulatable	page	229
Humanness,	page	16	Ladylikeness,	page	235
Heroicness,	page	do.	Electricalness,	page	206
Perfectest,	page	41	Ardentest,	page	193
Imaginariness,	page	193	Unsystemizable	page	191
Insolubleness,	page	188	Youngness,	page	190
Recallable,	page	186	Unemigrating,	page	470
Entangledly,	page	262	Unrunagate,	page	do.
Intermarryingly,	page	151	Undoffable,	page	do.
Magnifiedly,	page	472			

After such a list, what shall we say? Shall we leave Mr. Melville to the tender mercies of the Purists, or shall we execute vengeance upon him ourselves? We would gladly pursue the latter course if we only knew how to accomplish it. As to destroying or abusing the book, we cannot make it appear worse than it is; and if we continue our remarks upon it, it is simply because we have a duty to perform by every improper work, which we have no right to leave unfinished. We shall, then, instead of turning executioners, simply assume the post of monitors, and warn all our little authors who are just now learning to imitate the last celebrity, to avoid Mr. Melville and his book, as they would some loathsome and infectious distemper.

Perhaps one of the most remarkable features in *Pierre,* is the boldness of the metaphors with which it is so thickly studded. Mr. Melville's imagination stops at nothing, and clears a six-barred simile or a twenty-word antithesis with equal dexterity and daring. It is no light obstacle that will bring him up in his headlong course, and he scoffs alike at the boundaries of common sense and the limits of poetical propriety. We have just caught an image which will serve our purpose, and transfix it, butterfly-like, on our critical pin, for the admiration of scientific etymologists. It is a fine specimen, and quite perfect of its kind. Fortunately for the world, however, the species is very rare:

An infixing stillness now thrust a long rivet through the night, and fast nailed it to that side of the world!—Page 219.

This is a grand and simple metaphor. To realize it thoroughly, all we have to do is to imagine some Titanic upholsterer armed with a gigantic nail, and hammer to match, hanging one hemisphere with black crape.

His description of a lady's forehead is equally grand and incomprehensible. He says, "The vivid buckler of her brow seemed as a magnetic plate." Trephining is rather an uncommon operation, but we fancy that this lady's head must have undergone some such treatment, in order to warrant her forehead being likened to a "vivid buckler."

Mr. Melville, among other improvements, has favored us with a new substantive of his own invention. We are very grateful to him for this little attention, but our thankfulness would be rendered still more willingly if he had appended a little note explaining the meaning of this—no doubt very forcible—word. At page 242 we find the following sentence: "Thy *instantaneousness* hath killed her." On a first reading of this we hurriedly came to the conclusion that "instantaneous-ness" must be either some very old or some very new weapon of destruction. We judged simply from the fatal results attributed to it in the sentence. Can it be possible, thought we to ourselves, that the reign of the sanguinary Colt is over? that revolvers are gone out of fashion and "instantaneousnesses" come in? What can these new weapons be like? Have they six barrels, or are they worked by steam? In the midst of these perplexities we were still further bewildered by coming suddenly upon this passage, at page 248:

The strange, imperious *instantaneousness in* him.

Here in an instant was our whole theory upset. The hieroglyph on the Rosetta stone was not more puzzling than this noun of Mr. Melville's. It was eivdent from the context in the last sentence that it could not be a weapon of destruction, so we immediately formed a conception that it must be some newly discovered magnetic power, which resided *in* the man, but could be used with fatal effect if necessary. Upon this hypothesis we were proceeding to build another theory, far more magnificent than our first, when we lit upon a *third* sentence that sent to the winds all previous speculations. It ran as follows:

> That *instantaneousness* now impelled him.—Page 252.

Eureka! we shouted, we have it. Success has crowned our toil, and the enigma is for ever solved. "Instantaneousness" is a new motive power! We leave our readers to brood over this discovery.

Mr. Melville's lingual improvements do not stop here. He discards all commonplace words, and substitutes much better ones of his own in their stead. He would not for the world call the travelling from one place to another "a journey"—*that* would be far too common. In Mr. Melville's refined diction it becomes "a displacement." Every thing that is dim is with him "nebulous." Hence we have nebulous stories, nebulous landscapes, nebulous meanings, and though last, not least, Mr. Melville himself has given us a very nebulous book!

His descriptive passages are very vivid. The following "night piece" is somewhat after the manner of Callot:

> The obscurely open window, which ever and anon was still softly illumined by the mild heat-lightning and ground lightning, that wove their wonderfulness without, in the unsearchable air of that *ebonly warm* and most noiseless summer night.—Page 203.

In the same page, a little further on, we find that

> The casement was suddenly and *wovenly* illumined.

This is no doubt fine to those that understand, but, strange as the confession may appear, we are foolhardy enough to acknowledge that we have not the remotest conception of what it all means. We cannot, by any mental process hitherto discovered, induce our reasoning faculties to accept "ebonly warm" and "wovenly illumined" as conveying any tangible idea. The first two words we do not recognize as belonging to any known language, and we have a shrewd suspicion that the idea—if the author intended any—is quite as undiscoverable.

Again, he hits off a lady's eyes after the following fashion. It may be poetical, but we cannot call it complimentary:

> Her dry burning eyes of long-fringed fire.—Page 202.

This young lady must have been the original performer of the "lightning glance" and the "look of flashing scorn," once used so freely by a certain class of novel-writers.

At page 60 we find the following singular expression:

> It was no wonder that Pierre should flush a bit, and *stammer in his attitudes* a little.

It was an old-fashioned idea that the disease of stammering was usually confined to the organs of speech. In modern times, however, it seems to embrace a wider sphere; and we shall, no doubt, soon hear of "stuttering legs" and "a man with a hesitation in his arm." Nor do we see why the converse should not be adopted, or why a man should not have a "club tongue," or "bunions upon his conversation!"

We have been so far particular in pointing out Mr. Melville's faults. We have attached a certain degree of importance to each of them, from the fact that we are obliged to look upon him in the light of an experienced author, and cannot allow him that boyish license which we are always ready to grant to tyros who lose themselves for the first time amid the bewildering paths of literature. Mr. Melville has written good books, and tasted largely of success, and he ought to have known better. . . .

We have dwelt long enough upon these *Ambiguities*. We fear that if we were to continue much longer, we should become ambiguous ourselves. We have, we think, said sufficient to show our readers that Mr. Melville is a man wholly unfitted for the task of writing wholesome fictions; that he possesses none of the faculties necessary for such work; that his fancy is diseased, his morality vitiated, his style nonsensical and ungrammatical, and his characters as far removed from our sympathies as they are from nature.

Let him continue, then, if he must write, his pleasant sea and island tales. We will be always happy to hear Mr. Melville discourse about savages, but we must protest against any more Absurdities, misnamed *Ambiguities*.

Notes

1. Mr. Cornelius Mathews was, we believe, the first to designate this prurient taste under the happy and specific head of "the ballet-feeling."

—Unsigned, "Pierre, or The Ambiguities"
American Whig Review, November 1852, pp. 446–54

Anonymous "New Novels" (1852)

This unnamed reviewer recoils at what he calls Melville's "Germanism"— the importation, as the reviewer would have it, of un-American, metaphysical "ambiguities." Readers investigating the infamous failure of *Pierre*, or students looking into Melville's scathing, embedded, and extensive critique of the American literary marketplace (consult, in particular, Book XVII, "Young America in Literature"), might find this review and the one from *Graham's Magazine* a strong place to start.

This volume is a would-be utterance of 'Young Yankee' sentimentalism:— but beyond that its writer may be a subject of the States, we can discern nothing either American or original in its pages. It reads like an "upsetting" into English of the first novel of a very whimsical and lackadaisical young student at the University of Gottingen.

It is one of the most diffuse doses of transcendentalism offered for a long time to the public. When he sat down to compose it, the author evidently had not determined what he was going to write about. Its plot is amongst the inexplicable "ambiguities" of the book,—the style is a prolonged succession of spasms,—and the characters are a marrowless tribe of phantoms, flitting through dense clouds of transcendental mysticism. "Be sure," said Pope to a young author, "when you have written any passage that you think particularly fine—to *erase it*." If this precept were applied to *Pierre; or, the Ambiguities,*—its present form would shrink into almost as many pages as there are now chapters. German literature with its depths and shallows is too keenly appreciated in this country for readers to endure Germanism at second hand. We take up novels to be amused—not bewildered,—in search of pleasure for the mind—not in pursuit of cloudy metaphysics; and it is no refreshment after the daily toils and troubles of life, for a reader to be soused into a torrent rhapsody uttered in defiance of taste and sense. . . .

That many readers will not follow "the moody way" of Pierre, is in our apprehension not amongst the "ambiguities," of the age. The present chaotic performance has nothing American about it, except that it reminds us of a prairie in print,—wanting the flowers and freshness of the savannahs, but almost equally puzzling to find a way through it.

—Unsigned, "New Novels," *Athenaeum*, November 20, 1852, pp. 1265–66

Julian Hawthorne
"The American Element in Fiction"
(1886)

Here, Julian Hawthorne, Nathaniel's son, writing much later, underlines the invective that characterized much of *Pierre* scholarship before the Melville revival. *Pierre* is a difficult book, and many critics still consider it deeply flawed, so frustration is to be expected. Still, these extracts are curiously representative of how their authors present little evidence of having ever actually read the book.

... his only novel or romance, whichever it be, was also the most impossible of all his books, and really a terrible example of the enormities which a man of genius may perpetrate when working in a direction unsuited to him. I refer, of course, to *Pierre, or the Ambiguities*.

—Julian Hawthorne, "The American Element in Fiction,"
North American Review, August 1886, p. 175

THE PIAZZA TALES

After *Pierre*, Melville turned increasingly to the tale form. He wrote at least seventeen, many of them appearing in *Putnam's* and *Harper's*. The three short reviews below address the arrival of *The Piazza Tales*, Melville's 1856 attempt to collect many of his shorter works under one cover. He is recommended as keeping good company with several American Romantics, and also as a writer delivering "a weirdness of conceit." For the second reviewer, "Melville is a kind of wizard," a writer of "strange and mysterious" places and things.

These three reviews are significant because they remind contemporary readers that Melville rebounded after the harsh reception that greeted *Pierre*. Besides the sometimes long collected tales and sketches, Melville was also at work on *Israel Potter* and *The Confidence Man* during this period. These reviews underline the fact that Melville's substantial foray into the shorter form of fiction, while noticeably difficult for these reviewers to pin down, was generally well received. Students discussing the tales may want to compare the slight appreciation recorded here with the robust critical take on the tales that has erupted since the modernist era.

Anonymous (1856)

For some time the literary world has lost sight of Herman Melville, whose last appearance as an author, in *Pierre or the Ambiguities*, was rather an unfortunate one, but he 'turns up' once more in *The Piazza Tales* with much of his former freshness and vivacity. Of the series of papers here collected, the preference must be given to the *Encantadas, or the Enchanted Islands*, in which he conducts us again into that 'wild, weird clime, out of space, out of time,' which is the scene of his earliest and most popular writings. 'The Lightning Rod Man' is a very flat recital which we should never have suspected Melville of producing, had it not been put forth under the sanction of his name.

—Anonymous, *Southern Literary Messenger*, 22, June 1856, p. 480

Anonymous (1856)

The author of *Typee* and *Omoo* is so well known to the public, that something good is expected by it, when his name appears on the titlepage of a book—not only expected but in the case of the present work, the *Piazza Tales*, is realized. Mr Melville tells us very pleasantly in his introduction all about his piazza on his house, how and why he built it, and describes in an exceedingly pleasant manner the scenery that he saw therefrom. But he does not tell us that this house was on the edge of the beautiful town of Pittsfield, one of the most lovely of all the Berkshire towns, and that his piazza looked out upon the Berkshire hills, in the midst of all that wonderful scenery. Such, however, is the fact. In the *Piazza Tales*, there are stories of all descriptions, tales of the sea and of the city, some of which are told with due gravity, like that of 'Benito Cereno,' and others, such as 'the Encantadas' with that copiousness of fancy and gentility of imagination, which resemble Melville more nearly to Charles Brockden Brown, the great novelist than to either of our other American story-tellers. Hawthorne is more dry, prosaic and detailed, Irving more elegant, careful and popular, but Melville is a kind of wizard, he writes strange and mysterious things that belong to other worlds beyond this tame and everyday place we live in. Those who delight in romance should get the *Piazza Tales*, who love strange and picturesque sentences, and the thoughtful truth of a writer, who leaves some space for the *reader* to try his own ingenuity upon,—some rests and intervals in the literary voyage.

—Anonymous, New Bedford *Daily Mercury*, June 4, 1856

Anonymous (1856)

The Piazza Tales of Herman Melville, published in New York by Dix & Edwards, form one of the most delightful books of the season. Marked by a delicate fancy, a bright and most fruitful imagination, a pure and translucent style, and a certain weirdness of conceit, they are not unlike, and seem to us not inferior, to the best things of Hawthorne. The introduction is one of the most graceful specimens of writing we have seen from an American pen. It is a poem—essentially a poem—lacking only rhythm and form. The remainder of the volume is occupied by fine stories, respectively entitled 'Bartleby,' 'Benito Cereno,' 'The Lightning-Rod Man,' 'The Encantadas' and 'The Bell-Tower.' It can be obtained of Chapin, Bridgman & Co.

—Anonymous, Springfield *Republican*, July 9, 1856

THE CONFIDENCE MAN

Students seeking to make sense of what critics today often hail as Melville's most problematic prose work will find little help in the reviews collected here. This excerpt represents the sense of profound puzzlement this work prompted among its initial readers.

Anonymous (1857)

In this book, also, philosophy is brought out of its cloisters into the living world; but the issue raised is more simple:—whether men are to be trusted or suspected? Mr Melville has a manner wholly different from that of the anonymous writer who has produced *The Metaphysicians*. He is less scholastic, and more sentimental; his style is not so severe; on the contrary, festoons of exuberant fancy decorate the discussion of abstract problems; the controversialists pause over and anon while a vivid, natural Mississippi landscape is rapidly painted before the mind; the narrative is almost rhythmic, the talk is cordial, bright American touches are scattered over the perspective—the great steamboat deck, the river coasts, the groups belonging to various gradations of New World life. In his Pacific stories Mr Melville wrote as with an Indian pencil, steeping the entire relation in colours almost too brilliant for reality; his books were all stars, twinkles, flashes, vistas of green and crimson, diamond and crystal; he has now tempered himself, and studied the effect of neutral tints. He has also added satire to his repertory, and, as he uses it scrupulously, he uses it well. His fault is a disposition to discourse upon too large a scale, and to keep his typical characters too long in one attitude upon the stage. Lest we should seem to imply that the masquerade is dramatic in form, it is as well to describe its construction. It is a strangely diversified narration of events taking place during the voyage of a Mississippi river boat, a cosmopolitan philanthropist, the apostle of a doctrine, being the centre and inspiration of the whole. The charm of the book is owing to its originality and to its constant flow of descriptions, character-sketching, and dialogue, deeply toned and skilfully contrasted.

—Anonymous, *Leader*, April 11, 1857, p. 356

ANN SOPHIA STEPHENS (1857)

Ann Sophia Stephens started *Mrs. Stephens' Illustrated New Monthly Magazine* in 1856, and besides being a harsh critic of Melville she was the author of serial melodramatic stories that appeared in several popular women's magazines. Students interested in the difference between the popular fiction of the era and what Melville delivers in *The Confidence Man* may find her consternation and dismissal relevant.

Mr Herman Melville has also issued a new book, through the publishing house of Dix, Edwards & Co. It is called *The Confidence Man*. It is the most singular of the many singular books of this author. Mr Melville seems to be bent upon obliterating his early successes. *Typee* and *Omoo* give us a right to expect something better than any of his later books have been. He appears now, to be merely trying how many eccentric things he can do. This is the more to be condemned, because in many important points he has sensibly advanced. His style has become more individualized—more striking, original, sinewy, compact; more reflective and philosophical. And yet, his recent books stand confessedly inferior to his earlier ones. As to *The Confidence Man*, we frankly acknowledge our inability to understand it. The scene is laid upon a Mississippi steamboat, on a voyage from St Louis to New Orleans. In the course of the voyage The Confidence Man assumes innumerable disguises—with what object it is not clear—unless for the sake of dogmatizing, theorizing, philosophizing, and amplifying upon every known subject; all of which, philosophy, we admit to be sharp, comprehensive, suggestive, and abundantly entertaining. But the object of this masquerade? None appears. The book ends where it begins. You might, without sensible inconvenience, read it backwards. You are simply promised in the last line, that something further shall be heard of the hero; until which consummation, the riddle must continue to puzzle you unsolved.

—Ann Sophia Stephens, *Mrs. Stephens' Illustrated New Monthly Magazine,* June 2, 1857, p. 288

Anonymous (1857)

This review was most likely written in London, and in it readers first meet a somewhat sustained attempt at criticism. Here the steamboat may be "that epitome of the American world," and Melville's "puppet-show" perhaps allegorizes and satirizes "the gullibility of the great Republic." The writer's contention that Melville's "view of human nature is severe" jogs with most recent appreciations of this complex book. This critic also finds "the absence of humor" where there is certainly some form of tortured humor. He does not help us understand the strangely episodic and perplexing plot and structure of the book. Nor does he explore the story's use of allegory, allusion, and myth. For meaning in *The Confidence Man* students will need to look to twentieth-century criticism. The book is essential reading for anyone wanting to understand Melville's compressed and last prose consideration of the human condition published in his lifetime.

We are not among those who have had faith in Herman Melville's South Pacific travels so much as in his strength of imagination. The *Confidence-Man* shows him in a new character—that of a satirist, and a very keen, somewhat bitter, observer. His hero, like Mr Melville in his earlier works, asks confidence of everybody under different masks of mendicancy, and is, on the whole, pretty successful. The scene is on board an American steamboat—that epitome of the American world—and a variety of characters are hustled on the stage to bring out the Confidence-Man's peculiarities: it is, in fact, a puppet-show; and, much as Punch is bothered by the Beadle, and calmly gets the better of all his enemies, his wife in the bargain, the Confidence-Man succeeds in baffling the one-legged man, whose suspicions and snappish incredulity constantly waylay him, and in counting a series of victims. Money is of course the great test of confidence, or credit in its place. Money and credit follow the Confidence-Man through all his transformations—misers find it impossible to resist him. It required close knowledge of the world, and of the Yankee world, to write such a book and make the satire acute and telling, and the scenes not too improbable for the faith given to fiction. Perhaps the moral is the gullibility of the great Republic, when taken on its own tack. At all events, it is a wide enough moral to have numerous applications, and sends minor shafts to right and left. Several capital anecdotes are told, and well told; but we are conscious of a certain hardness in the book, from the absence of humour, where so much humanity is shuffled into close neighbourhood. And with the absence of humour, too, there is an absence of kindliness. The view of human nature is severe and sombre—at least, that is the impression left on our mind. It wants relief, and is written too much in the spirit of Timon; who, indeed, saw life as it is, but first wasted his money, and then shut his heart, so that for him there was nothing save naked rock, without moss and flower. A money-less man and a heartless man are not good exponents of our state. Mr Melville has delineated with passable correctness, but he has forgotten to infuse the colours that exist in nature. The fault may lie in the uniqueness of the construction. Spread over a larger canvas, and taking in more of the innumerable sides of humanity, the picture might have been as accurate, the satire as sharp, and the author would not have laid himself open to the charge of harshness. Few Americans write so powerfully as Mr Melville, or in better English, and we shall look forward with pleasure to his promised continuation of the masquerade. The first part is a remarkable work, and will add to his reputation.

—Anonymous, *Westminster and Foreign Quarterly Review*, n.s. 12, July 1857, pp. 310–11

POETRY

As with the preceding criticism of *The Confidence Man*, critical reaction to Melville's poetry in his own time seems to have suffered from a lack of any patient attempt at understanding. Students of Melville's powerful poetry should note that this has since changed. These three reviews, one of *Battlepieces* and two of *Clarel*, are representative of the scant notice engendered by Melville's late turn to verse. While the brief anonymous review of *Battlepieces* written from New York entirely avoids engaging in a close reading of the many wonderful poems that make up the book, it may be of interest to students considering Melville's politics, especially his complexly disengaged stance on the Civil War. In the "supplement" that closes *Battlepieces,* Melville writes that he "never was a blind adherent," and advocates for healing, or "re-establishment." This desire is built into the very structure of the book, something also not addressed until much more recent criticism. Students comparing Whitman's *Drum-Taps* (or *Sequel to Drum-Taps*) to Melville's *Battlepieces* may find this review of use.

The two responses to *Clarel* might be compared (by students of Melville's reception history) with several other instances of critical befuddlement evident in this volume. Readers could turn especially to the reviews of *The Confidence Man* and *Pierre* collected here. What is it about Melville in his time that engendered such responses?

Anonymous (1866)

A rough time of it the country had during our four years' war, and many of the lines in which Herman Melville, in his new character as a poet, commemorates it are not inappropriately rugged enough. The beginning of one of his 'Battle Pieces' characterizes his poetical style:—

Plain be the phrase, not apt the verse,
   More ponderous than nimble.

In a prefatory note he says:—'I seem, in most of these verses, to have but placed a harp in a window and noted the contrasted airs which wayward winds have played upon the strings.' But we wish to direct special attention to the 'supplement' which Mr Melville has added, in obedience to a claim overriding all literary scruples—a claim urged by patriotism not free from solicitude. So far from spoiling the symmetry of the book, this supplement completes it, and converts it into what is better than a good book—into a good and patriotic action. The writer sees clearly that there is no reason why patriotism and narrowness should go together, or why intellectual impartiality should be confounded with political trimming, or why serviceable truth should keep cloistered because not partisan. And therefore, 'in view of the infinite desirableness of re-establishment, and considering that, so far as feeling is concerned, it depends not mainly on the temper in which the South regards the North, but rather conversely. One who never was a blind adherent feels constrained to submit some thoughts, counting on the indulgence of his countrymen.' We are confident that 'the second sober thought' of his countrymen will endorse his views. We welcome these 'words in season,' not only as the deliberate, impartial testimony of a highly cultivated individual mind, but as hopeful signs of a change in public opinion and sentiment.

—Anonymous, New York *Herald,* September 3, 1866

Richard Henry Stoddard (1866)

The reader who undertakes to read a poem of 600 pages in length, thirty-five lines to the page, is more than apt to receive the reward given by Jupiter to the man whom he caused to seek a grain of wheat in a bushel of chaff—to wit, the chaff. Good lines there must be, but they and their effect will alike be lost in the overwhelming tide of mediocrity. There are very few themes capable of such expansion, and the theme being found, very, very few authors capable of conducting it successfully to the close. In the present instance Mr Melville has for subject the story of a short pilgrimage in the Holy Land, and as characters an old religious enthusiast of Yankee birth; a Swede; an English clergyman; a Greek; a Jewish girl, Ruth; a very nondescript genius, Vine; and another, Rolfe, who

> Was no scholastic partisan
> Or euphopist of Academe,
> But supplemented Plato's theme
> With daedal life in boats and tents,
> A messmate of the elements.

Last comes the hero who gives the name to the poem, Clarel, a doubting, dreaming student. There is no particular reason why these characters should be assembled, but they are. Clarel falls in love with Ruth at Jerusalem, leaves her for a brief tour through the Holy Land, and returns to, as the French would say, assist at her funeral by torchlight, the book concluding with a description of Passion Week, and the characters vanish with about as much reason as they had for appearing at the first. There is thus no plot to sustain the interest of the reader, but there is a constant opportunity, fatal to such a facile writer as Mr Melville, for digression, discussion, and, above all, description. Given these characters and that scene, there is no earthly reason why the author should have turned the faucet and cut off his story at 21,000 lines instead of continuing to 221,000. Not being in his confidence we cannot of course say why he wrote the book, and what he intended it to mean, whether it has any cause or object. In the absence of this information, the reader is harassed by constant doubt whether the fact that he hasn't apprehended its motive and moral is due to his own obtuseness, or—distracting thought!—to the entire absence of either. The style is just as provoking. After a lot of job-trot versifying—Mr Melville rhymes 'hand' and 'sustained,' and 'day' and 'Epiphany' in the first ten lines—and just as he is prepared to abandon the book as a hopeless case, he stumbles on a passage of striking original thought, or possessing the trite lyrical ring and straightway is lured over another thousand lines or so, the process being repeated till the book ends just where it began. There has been much action but nothing has been accomplished. There is some very break-neck reading, as for instance:

> 'The chiffonier!' cried Rolfe. 'e'en grim
> Milcom and Chemosh scowl at him,
> Here nosing underneath their lee
> Of pagod heights.'

The philosophizing of the book is its least agreeable part, nor can the analyzations of character—or what appear to be intended therefor—receive much higher praise. Its best passages, as a rule, are the descriptive ones, which, notwithstanding frequent turgidness and affectation, are frequently bold, clear, and judicious. On the whole, however, it is hardly a book to be commended, for a work of art it is not in any sense or measure, and if it is an attempt to grapple with any particular problem of the universe, the indecision as to its object and processes is sufficient to appall or worry the average reader.

—Richard Henry Stoddard,
New York *World*, October 19, 1866

Edmund Clarence Stedman (1876)

After a long silence, Mr Herman Melville speaks again to the world. No more a narrator of marvelous stories of tropical life and adventure, no more a weird and half-fascinating, half-provoking writer of romances, but now as a poet with a single work, in four parts, and about 17,000 lines in length. We knew already that Mr Melville's genius has a distinctly poetical side; we remember still his stirring lines on Sheridan's Ride, commencing:

> Shoe the steed with silver,
> That bore him to the fray!

But the present venture is no less hazardous than ambitious. A narrative poem of such a length demands all the charms of verse, the strength and interest of plot, the picturesque of episode, and the beauty of sentimental or reflective digression which the author's art is capable of creating; and even then it may lack the subtle spell which chains the reader to its perusal. *Clarel*, we must frankly confess, is something of a puzzle, both in design and execution. A short excursion in Palestine—the four parts of the poem being entitled Jerusalem, the Wilderness, Mar Saba, and Bethlehem—gives a framework of landscape and incident to the characters, who are Clarel, a student, a doubter and dreamer; Nehemiah, an old Rhode Island religious enthusiast; Vine, a problematic character; Rolfe, 'a messmate of the elements;' Derwent, an English clergyman; Glaucon, a Smyrniote Greek; and Mortmain, an eccentric Swede. After a love-passage between Clarel and Ruth, a young Jewish girl, in Jerusalem, the above characters make up a party for Jericho, the Jordan and the Dead Sea, returning by way of the Greek monastery of Mar Saba and Bethlehem. The excursion lasts but a few days: they return to Jerusalem by night, and find Ruth dead and about to be buried by torch-light. Passion Week follows, and with it the poem closes. Clarel with his grief, and the other characters with their several eccentricities, disappear suddenly from our view.

There is thus no plot in the work; but neither do the theological doubts, questions, and disputations indulged in by the characters, and those whom they meet, have any logical course or lead to any distinct conclusions. The reader soon becomes hopelessly bewildered, and fatigues himself vainly in the effort to give personality to speakers who constantly evade it, and connections to scenes which perversely hold themselves separate from each other. The verse, frequently flowing for a few lines with a smooth, agreeable current, seems to foam and chafe against unmanageable words like a brook in a stony glen: there are fragments of fresh, musical lyrics, suggestive both of Hafiz and of William Blake; there are passages so rough, distorted, and commonplace withal, that the reader impatiently shuts the book. It is, in this respect, a medley such as we have rarely perused,—a mixture of skill and awkwardness, thought and aimless fancy, plan shattered by whim and melody broken by discords. It is difficult to see how any one capable of writing such excellent brief passages should also write such astonishingly poor ones—or the reverse.

The descriptive portions of the poem are often bold, clear, and suggestive of the actual scenes. We might make a collection of admirable lines and couplets, which have the ring and sparkle of true poetry. On the other hand it would be equally easy to multiply passages like the following, the sense of which is only reached with difficulty, and then proves to be hardly worth the trouble of seeking.

> But one there was (and Clarel he)
> Who, in his aspect free from cloud,
> Here caught a gleam from source unspied,
> As cliff may take on mountain-side,
> When there one small broom cirque ye see,
> Lit up in mole, how mellowly,
> Day going down in somber shroud—
> October pall.
>   But tell the vein
> Of new emotion, inly held
> That so the long contention quelled—
> Languor and indecision, pain.
> Was it abrupt resolve? a strain
> Wiser than wisdom's self might teach
> Yea, now his hand would boldly reach
> And pluck the nodding fruit to him,
> Fruit of the tree of life.

As a contrast, we take at random a few of the lyrical passages scattered through the work:

> Noble gods at the board,
>   Where load unto lord
>
> Light pushes the care-killing wine.
>   Urbane in their pleasure,
>   Superb in their leisure—
>   Lax ease—
> Lax ease after labor divine!

> With a rose in thy mouth
>   Through the world lightly veer,
> Rose in the mouth
>   Makes a rose of the year!

> But through such strange illusions have they passed
>   Who in life's pilgrimage have baffled striven—
> Even death may prove unreal at the last,
>   And stoics be astounded into heaven.

The ordinary reader will find himself in the position of one who climbs over a loose mound of sliding stones and gravel, in the search for the crystals which here and there sparkle from the mass. Some may suspect a graver enigma hidden in the characters of the story, and study them with that patience which the author evidently presupposes; but all will agree that a little attention to the first principles of poetic art would have made their task much more agreeable. An author has the right, simply as an individual, to disregard those principles, and must therefore be equally ready to accept the consequences. There is a vein of earnestness in Mr Melville's poem, singularly at variance with the carelessness of the execution; but this only increases the impression of confusion which it makes.

—Edmund Clarence Stedman,
New York *Tribune*, June 16, 1876

BILLY BUDD

Billy Budd was left in unfinished manuscript form in the writer's New York home at the time of his death in September 1891. He had apparently been working on the text since 1888. It was not until during the revival, in 1921, that Raymond Weaver became the first to write about the manuscript (in his now classic life of the author, titled *Herman Melville: Mariner and Mystic*). Weaver also brought the manuscript out in its first published form in 1924.

E.L. Grant Watson
"Melville's Testament of Acceptance" (1933)

E.L. Grant Watson was an anthropologist, novelist, and critic who wrote prolifically about the natural world as a window to the spiritual realm. He wrote "Melville's Testament of Acceptance" about a decade after the first Weaver edition of *Billy Budd*. His general thesis, that the text bore evidence of Melville's coming to terms with God, or universal necessity, came to dominate readings of the book for many years. Early on, Watson names *Billy Budd* Melville's "gospel story," and in so doing both reflects and foreshadows the many critical readings that have considered biblical content in the book. Watson asserts that, after struggling with ultimacies in *"Mardi, Moby Dick, and Pierre,"* the Melville of 1888–91 "is no longer a rebel." In both Billy and Captain Vere, Watson finds a "supreme quality of acceptance"—even as they are confronted with the inexplicable malignity of Claggart, with the Master at Arms' "bitter perversion of love."

Students writing about the influence of scriptural allegory on Melville will find Watson essential reading. Billy is "simple" and "everyday" and in these traits returns a version of Christ's humility. Captain Vere aligns subtly with Pontius Pilate. Watson offers a strong example of academic typological reading—an antique yet still powerful critical mode of reading where, as Watson asserts, "The critic's function is . . . to hint at what lies beneath—hidden, sometimes, under the surface." Watson is also notable for his early assessment, through Freud, of latent homosexual content in the story. Students may want to explore the long critical conversation over *Billy Budd* that arguably has its genesis in Watson's essay. Numerous later critics have split into camps, those aligning with Watson, reading the story as Melville's' "testament of acceptance," and those finding Melville still worrying in prose over the nature of divine intention in the world of men. Students concerned with the lifelong course of Melville's religious beliefs can read Watson against the Hawthorne letters included in the first section of this volume. There, Hawthorne logs anything but Melville's "acceptance" of God's ways toward man.

The title *Billy Budd* is not without significance, and would strike some readers in its crude simplicity as proof that Melville was lacking in a sense of humor. How could any man, they would argue, write a tragedy and call it *Billy Budd*? But a sense of humor, like almost everything else, is relative. Melville certainly lacked it in the crude form; but he was always conscious of those occasions when he might seem, to a superficial view, to be wanting it. He is particularly conscious of the obvious, but not in the obvious manner; and when he uses such a name as *Billy Budd* to set as the hub round which his own philosophy of life must revolve, he does so consciously, choosing the obvious to carry the transcendental. 'I have ever found the plain things, the knottiest of all,' he has written; and so he has made the simple man, the everyday Billy, the handsome sailor, the hero of a tragedy. Humor is appreciated most easily when larger things contract suddenly to smaller things—as when a man slips on a piece of orange-peel, thus converting his intention of going about his business to the abrupt act of falling on his back-side. Yet a more imaginative intelligence might, with a sense of humor just as true, see in this fall, the destiny of man, with full chorus of pities and ironic spirits. The easy contraction will seem to the sophisticated too facile to provoke a smile, a larger humor is found in the reverse process, namely in a filling in, in an exaggeration from the particular to the general. With such an added pinch of imagination, the obvious thing becomes the centre of mystery. And so, with a sense of humor which perceived both the obvious and the peculiar quality of the name, Melville deliberately chose 'Billy Budd.' Moreover, he made the hero of this, his gospel story (as it might well be called), a foundling of uncertain parentage, whose 'entire family was practically invested in himself.'

It is a mistake for critics to try to tell stories which authors must have told better in their texts. The critic's function is rather to hint at what lies beneath—hidden, sometimes, under the surface. Melville called his story 'an inside narrative,' and though it deals with events stirring and exciting enough in themselves, it is yet more exciting because it deals with the relation of those principles which constitute life itself. A simple-mindedness unaffected by the shadow of doubt, a divine innocence and courage, which might suggest a Christ not yet conscious of His divinity, and a malice which has lost itself in the unconscious depths of mania—the very mystery of iniquity—these opposites here meet, and find their destiny. But Melville's theme is even larger. All the grim setting of the world is in the battleship *Indomitable*, war and threatened mutiny are the conditions of her existence. Injustice and inhumanity are implicit, yet Captain Vere, her commander, is the man who obeys the law and yet understands the truth of the spirit. It is significant of Melville's development since the writing of *Moby-Dick* and *Pierre*, that he should create this naval captain—wholly pledged to the unnaturalness of the law, but sufficiently touched, at the same time, by the divine difference from ordinary sanity (he goes by the nick-name of 'Starry Vere'), as to live the truth *within* the law, and yet, in the cruel process of that very obedience, to redeem an innocent man from the bitterness of death imposed by the same law. A very different ending this from the despairing acts of dissolution which mark the conclusions of the three earlier books: *Mardi*, *Moby-Dick* and *Pierre*.

Melville is no longer a rebel. It should be noted that Billy Budd has not, even under the severest provocation, any element of rebellion in him. He is too free a soul to need a quality which is a virtue only in slaves. His nature spontaneously accepts whatever may befall. When impressed from the merchant-ship, the *Rights of Man*, he makes no demur to the visiting lieutenant's order to get ready his things for trans-shipment. The crew of the merchant-ship are surprised and reproachful at his uncomplaining acquiescence. Once aboard the battleship, the young sailor begins to look around for the advantages of chance and adventure. Such simple power to accept gives him the buoyancy to override troubles and irritations which would check inferior natures.

Yet his complete unconscious of the attraction, and consequent repulsion, that his youthful beauty and unsophisticated good-fellowship exercise on Claggart, make it only easier for these qualities to turn envy into hatred. His very virtue makes him the target for the shaft of evil, and his quality of acceptance provokes to action its complementary opposite, the sense of frustration that can not bear the consciousness of itself, and so has to find escape in mania. Thus there develops the conflict between unconscious virtue (not even aware of its loss of Eden and unsuspecting of the presence of evil) and the bitter perversion of love which finds its only solace in destruction.

And not only Billy Budd is marked by this supreme quality of acceptance. Captain Vere, also, possesses it, but with full consciousness, and weighted with the responsibility of understanding the natural naturalness of man's volition and the unnatural naturalness of the law. . . .

In Captain Vere we find a figure which may interestingly be compared to Pontius Pilate. Like Pilate, he condemns the just man to a shameful death, knowing him to be innocent, but, unlike Pilate, he does not wash his hands, but manfully assumes the full responsibility, and in such a way as to take the half, if not more than the half, of the bitterness of the execution upon himself. We are given to suppose that there is an affinity, a spiritual understanding between Captain Vere and Billy Budd, and it is even suggested that in their partial and separate existences they contribute to essential portions of that larger spirit which is man. Such passages as that quoted lie on the surface of this story, but they indicate the depths beneath. There are darker hints: those deep, far-away things in Vere, those occasional flashings-forth of intuition—short, quick probings to the very axis of reality. Though the book be read many times, the student may still remain baffled by Melville's significant arrangement of images. The story is so solidly filled out as to suggest dimensions in all directions. As soon as the mind fastens upon one subject, others flash into being.

Melville reported in *Pierre* how he fished his line into the deep sea of childhood, and there, as surely as any modern psychoanalyst, discovered all the major complexes that have since received baptism at the hands of Freudians. He peered as deep as any into the origins of sensuality, and in conscious understanding he was the equal of any modern psychologist; in poetic divination he has the advantage of most. No doubt the stresses of his own inner life demanded this exceptional awareness. In this book of his old age, the images which he chose for the presentation of his final wisdom, move between the antinomies of love and hate, of innocence and malice. From behind—from far behind the main pageant of the story—there seem to fall suggestive shadows of primal, sexual simplicities. In so conscious a symbolist as Melville, it would be surprising if there should be no meaning or half-meaning in the spilling of Billy's soup towards the homosexually-disposed Claggart, in the impotence of Billy's speech in the presence of his accuser, in his swift and deadly answer, or the likening of Claggart's limp, dead body to that of a snake.

It is possible that such incidents might be taken as indications of some unresolved problem in the writer himself. This may be, but when we remember how far Melville had got in the process of self-analysis in *Pierre*, and when we have glanced at the further analysis that is obvious in the long narrative poem *Clarel*, it seems likely that this final book, written nearly forty years after *Pierre*, should contain a further, deeper wisdom. And as the philosophy in it has grown from that of rebellion to that of acceptance as the symbolic figures of unconscious forces have become always more concrete and objective, so we may assume that these hints are intentional, and that Melville was particularly conscious of what he was doing. . . .

Here is Melville at his very best, at his deepest, most poetic, and therefore at his most concentrated, most conscious. Every image has its significant implication. The very roll of the heavily-cannoned ship so majestic in moderate weather—the musket in the ship-armourer's rack; and Billy's last words are the triumphant seal of his acceptance, and they are more than that, for in this supreme passage a communion between personality at its purest, most-God-given form, and character, hard-hammered from the imperfect material of life on the battleship *Indomitable*, is here suggested, and one feels that the souls of Captain Vere and Billy are at that moment strangely one.

In this short history of the impressment and hanging of a handsome sailor-boy, are to be discovered problems almost as profound as those which puzzle us in the pages of the Gospels. *Billy Budd* is a book to be read many times, for at each reading it will light up, as do the greater experiences of life, a beyond leading always into the unknown.

—E.L. Grant Watson, "Melville's Testament of Acceptance,"
New England Quarterly, 6, June 1933, pp. 319–27

Karl E. Zink "Herman Melville and the Forms—Irony and Social Criticism in *Billy Budd*" (1952)

Karl E. Zink's text is a powerful and critically confident reading of *Billy Budd*. Zink reads *Billy Budd* as "ironic social criticism, not acceptance," thereby challenging the enduring critical legacy of Watson and critics like him. Zink restricts his scope in order to emphasize why he thinks years of reading *Billy Budd* as a "testament of Acceptance" have been wrong. Melville, he thinks, writes *Billy Budd* to rail against repressive social "forms." The tale, read correctly, contains unequivocal meaning: "Claggart is aggressive evil; Billy is passive good." Captain Vere is "a third symbolic character, . . . the enlightened mediator, symbol of Authority." Zink unpacks Melville's reading of these repressive social forms, leaving little room for the sort of rich ambiguity appreciated by other, later critics of the tale. His most powerful and inventive move is to read the crew of the *Indomitable* as "a fourth character." The crew is essential as, in its "undiscriminating docility" before "forms" of authority, Zink discloses Melville's tragic assessment of life toward the end of the century. *Billy Budd* is best read as an "allegory," Zink charges, an allegory of how "civilization has come to compromise men's cherished natural integrity and constitutes a threat to itself."

Billy Budd, Foretopman is a social allegory, the last of Herman Melville's criticisms of social injustice as he saw it in nineteenth century America. . . .

Billy Budd is a tragedy of society; not a tragedy of 'hope and triumph in death,' as Mr Freeman asserts in summarizing his critique of the novel[1] nor of 'passive acceptance,' or 'necessity,' as some thirty years of American criticism have uniformly reiterated.[2]

1

Despite its apparent historical authenticity, *Billy Budd* is not a realistic novel of events. It is rather heavy social allegory. The characters and situations operate clearly as symbols. Against the social frame of the ship—the man-of-war society—it develops anew the old struggle between the force for good and the force for evil, with a special ugly twist brought into being (Melville feels) by the inherent evil of the social machinery. Billy and John Claggart are the complex symbols for these forces. Claggart is aggressive evil; Billy is passive good, a comprehensive symbol of the sort of natural goodness that Adam lived before his fall, in large part only the ignorance of evil. He is possibly an agent of Divine justice. Evil in the world has the edge; it enjoys a strong survival factor, not because of greater power[3] but because it is nurtured and protected by the 'forms' (potentially evil) by which the culture governs itself. A third symbolic character is Captain Vere, the enlightened mediator, symbol of Authority, who phrases and ponders the philosophical problem involved in Billy's fatal clash with Claggart, but who defends the harshness of the social code as ultimately best for the common good. It is Vere, as much as Billy, who dramatizes the awful power and blind impersonality of the forms. For although he, a *good* man, sensitive and intelligent, is fully aware (where Billy is not) of the injustice of the trial and the execution, he is too enmeshed in the forms himself not to enforce them. His dilemma is, of course, acute—he is many days away from the jurisdiction of the fleet admiral; the recency of the great mutinies is still an ever present threat to all naval authorities. The letter of the law simplifies; it softens the sting to the conscience of disturbing moral considerations. He too dies, soon after Billy, trammelled in his own fashion among the forms. And though Billy's name is on his lips when he dies he apparently does not regret his decision.

A fourth character, apparently overlooked for many years, is the crew of the *Indomitable*, the mass of mankind, dominated easily, often brutally, by an authority they have learned to fear and respect. The symbolic behavior of the crew in response to the hanging has been long overlooked. Prior to Billy's hanging the crew do not act as a group; they enjoy no dynamic identity. But the execution of Billy galvanizes them into action and identity. They respond immediately as a mass, integrated by instinctive resistance to injustice. We shall see that in this instinctive, but pathetically abortive, reaction of the crew to the hanging Melville asserts his final judgment of nineteenth century America's dangerously immoral inclination.

2

Through the Christ imagery which surrounds Billy, Melville makes possible many ironic parallels between the story of Christ, fouled in the forms of pre-Christian Roman colonial administration, and the story of Billy Budd, nineteenth century man, helplessly fouled in the social machinery of his own century. In both cases, we remember, a force for good among men ran afoul of arbitrary rules for mass conduct and was destroyed inevitably in the meeting. Both men were accused of agitating, of questioning the status quo. Both were executed as an 'admonitory spectacle' for the mob, each a warning against breaking the rules. Both were simple, 'good' men, who suffered violent death passively. Both uttered before their death a benediction for the authority they had offended. In both cases an individual was sacrificed to inflexible forms by which men had chosen to live.

Melville deliberately points up this complex comparison with the illusion of Billy's glorification in 'the full rose of the dawn'—his hanging is an apparent 'ascension,' an acceptance, a moral victory. But in the light of the crew's reaction to the hanging and the material presented in the following several chapters, Billy's 'ascension' becomes a climactic irony. For the still figure at the yard end dramatizes more fittingly the evil of the forms, the awful impersonality that could thus shove goodness and innocence out of the world; that for the sake of immediate comfort, in order to frighten men into more complete docility, could perpetrate an injustice against man and God. Melville allows the Christ-like Billy to 'accept' the necessity of his fate. But we are mistaken if we assume that Melville himself accepted it.

3

Every development which follows the hanging is an ironic comment on that event and underscores the final triumph of the forms: (1) the unusual behavior of the crew—at the pronouncement of sentence, at the hanging, and at the burial; (2) the 'something of a sequel' in the last three chapters, which records the death of Vere, the falsified official account of the story, the history of the spar Billy died on; and (3) the ballad.

(1) This crucial sequence of events begins, in fact, just before the hanging, when Vere summons all hands during the second dog-watch to pronounce sentence. The men betray an immediate, instinctive reaction against his announcement of Billy's fate. But their impulse is quickly overpowered by Authority:

> Their Captain's announcement was listened to by the throng of standing sailors in a dumbness like that of a seated congregation of believers in hell listening to the clergyman's announcement of his Calvinistic text.
>
> At the close, however, a confused murmur went up. It began to wax. All but instantly, then, at a sign, it was pierced and suppressed by shrill whistles of the Boatswain and his mates piping down one watch.[4]

We must note the beginning here of characteristic terms for the description, on the one hand, of Authority, and, on the other, of the unorganized mass:

the *dumbness*, the *confused murmur* of the men *is pierced and suppressed* by *shrill whistles, piping*.

Later, only seconds after the awful moment of the execution, with Billy still warm and quiet against the yard, Melville is at pains to describe a second sullen murmur from the men; this too is firmly and efficiently silenced by Authority:

> The silence at the moment of execution and for a moment or two continuing thereafter, a silence but emphasized by the regular wash of the sea against the hull or the flutter of a sail caused by the helmsman's eyes being tempted astray, this emphasized silence was gradually disturbed by a sound not easily to be here verbally rendered. Whoever has heard the freshet-wave of a torrent suddenly swelled by pouring showers in the tropical mountains, showers not shared by the plain; whoever has heard the first muffled murmur of its sloping advance through precipitous woods, may form some conception of the sound now heard. The seeming remoteness of its source was because of its murmurous indistinctness since it came from close by, even from the men massed on the ship's open deck. Being inarticulate, it was dubious in significance further that it seemed to indicate some capricious revulsion of thought or feeling such as mobs ashore are liable to in the present instance possibly implying a sullen revocation on the men's part of their involuntary echoing of Billy's benediction. But ere the murmur had time to wax into clamor it was met by a strategic command, the more telling that it came with abrupt unexpectedness.
>
> 'Pipe down the starboard watch, Boatswain, and see that they go.'
>
> Shrill as the shriek of the sea-hawk the whistles of the Boatswain and his Mates pierced that ominous low sound, dissipating it; and yielding to the mechanism of discipline the throng was thinned by one half. For the remainder most of them were set to temporary employments connected with trimming the yards and so forth, business readily to be got up to serve occasion by any officer-of-the-deck.[5]

Again, the instinctive feelings of the group are quelled. Note they are described as *indistinct, inarticulate, murmurous*; it is *the mechanism of discipline* which thins the throng.

When Billy's shotted hammock is dropped over the side a few moments later (all hands called again, this time to witness burial), a third strange human murmur is heard, blended this time with another 'inarticulate' sound—that of the great sea fowl hovering hungrily over the spot, 'circling it low down with the moving shadow of their outstretched wings and the cracked requiem of their cries.' This motion was seen by the superstitious sailors as 'big with no prosaic significance'—nature too rebelled—and immediately

> An uncertain movement began among them, in which some encroachment was made. It was tolerated but for a moment. For suddenly the drum beat to quarters, which familiar sound happening at least twice a day, had upon the present occasion some signal peremptoriness in it. True martial discipline long continued superinduces in an average man a sort of impulse of docility whose operation at the official sound of command much resembles in its promptitude the effect of an instinct.[6]

This time it is the drum beat that dissipates the angry mood of the massed men. The movement is characteristically *uncertain*, but Authority as usual is brisk and sure. For the third time Melville has driven home his belief in the natural though inarticulate revulsion which the mass of men feel against the tyranny of the forms, and for the third time we have seen their vague 'murmur' expertly quelled. He is most specific at this point that the average man has developed an impulse of docility in the face of Authority that is practically instinctive.

Captain Vere immediately justifies the drumbeat to quarters (it is an hour earlier this Sunday morning) as necessary to counteract the temporary mood of his men:

> 'With mankind' he would say 'forms, measured forms are everything: and that is the import couched in the story of Orpheus with his lyre spellbinding the wild denizens of the woods.'[7]

This is the climactic, ironic cap to their *inarticulate* feelings of outrage—this easy, learned explanation, heightened by the classical allusion which betrays the great age of the entrenched power of the forms. For 'Orpheus' read *Vere*; for 'lyre' read *Boatswain's pipe, drum*; 'spellbinding' and 'wild denizens' have overtones which are immediately apparent. In the following paragraph the Chaplain conducts the customary morning service, the drum beats the retreat, and 'toned by music and religious rites subserving the discipline and purpose of war, the men in their wonted orderly manner dispersed to the places allotted them when not at the guns.'[8] Note the terms *wonted, orderly, allotted*. The forms have won out.

4

(2) According to Mr Freeman's editing of the *Billy Budd* manuscripts, the short story, *Baby Budd, Sailor*, ends at this point, the burial, with the men dispersed and quieted. It is thus apparent that even in his initial conception of the tale, Melville included the crew's instinctive revulsions against the authority of the forms. To the novel Melville added three short chapters and the ballad, 'Billy in the Darbies.' These final chapters trace Billy's story forward in time and amplify Melville's final criticism of the forms. The first of these records the death of Captain Vere in the act of destroying the *Athéiste*.[9] The second records the further triumph of the impersonal forms in the ironic reversal of character and fact which was preserved in the authorized weekly naval chronicle called *News from the Mediterranean*—'all that hitherto has stood in human record,' Melville says with characteristic irony, 'to attest what manner of men respectively were John Claggart and Billy Budd.' For here, it will be remembered, John Claggart was 'vindictively stabbed to the heart by the suddenly drawn sheath knife of Budd,' whom he accused of 'some sort of plot . . . among an inferior section of the ship's company.' Because he used a knife, Billy is presumed no Englishman but an 'assassin' of foreign origin serving in the English Navy. The 'enormity' of his crime and the 'extreme depravity of the criminal' are deplored. The exemplary character of Claggart is there said to refute Dr Johnson's 'peevish saying' that patriotism is the last refuge of a scoundrel. 'The promptitude of the punishment has proved salutary. Nothing amiss is now apprehended aboard the *H.M.S. Indomitable*.'[10] Authority speaks. Through the high impersonality and indifference of the forms to the individual lives they dominate Billy dies unjustly and his character in the annals of men is unjustly and carelessly defamed.

The last chapter briefly traces the history of the yard from which Billy hung, how chips of it came to be cherished as pieces of the Cross, and records the composition of the ballad and how it was in time printed at Portsmouth. But this perspective, too, only reiterates man's subservience to the forms, his docility. This is manifest in the uncritical, paradoxical feeling of the men regarding the rightness of the execution:

> Ignorant though they were of the secret facts of the tragedy, and not thinking but that the penalty was somehow unavoidably inflicted from the naval point of view, for all that they instinctively felt that Billy was a sort of man as incapable of mutiny as of willful murder.[11]

Though they cherished splinters from his spar and in their hearts felt him incapable of murder and mutiny, somehow his execution must have been justified 'from the naval point of view.' The murmur grows weaker.

(3) There remains the folk record, the ballad, 'Billy in the Darbies,' which brings Melville's story of Billy Budd to a close. Composed by a watchmate of Billy's (a man who should have known him well), it is said to preserve 'the general estimate of his nature and its unconscious simplicity.'[12] But in no satisfactory sense does it do this. This folk record tells us as little about the Billy Budd the reader knows as did the organ of the forms, *News from the Mediterranean*.

It preserves the last reflections of the condemned man on the night before he was hanged (a longer speech than Billy made anywhere in the novel), not his narrative, as might be expected, or any suggestion of his symbolic or spiritual meaning. Rough as it is, there is about it a sophistication, a bizarre humor, grim puns, that no one who knew him well could have attributed to him. Preoccupation with the ugly details of death by halter and sea burial do not bespeak the undisturbed boy who slept like a baby before his hanging. It is even doubtful that Billy ever gave an ear-drop to Bristol Molly. The ballad is too passive, for one thing, and too noncommittal. If the facts of his story—and his spiritual significance, as well—are thus blurred in the folk mind as well as in the official record, then mankind's immersion in the forms is blind and dark indeed. Something is missing in a ballad which generations of sailors are supposed to have sung in memory of a hero. What is missing, I suggest, is the outraged murmur which sought articulation first when sentence was pronounced, again when Billy ascended to the yard, and again when he was dropped into the sea. No spark of that 'instinctive,' 'inarticulate,' 'uncertain' but genuine outrage which the massed crew had intuitively felt and abortively expressed aboard ship appears even by implication in the folk record—where it belongs. We should expect their murmur at his death to survive. But it does not. Only blurred, sympathetic feelings survive. Inasmuch as the ballad is no more valuable a record of the real Billy and no more sensitive to the spiritual Billy than it is, Melville's implication, his irony, seems clear. The men were incapable of understanding—incapable of realizing just how rare, and how innocent, and how important Billy was to the ship and to themselves. We know that Authority withheld the central facts. The several mass reactions we see the crew make are all non-rational, intuitive. (The crew's echo of Billy's benediction of Vere is irrational, coming as it does between clear manifestations of revolt.) Because their response to the injustice of the hanging was intuitive and inarticulate, it could be controlled. Melville stresses this. Apparently the men were no more capable of a vital, resistant articulation in words, than they were in action. And thus Authority perpetuates itself. This is the last of the chain of ironies following the hanging which illuminate the brute, insidious power of the forms—the great danger to the individual resident in the machinery by which the group manages itself.

5

We have seen resistance to the forms grow weaker with each remove from the deck of the *Indomitable*. Vere dies convinced that his decision was justified—his last words, 'Billy Budd,' were not the 'accents of remorse.' The only official documentary record of Billy's story was hopelessly distorted. His mates, cherishing splinters from his spar, knowing in their hearts he was incapable of murder and mutiny, docilely accepted the penalty as 'unavoidably inflected from the naval point of view.' And, finally, the ballad, the folk record, is also a distortion, which betrays subtly the undiscriminating docility of the pliable crew. This is Melville's final irony. The murmur has been lost. The triumph of the forms is complete. And Melville's tragic allegory of nineteenth century American society is finished.

That Billy Budd had to die is to the eternal shame of the inflexible machinery that could shove him off. For it was 'the forms' that nurtured and protected the evil Claggart, and an apologist for the forms (Vere) who, fully awake to Billy's moral innocence, condemned the man to die who had rid the world (symbolically) of natural evil. Mr Schiffman reminds us of the terrible dramatic irony of Billy's benediction of Captain Vere. And there is deep irony in the repetition of Billy's words—'God bless Captain Vere'—by the 'wedged mass of upturned faces,' the docile crew, inured to passive acceptance of the rules, to worship, almost of their administrators. 'God bless Captain Vere' is the last thing they would knowingly have uttered. But with Billy alone in their hearts and in their eyes, their emotional identification with him is so complete that momentarily they too reflect his own special innocence of their true dilemma. The lesson is not that Billy learns to accept the necessary harshness of the forms, but that in their high impersonality there is a dangerous lack of discrimination—dangerous to the individual and to the social structure itself. For in justifying Billy's death, the structure deprived itself symbolically of the force for good. And part of the lesson is that men tolerate this inherent evil of the structure passively, uncritically. Moral integrity is often, unhappily, endangered by or sacrificed to the impersonal dicta of the forms. Civilization has come to compromise men's cherished natural integrity and constitutes a threat to itself. Something like this, it seems to me, is the tenor of Melville's thought in *Billy Budd*. It is ironic social criticism, not acceptance.

Notes

1. F. Barron Freeman, *Melville's Billy Budd*. Cambridge: Harvard University Press, 1948.
2. See Joseph Schiffman, 'Melville's Final Stage, Irony: A Re-examination of *Billy Budd* Criticism.' *American Literature* (May, 1950), for a long overdue re-appraisal of this century's criticism of *Billy Budd*, and a brief analysis of the essential irony of this novel.
3. Billy always triumphs over evil until he runs afoul of the forms. Red Whiskers, the Afterguardsman, and Claggart are experiences with evil of increasing degrees of complexity. Claggart is his most complex experience of evil short of the social code that hangs him, against which he has not the necessary 'touch of defensive ugliness.'
4. Freeman, pp. 254–5.
5. Freeman, pp. 269–270.
6. Freeman, pp. 271–2.
7. Freeman, p. 272.
8. Freeman, pp. 272–3.
9. The old St Louis had been rechristened *Athéiste* under the Directory. Vere dies, interestingly enough, in the glorious act of destroying the *Athéiste*, a ship fighting in a cause which sought to eradicate a system of entrenched forms. It is thus, symbolically, the 'natural' enemy of the *Indomitable* which has just rationalized a shocking injustice to a Christ-like sailor in the name of law and order and authority. We are reminded here of the terrible paradox that the brute *Indomitable* bore the 'Minister of the Prince of Peace' aboard, the military chaplain, 'serving in the host of the God of War—Mars.' 'Why is he there?' Melville asks bitterly. 'Because he indirectly subserves the purpose attested by the cannon; because too he lends the sanction of the religion of the meek to that which practically is the abrogation of everything but brute force.' (Freeman, p. 262).
10. Freeman, p. 277.
11. Freeman, p. 278.
12. Freeman, pp. 278–279.

—Karl E. Zink, "Herman Melville and the Forms—
Irony and Social Criticism in *Billy Budd*,"
Accent, 12, 3, Summer 1952, pp. 131–39

Wendell Glick "Expediency and Absolute Morality in *Billy Budd*" (1953)

Here Glick differs from Zink in reading Melville as not railing against social "forms," but rather siding without irony (rather, with a sense of tragic acceptance) on the side of social expediency. Glick begins and ends by considering the digression in *Billy Budd* about the death of Lord Nelson. What does it mean? Why does Melville include it? Glick believes Melville intended to show that Nelson's death was not foolhardy, but an act deeply expedient, as it "inspired posterity to [further] deeds of greatness." Billy is no Nelson, though. According to Glick, his "noble devotion to absolute justice and right throughout the novel made him a sort of personification of the moral law"—a law Melville had come to find "simply unworkable when applied to complex social relationships." The essay is fascinating in how it challenges Zink's thesis by returning to the general structure of Watson's "acceptance" essay, revising that position to take up social, rather than theological, issues. Students considering Captain Vere, especially students writing about whether he is a villain or the moral center of the story, will find in Zink and Glick essential reading. Students focusing on even later critical repercussions of the important Watson/Zink opposition over meaning in Melville's last work should read Barbara Johnson's rich and influential essay "Melville's Fist; The Execution of *Billy Budd*."

'Resolve as one may to keep to the main road,' Melville wrote in *Billy Budd*, 'some bypaths have an enticement not readily to be withstood. Beckoned by the genius of Nelson, knowingly, I am going to err in such a bypath.'[1] With these words of caution to the reader who might object to the 'literary sin' of digression, the author of *Moby Dick* launched into a spirited encomium upon the heroism of Lord Nelson, defending the Admiral against any 'martial utilitarians' and 'Benthamites of war' who might interpret his acts of 'bravado' at Trafalgar which had resulted in his death to have been foolhardy and vain. For what reason, the question arises, did Melville feel that the eulogy on Nelson could justifiably be included in *Billy Budd*? What is the meaning of the attack upon Benthamites and utilitarians? This was no potboiler which required padding; surely his inclusion of the highly emotional defense of Nelson is significant for other reasons than that the chapter makes 'more understandable Melville's hearty interest in martial exploits, sayings, and songs.'[2]

At the time Melville was writing and revising *Billy Budd* he was in no mood to trifle with peccadilloes. 'My vigor sensibly declines,' he had written to Archibald MacMechan on 5 December 1889: 'What little of it is left I husband for certain matters yet incomplete, and which indeed, may never be completed.'[3] He could hardly have been husbanding his strength to communicate his 'hearty interest in martial exploits'; his digression away from his narrative in order to praise Nelson must have served in his mind the more serious purpose of clarifying one of the 'truths' for which, as he pointed out, *Billy Budd* was but the vehicle. The purpose of this article is to call attention to an aspect of one of these truths, heretofore unnoticed. Although it is much more, *Billy Budd* is the cogent fruition of a lifetime of observation and study of the eternal conflict between absolute morality and social expediency; and the digression on Nelson, though it intrudes upon the plot, is central to an understanding of Melville's final resolution of this crucial problem.

In writing *Billy Budd*, Melville made clear at the outset of his novel, he was writing no 'romance'; he would not be bound, consequently, in his delineation of the 'Handsome Sailor,' by any of the conventions usually followed in depicting a romantic hero. Nor would he be bound to refrain from digressing if digression served his purposes. His interest was less in art than in 'Truth uncompromisingly told' (pp. 149 and 274). He was quite willing, he asserted, to sacrifice 'the symmetry of form attainable in pure fiction' and to risk 'ragged edges' on his final work if by so doing he could tell a story 'having less to do with fable than with fact' (p. 274). Thus relieved both from the conventional restrictions usually imposed by art and from the financial exigencies which had dictated the content of some of his early works, he would be free to deal forthrightly and honestly with issues far too serious to be treated cavalierly.

For his *raisonneur* Melville chose Captain 'Starry' Vere, a clear-headed realist possessed of sufficient perspective as a result of broad human experience and extensive reading to enable him to weigh the most difficult alternatives and choose rationally between them. No person with lesser qualifications would serve. For the choice which Captain Vere had to make involved more than a simple distinction between blacks and whites; instead it was a choice between two standards of human behavior, to each of which man owed unquestioning loyalty. The Captain's decision, moreover, was to be Melville's as well; and Melville felt no disposition in the waning years of his life to trifle with reality and call the process truth-seeking.

Melville sympathized with Billy Budd as completely as did Captain Vere. He appreciated with the Captain the stark injustice of a situation which finds the individual condemned for adherence to a standard of behavior most men would consider noble and right. But he agreed with the Captain that justice to the individual is not the ultimate loyalty in a complex culture; the stability of the culture has the higher claim, and when the two conflict, justice to the individual must be abrogated to keep the order of society intact. Turning their backs upon one of the most cherished systems of ideas in the American tradition, a system typified by such individualists as Thoreau and Emerson, Melville and Captain Vere brought in the verdict that the claims of civilized society may upon occasion constitute a higher ethic than the claims of 'natural law' and personal justice (p. 245). The ultimate allegiance of the individual, in other words, is not to an absolute moral code, interpreted by his conscience and enlivened by his human sympathies, but to the utilitarian principle of social expediency.

To isolate his problem, to strip it of all irrelevant issues preparatory to making a critical examination of it, Melville chose as his setting a British vessel at sea. The ship-of-the-line *Indomitable*, a smooth-functioning microcosm of society as a whole, was threatened with mutiny. Though the threat was remote, whatever would contribute to the end of knitting together the diverse individuals who made up the crew into a homogeneous unit which would act efficiently in an emergency was fully justified; conversely, that which jeopardized even slightly the clock-like functioning of the crew it was necessary to stamp out ruthlessly. His highest obligation, as Captain Vere conceived of it, was the preservation of the tight little society into which the crew had been welded, and the prevention of anything resembling anarchy. The transcendent responsibility of the leaders of the English nation, moreover, was the same as his own, writ large. An intensive study of history had confirmed his 'settled convictions' against 'novel opinion, social, political, and otherwise, which carried away as in a torrent no few minds in those days'; and he was 'incensed at the innovators,' not because their theories were inimical to the private interests of the privileged classes of which he was a member, but because such theories 'seemed to him incapable of embodiment in lasting institutions,' and 'at war with the peace of the world and the good of mankind' (pp. 163–164). The world as he viewed it was ruled by 'forms'; 'with mankind,' Melville quotes him as saying, 'forms, measured forms, are everything'; that was the import which he saw 'in the story of Orpheus, with his lyre, spellbinding the wild denizens of the woods' (p. 272). To preserve the ordered functioning of his crew Captain Vere was willing to sacrifice even the ideal of justice when the absolute necessity arose. What he objected to in Claggart was not that Claggart was remiss in his 'duty of preserving order' but that the Master at Arms abridged the ideal of justice unnecessarily, even when the autonomy and general good of the crew were not at stake. Still, the maintenance of order came first, and it was rigorously safe-guarded on the *Indomitable* 'almost to a degree inconsistent with entire moral volition' (pp. 172–173).

To the idea that order in society should be maintained at all cost Captain Vere adhered 'disinterestedly,' not because he desired such a regimented society, but because he believed it to be a practical necessity of this world. Like Plotinus Plinlimmon of *Pierre*, he preferred Christian ('Chronometrical') standards of absolute morality to the more mundane, utilitarian standard of expediency; but like Plinlimmon, he had concluded that Christian ideals were unworkable in everyday situations. He was fully aware that a regimented society abridged many private rights, but he realized also that in the absence of such a society a state of anarchy and chaos inevitably arose in which every human right was sacrificed. An ordered society at least guaranteed the preservation of *some* rights; and though this fell far short of the ideal of the preservation of *all*, it was far better than the sort of 'society' which, in the idealistic attempt to guarantee all rights, degenerated into chaos and so permitted their complete and total destruction. It was not a question of insuring all individual rights or a part of them; the choice was between insuring a part of them or none. The ideal society which abridged no prerogatives and guaranteed all private liberties was, in the considered opinion of Captain Vere, a figment of the imagination.

Recent events, Melville makes abundantly plain, had been responsible for the Captain's position. The Nore Mutiny, though it had been precipitated by the failure of the authorities to redress the legitimate grievances of the seamen, had threatened the military usefulness of the 'indispensable fleet' upon which the stability of the entire English nation depended, and consequently had been ruthlessly suppressed (pp. 150–153). The cataclysmic French Revolution had taught its bitter lesson, both to Captain Vere and to his creator. To the Captain the principle involved in the two events was the same: the English sailors at Nore, in running up 'the British colors with the union and cross wiped out,' had transmuted 'the flag of founded law and freedom defined' into 'the red meteor of unbridled and unbounded revolt' of the French. 'Reasonable discontent,' Melville pointed out, 'growing out of practical grievances in the fleet had been ignited into irrational combustion as by live cinders blown across the Channel from France in flames' (p. 151). No price was too great to pay to keep such unhinging forces of anarchy in check; in giving his life to destroy the *Athéiste*, Captain Vere sacrificed himself in defense of the *sine qua non* of civilized existence and in opposition to the false, unworkable doctrines of the French Revolution. The triumph of the *Indomitable* over the *Athéiste* was the triumph of order over chaos.

Yet how staggering was the cost of a stable society! Having decided upon the absolute necessity for maintaining unweakened the strength of the social fabric, Melville shuddered when he contemplated the price exacted in terms of human values; and *Billy Budd* became the balance-sheet upon which he reckoned the price men have to pay for the ordered society which they have to have. The most obvious price was the destruction of 'Nature's Nobleman,' the superlatively innocent person: every Billy Budd impressed by an *Indomitable* is forced to leave his *Rights-of-Man* behind. To the destruction of innocent persons, moreover, it was necessary to add the mental suffering of the individual forced to make moral judgments. But the total cost is not met even by the sacrifice of Billy Budds and the suffering of Captain Veres; social stability based upon expediency is paid for also with a general, blighting, human mediocrity. The standards of any civilized society are the standards of the great mass of men who make up its bulk; and when maintenance of the stability of society becomes the supreme obligation of every person, the result is a levelling of the superior persons down to the level of the mass. The chief personal virtue becomes 'prudence'; the end most worth seeking for becomes 'that manufacturable thing known as respectability,' so often allied with 'moral obliquities' (p. 147), and occasionally, as in the case of Claggart, indistinguishable even from 'natural depravity.' 'Civilization,' Melville remarks categorically, 'especially of the austerer sort, is auspicious' to natural depravity because natural depravity 'folds itself in the mantle of respectability' by avoiding 'vices or small sins' and by refraining from all excesses; in short, by exhibiting the prudence which is the only virtue society demands. The natural depravity of Claggart was so insidious because it lacked the trappings in which society expects to see evil garbed, and instead, prudently enfolded itself in 'the mantle of respectability' (pp. 185–186). Prudence, while being the mark of the socially adjusted man who rigidly adheres to the utilitarian principle of expediency, may also be the last refuge of scoundrels.

But even when prudence did not take the extreme form of moral obliquity, even when it was not 'habitual with the subtler depravity' (p. 195), as it proved to be in the case of Claggart, it left its mark upon the people in the world of Billy Budd. The most 'prudent' characters discharged faithfully their 'duty' to their king even when to do so clashed with moral scruple, but they fell far short of the personal heroism which inspires others and vitalizes them into acts. Captain Graveling of the *Rights-of-Man* was 'the sort of person whom everybody agrees in calling "a respectable man"'; he was a lover of 'peace and quiet' and the possessor of 'much prudence' which caused 'overmuch disquietude in him,' but he was by and large a pedestrian individual who could hardly be depended upon to make any signal contribution to human progress (p. 137). The old ascetic Dansker had learned from experience a 'bitter prudence' which had taught him never to interfere, never to give advice, in other words, to solve the problem of his social responsibility by escaping into a shell of cynicism, and by so doing had disqualified himself for service to society (p. 205). The *Indomitable*'s 'prudent surgeon' was singularly unequipped to pass moral judgments and would have 'solved' the problem of Billy's murder of Claggart by dropping the whole affair into the lap of the Admiral (pp. 229, 231). Even Captain Vere, who possessed in eminent measure the 'two qualities not readily interfusable' demanded of every English sea-commander at the time 'prudence and rigor' (p. 234), did not earn Melville's highest accolade as a member of 'great Nature's nobler order' until he let himself 'melt back into what remains primeval in our formalized humanity'; in short, until he forgot temporarily his 'military duty,' his prudence, and acted in a manner difficult to reconcile with strict social expediency (p. 252).[4]

To what do these examples of prudence, the highest ethic of utilitarian philosophers, add up? Simply this: in making social expediency an ethic superior to absolute morality, Melville found himself pushed perilously close to a *Weltanschauung* which would admit slight, if any, possibility of personal greatness. Could prudence ever be truly heroic? A society which elevated prudence above all other virtues seemed to be anathema to the sort of moral adventuresomeness which Melville loved, and which for him set the great man off from the mediocre one. Yet such a society seemed to be the only sort which could safeguard men from the perils of 'irrational combustion' which followed hard upon an idealism permitted to run its free course unrestrained. Here lay a crucial dilemma: was the race doomed to accept mediocrity as the price of its self-preservation, or was it still possible in a complex society for great private virtues to generate and grow?

Emotionally unequipped to reconcile himself to the bleaker alternative toward which both his experience and his reason had led him, Melville turned to history in the hope of discovering a figure of heroic dimensions whose life would free him from his impasse. Having played the role of champion of man's dignity and greatness for a lifetime, he did not feel that he could relinquish it now; and in the person of Nelson, 'the greatest sailor since the world began,' he found his answer.[5] Though he recognized that many changes had taken place since Trafalgar, that the 'symmetry and grand lines' of Nelson's *Victory* seemed obsolete in a world of '*Monitors* and yet mightier hulls of the European ironsides,' he nonetheless insisted that 'to anybody who can hold the Present at its worth without being inappreciative of the Past,' the 'solitary old hulk at Portsmouth' spoke eloquent truth. If he could no longer embrace the simple faith of his youth when he had believed in a law 'coeval with mankind, dictated by God himself, superior in obligation to any other,' when he had advocated the abolition of flogging on the grounds that 'it is not a dollar-and-cent question of expediency; it is a matter of *right and wrong*';[6] if the corrosive years had eaten away for him such immutable standards, he could at least salvage somehow a foundation for personal greatness and heroism. Nelson was the man he needed.

He admitted that strict 'martial utilitarians,' believers in the rigorous application of an inexorable social expediency to every particular situation, would be inclined to take issue with his estimate of Nelson's greatness, even perhaps 'to the extent of iconoclasm.' For Nelson's exposure of his own person in battle at Trafalgar appeared on the surface to have been militarily inexpedient, even vain and foolhardy; his value to the cause for which he fought was so great that he should have sacrificed his natural desire for personal heroism to the higher principle of preserving a life which was indispensable to the general good. Had his life been preserved and his command of the fleet therefore been retained, the mistakes made by his successor in command might have been avoided; and his sagacity might well have averted the shipwreck with its horrible loss of life which followed the battle. So the 'Benthamites of war' argued, and, Melville admitted, with some plausibility; using only the immediate circumstances of the engagement as their criteria they could convict Nelson of behavior out of harmony with the general good, and on these grounds strip him of the glory with which Englishmen had invested him.

But to this sort of iconoclasm Melville would not accede for a moment. 'Personal prudence,' he countered, 'even when dictated by quite other than selfish considerations, is surely no special virtue in a military man; while an excessive love of glory, exercising to the uttermost heartfelt sense of duty, is the first.' The Benthamites were wrong; in applying their principle of social expediency to Nelson's deed 'of foolhardiness and vanity' they failed to calculate the strength of purpose which such a 'challenge to death' injects into the arteries of a nation. Nelson's deed was 'expedient' to a degree they lacked the vision to perceive; his name had become a 'trumpet to the blood' more stimulating even to the hearts of Englishmen than the name of Wellington;

the act which on the surface seemed sheer 'bravado' still inspired posterity to deeds of greatness.

Unless, Melville argued, Nelson's 'challenge to death' could be considered an act of supreme heroism, conformable to the highest ideals governing human behavior, no deed could be truly heroic; and this possibility he refused to entertain. The vitality of Nelson's example was immortal. In 1891, shortly after he had made his own will, Melville composed this enthusiastic tribute to another great man who had also glimpsed a premonition that death was near:

> At Trafalgar, Nelson, on the brink of opening the fight, sat down and wrote his last brief will and testament. If under the presentiment of the most magnificent of all victories, to be crowned by his own glorious death, a sort of priestly motive led him to dress his person in the jewelled vouchers of his own shining deeds; if thus to have adorned himself for the altar and the sacrifice were indeed vainglory, then affectation and fustian is each truly heroic line in the great epics and dramas, since in such lines the poet but embodies in verse those exaltations of sentiment that a nature like Nelson, the opportunity being given, vitalizes into acts. (p. 157)

The question naturally arises whether Melville intended the digression on Nelson to illuminate the final scene of the novel. Might the answer be that the hanging of Billy Budd is Melville's final commentary upon the theme of the impracticability of absolute standards in a world necessarily ruled by expediency? Billy's noble devotion to absolute justice and right throughout the novel made him a sort of personification of the moral law; his death must have meant for Melville, consequently, that the standard of behavior to which Billy gave his allegiance, though a noble one, is simply unworkable when applied to complex social relationships. There was something unearthly about the death of Billy Budd: he was 'an angel of God' (p. 229), returning without fear to his Maker; his pinioned figure at the yard-end behaved like that of no mortal man; to the sailors aboard the *Indomitable* the spar from which Billy's body had hung was thought of for some years as a piece of the Cross. The luminous night of the morning when Billy was to be hanged passed away like the prophet Elijah disappearing into heaven in his chariot and dropping his mantle to Elisha. Billy was too good for this world; he properly belonged to another, not to this; and the moral principles from which he acted were appropriate enough for the world to which he belonged. But in a society composed of men, not angels—in a society in which even Claggarts are to be found—an inferior standard, that of expediency, is the only workable one.[7]

Notes

1. Herman Melville, *Billy Budd*, ed. F. Barron Freeman (Cambridge, Mass., 1948), p. 154n. Citations to *Billy Budd* in the text of this article are to this, the best critical edition so far available.
2. For this reason, Freeman suggests, the digressions on Nelson are 'important' (p. 42).
3. Leon Howard, *Herman Melville* (Berkeley, 1951), p. 328.
4. Melville conjectures that this is what transpired while the Captain spoke with Billy privately in the cabin.
5. The scattered references to *Billy Budd* which follow are to Ch. iv, pp. 154–157, passim.
6. *White Jacket* (Boston, 1892), pp. 138, 139.
7. This article is peripheral to a study of the concept of 'expediency' in American thought, undertaken with the aid of a grant from the American Council of Learned Societies.

—Wendell Glick, "Expediency and
Absolute Morality in *Billy Budd*," *PMLA*, 68, 1,
March 1953, pp. 103–10

Chronology

1819	Herman Melville (or Melvill) is born August 1 in New York City. He is the third child of Allan Melville, an importer, and Maria Gansevoort Melville.
1825	Melville attends the New-York Male High School.
1830–32	Allan Melville's importing business fails, and he moves the family to Albany. Herman becomes a student at the Albany Academy until his father's death in 1832. Then he works at various jobs: bank clerk, helper on his brother Gansevoort's farm, assistant in Gansevoort's fur factory and store.
1835–38	He continues his education at various high schools, supplementing the family income by teaching at a district school.
1839	"Fragments from a Writing Desk" is published May 4 and May 18 in the *Democratic Press and Lansingburgh Advertiser*. Melville then works his way to Liverpool and back on the *Saint Lawrence,* a merchant ship.
1841–44	Melville leaves New Bedford, Massachusetts, as a sailor on the whaler *Acushnet,* bound for the South Seas. He jumps ship in the Marquesas Islands, where he lives among the native peoples for about a month. After a series of adventures, he enlists in the U.S. Navy and returns to the United States.
1846	He publishes *Typee*. His brother Gansevoort dies.
1847	Melville publishes *Omoo*. He marries Elizabeth Shaw, daughter of Chief Justice Lemuel Shaw of Boston.
1847–50	Melville tries to earn a living as a writer, producing occasional articles and reviews. He makes the acquaintance of George

	and Evert Duyckinck and other figures of the New York literary world.
1849	He publishes *Mardi* and *Redburn*. He travels to Europe. His son Malcolm is born.
1850	Melville publishes *White-Jacket*. He purchases Arrowhead, a farm near Pittsfield, Massachusetts. He begins his friendship with Nathaniel Hawthorne, who lives in nearby Lenox.
1851	He publishes *Moby-Dick*. He son Stanwix is born.
1852	Melville publishes *Pierre*.
1853	His daughter Elizabeth is born.
1852–56	He writes stories and sketches for *Putnam's Monthly Magazine* and *Harper's New Monthly Magazine*.
1855	Melville publishes *Israel Potter* as a book, after serialization in *Putnam's*. His daughter Francis is born.
1856	*The Piazza Tales* is published. Melville travels to Europe and the Middle East for his health.
1857	*The Confidence Man,* which Melville had left with his publisher before he began traveling, is finally released. Melville returns to the United States.
1857–60	Melville supports his family by lecturing on such topics as "Statues in Rome," "The South Seas," and "Traveling."
1863	Melville sells Arrowhead and moves his family to New York City.
1866	He publishes a collection of poems, *Battle-Pieces and Aspects of the War*.
1867	His son Malcolm shoots himself, after which son Stanwix runs away to sea.
1876	Melville publishes *Clarel*.
1886	His son Stanwix dies.
1888	*John Marr and Other Sailors* is privately printed.
1891	*Timoleon* is privately printed. Melville dies on September 28.
1924	*Billy Budd* is published for the first time.

Index

A

Adventures of Huckleberry Finn, The (Twain), xii
"After the Pleasure-Party," xii
Allison, Archibald, 18
American Literature
  criticism, 178–179
  history, 5–6, 118, 120–123, 134, 137, 140–141
  letters, 63
  marketplace, 161
  press, 155
  prose fiction, 29, 42, 51, 57, 77, 93–94, 98, 134, 141–142, 164, 167
  romances, 48, 139, 162, 164, 166
"American Literature" (Whipple), 29
Anthenaeum, 142
Aristarchus, 88
Aristotle, 40, 88
  formalism, 6

B

Bacon, Francis, 19
Barbour, James
  "The Composition of Moby-Dick," 138
Barrie, James, 105
"Bartleby the Scrivner," xii, 2
Bates, Katharine Lee
  on *Typee*, 53

Battle-Pieces and Aspects of the War, 2, 31
  criticism, 167–169
  incidents of the Civil war in, 41, 167–168
  language of, 32
  structure of, 168
"Bell-Tower, The," xii
"Benito Cereno," xii, 2, 163–164
Bentley, Richard, 74
Billson, James, 41
Billy Budd, Foretopman, 1, xii
  Billy in, 173–181, 183–185, 188, 191, 194
  bitter perversion of love in, 174
  Christ's humility in, 174–175, 179–180
  crew in, 178, 184, 189
  criticism, 173–195
  death of Lord Nelson in, 187–188, 192–194
  destiny of man in, 174–175, 180
  homosexual content in, 174, 177
  humor in, 174
  ironic social criticism, 178–179, 185–187, 189, 192
  John Claggart in, 176–179, 183, 185, 189, 191–192, 195
  man-of-war society in, 178
  narrative, 175, 184

Index

nature of evil, suffering, and
 authority in, 7
publication, 33, 173, 183
symbolism allegory of, 178–185
Transcendentalism in, xii, 174
Captain Vere in, 173–180, 182–
 185, 187–192
writing of, 188
Birds, Beast, and Flowers (Lawrence),
 117
Black and White (Stevenson), 44
Blake, William, 171
 Rime of the Ancient Mariner, 26
Bloom, Harold
 introduction, xi-xii
Boone, Daniel, 141
Brooklyn Daily Eagle, 54
Brown, Charles Brockden, 163
Browne, Thomas
 influence of, 43, 48, 102, 105, 108
 Urne Burial, 44
Browning, Robert
 "The Ring and the Book," 98
Buchanan, Robert, 34
 "Socrates in Camden, with a
 Look Round," 28, 42
Burke, Edmund, 90
Burton, Richard, 100, 102
Butler, William A.
 on *Moby-Dick*, 87–90

C

Call Me Ishmael (Olson), 138
Carlyle, Thomas, 17, 24
 influence of, 43–44, 46, 48, 61–
 62, 80, 82, 102, 134, 157
Cenci (Shelley), 155
Cervantes, Miguel de, xii, 23
Channing, William Ellery
 "The Island Nukuheva," 5
Chorley, Henry
 on *Moby-Dick*, 74–75
"City of Dreadful Night" (Thompson),
 41
Clarel, a Pilgrimage in the Holy Land,
 xii, 2

Clarel in, 169, 171–172
criticism, 167–173
Derwent in, 171
Glaucon in, 171
Mortmain in, 181
narrative, 177
Nehemiah in, 171
Passion Week in, 169
pilgrimage in, 41, 169, 171
plot of, 169, 171
Rolfe, 169, 171
Ruth in, 169, 171
Vine in, 169, 171
Classical American Literature
 (Lawrence), 117
Coan, Titus, 37–38
Colcord, Lincoln
 on *Moby-Dick*, 74, 103, 106–117
Coleridge, Samuel Taylor, 90
Columbus, Christopher, 80, 141
"Composition of Moby-Dick, The"
 (Barbour), 138
Confidence Man: His Masquerade, The
 characters and dialogue in, 165
 criticism, 164–167
 failure of, 39–40, 48
 human condition in, 164, 166–167
 Mark Winsome in, xi
 Mississippi steamboat in, 164–166
 publication, 165
 satire in, 2, 164, 166–167
 writing of, 162
Conrad, Joseph, 30, 107
 Heart of Darkness, 100
 Lord Jim, 100
 on *Moby-Dick*, 100–101
 The Secret Sharer, 101
Coverdale, Miles, 16
Cozzens, Frederick Swartwout
 on *White-Jacket*, 62–63
Crane, Stephen, 91

D

Dana, Richard Henry, 120, 124
 Two Years before the Mast, 47,
 62, 96

Dante, Alighieri, 102
Defoe, Daniel, 39, 60
    Robinson Crusoe, 55–56, 89
"Devil as Quaker," 68
Dickens, Charles
    style of, 19, 85–86, 156
Dickinson, Emily, xi
Doctor, The (Southey), 81
"Drum-Taps" (Whitman), 168
Duyckinck, Evert A.
    on *Moby-Dick*, 33, 77–83, 107, 138

E

Emerson, Ralph Waldo, 5, 24
    Essays, First and Second series, xii
    influence of, xi–xii, 62, 64, 82, 98, 118–119, 142, 189
"Encantadas, or the Enchanted Islands," xii, 163–164
Endymion (Keats), 13–15
Essays, First and Second series (Emerson), xii

F

Fielding, Henry, 105
Franklin, Benjamin, 121
Freud, Sigmund
    analysis, 118, 174, 176
Fuller, Margaret
    on *Typee*, 51–52

G

German, Jean Paul, 81
Glick, Wendell
    on *Billy Budd*, 187–195
Goethe, 16
    style of, 63, 67
    "Witches' Kitchen," 88
Golden Bowl, The (James, H.), xii
Graham's Magazine, 161
Greeley, Horace
    on *Moby-Dick*, 55, 83–85
    on *Omoo*, 55–57
Greene, Charles Gordon
    on *Omoo*, 54–55
Gulliver's Travels (Swift), 55, 89

H

Hamlet (Shakespeare), 34
Hardy, Thomas, xii
"Hawthorne and His Mosses," 77
Hawthorne, Julian
    on *Pierre*, 162
Hawthorne, Nathaniel, xi–xii, 162
    friendship with Melville, 5–6, 41, 46, 67–68, 80, 96, 107
    The House of Seven Gables, 66
    influence of, 115, 119, 139, 147, 156, 163–164
    journals, 7–9, 38
    letters to, 40, 47, 60, 63–71, 78, 114, 174
    on Melville, 1, 5–9, 46
    Mosses from an Old Manse, 63
    nature of, 33
    on *Typee*, 51–52
Hawthorne, Sophia, 71
    on Melville, 6–7
Hazlitt, William, 94
Heart of Darkness (Conrad), 100
"Herman Melville" (Strachey), 43–45
Herman Melville: Mariner and Mystic (Weaver), 173–174
Holmes, Oliver Wendell
    "The Last Leaf," 46
Homer, 14
House of Seven Gables The (Hawthorne), 66
Howard, Leon, 138
Hunt, Leigh, 94

I

"Island Nukuheva, The" (Channing), 5
Israel Potter: His Fifty Years of Exile, 2
    Franklin Jones in, 46
    narrative of, 39, 48
    Paul Jones in, 46
    writing of, 162

J

James, Henry, xii
    The Golden Bowl, xii
James, William, xii

John Marr and Other Sailors, 2
    publication, 41
Johnson, Barbara
    "Melville's Fist; The Execution of *Billy Budd*," 187
Johnson, Samuel, 52
Journal of a Cruise to the Pacific Ocean (Porter), 37

K

Kaloolah (Mayo), 89
Keats, John
    Endymion, 13–15
Kipling, Rudyard, 102

L

Lamb, Charles, 94, 105
Last Leaf, The (Holmes), 46
Lawrence, D.H., 94
    Birds, Beast, and Flowers, 117
    Classical American Literature, 117
    on *Moby-Dick*, 33, 117–133, 138
    Studies, 117–118
    Women in Love, 117
Leaves of Grass (Whitman), xi–xii, 54, 142
Leda, Jay
    The Melville Log, 93
"Lightning Rod Man, The," 163–164
Literary World, 148
London, Jack, 30
    on *Typee*, 53–54
Longfellow, Henry Wadsworth, 119
    influence of, 156
    on *Typee*, 52
Lord Jim (Conrad), 100
Lowell, James Russell
    on Poe, 29
    on *Typee*, 51, 53

M

Macbeth (Shakespeare), 92
MacMechan, Archibald, 188
    on Melville, 25
    on *Moby-Dick*, 93–100, 107, 118
Mardi and a Voyage Thither, 1, 175
    conclusion of, 39
    criticism, 13, 18, 57–60, 62, 80, 84, 134, 148, 173
    imaginative element of, 35
    garden of, 59
    language, 58–59, 85
    narrative, 35
    political satire in, 95
    rambling metaphysics of, 57
    romance and adventure, 14, 18–19, 45, 47–48
    sea allegory in, 57–58, 83, 150
    sinful voice of, 61
"Marquesan Melville" (Salt), 33–43
Marryat, Frederick, 39, 96
Masefield, John, 103
Massinger, Philip, 105
Mather, Frank Jewett Jr.
    on *Moby-Dick*, 101–103, 105
Mayo, William
    Kaloolah, 89
Melville, Elizabeth Shaw (wife), 1, 77, 96
Melville, Gansevoort, 51
Melville, Herman
    biography, 1–2
    chronology, 196–197
    death, 2, 30–31, 33–34, 43, 45, 48, 173
    early careers, 1–2, 35, 45–47, 85, 95–96
    family, 38, 41, 45, 48, 77, 141–142
    imagination of, 32, 46, 62, 74, 97, 103, 105, 111, 135, 140, 142, 157, 163–164, 166, 175
    influence of, 29–30, 32, 42
    lecture tours, 2
    on *Moby-Dick*, 63–71
    religion, 64, 68, 73–74, 141, 173–174
    reputation, 30–31, 33
    sexuality, 69
    sufferings, 7–8, 13, 29, 33, 40–41, 48, 69, 78, 107, 117, 120, 141
Melville Log, The (Leda), 93
"Melville's Fist; The Execution of *Billy Budd*" (Johnson), 187

"Melville's Testament of Acceptance" (Watson, E.L.), 173
Metaphysicians, The, 164
Milton, John
    influence of, 27, 86, 105, 157
    Paradise Lost, 82
Moby-Dick; or, The Whale, 1, 95
    Captain Ahab in, xi–xii, 24, 26, 38–39, 46, 73–74, 76, 79–82, 84, 91–92, 97–99, 101–104, 107–108, 111–114, 116–117, 122–123, 130–131, 135–136, 140, 142
    American seaports in, 72, 78
    Captain Bildad in, 73, 92, 101, 105, 112
    criticism, 14, 22–25, 33, 45, 48, 55, 63–143, 173
    Daggoo in, 123, 127
    Captain Deblois in, 78–80
    Feddallah in, 102
    Flask in, 92, 123
    Gayheader in, 92
    harpooners, 77, 102, 123, 125, 131, 134, 142
    hatred and revenge theme in, 39, 76, 91–92, 97, 101–102, 104, 108, 122–123, 125, 129, 135–136, 140–141
    Ishmael in, xi–xii, 40, 72–73, 82–84, 91, 97, 106, 112–113, 120–122, 134–135, 137, 142
    magic influence of the sea in, 38
    and masculinity in fiction, 69, 73, 121
    Moby Dick in, 19, 26, 38, 65, 73–74, 78, 80–81, 83–84, 87, 92–93, 96, 98, 100–101, 114–115, 119, 122, 125–126, 130–131, 133–136, 140, 142
    narrative, 26, 29, 46, 72, 74, 77–78, 81–82, 84, 89–92, 100, 104, 108, 110, 112–113, 115, 118, 121, 134, 137, 139
    Captain Peleg in, 73, 92, 101, 105, 112
    Pequod in, 26, 72–74, 76–77, 80, 82, 84, 96–97, 99, 102–103, 108–109, 111–115, 122–124, 126, 128, 130, 132–137
    Pip in, 130
    psychoanalytic interpretations of, 118
    publication, 46, 71, 74, 113, 133
    Queequeg in, xi, 19, 39, 73, 81, 97, 102, 112, 120–123, 125, 129–130
    romance of, 76, 81, 84, 87, 89–91, 103, 107, 110–111, 134–136
    satire in, 72
    sea story, 26–27, 30, 32, 44, 72–74, 79–80, 119–120
    sentimentalism in, 14
    Starbuck in, 19, 92, 102, 112–113, 117, 123, 125, 128
    structure of, 72, 97, 100–101, 106, 108, 113, 115
    Stubbs in, 19, 92, 102, 113, 123
    superstition in, 72, 84, 92
    symbolism and allegory in, 77, 80–81, 83, 99, 101–105, 116–118, 132, 135–136, 139
    Tashtego in, 81, 102, 123, 132
    Transcendentalism in, xii
    Turner in, 19
    writing of, 63, 65, 67, 70–71, 77, 112, 114, 117, 175
Modernism, 106, 138, 162
Morris, William
    Sigurd the Volsung, xii
Mosses from an Old Manse (Hawthorne), 63
Mrs. Stephens' Illustrated New Monthly Magazine, 165
Murray, John, 51, 53

N

National Intelligence, 87
Naturalism, 107

Nichols, Thomas Low
    on *Typee*, 51, 53
North, Christopher, 14

O

O'Brien, Fitz-James
    on Melville, 13–14
Olson, Charles
    Call Me Ishmael, 138
    on *Moby-Dick*, 33, 107, 138–142
Omoo: A Narrative of Adventures in the South Seas, 95, 163
    Bembo in, 17
    Captain Bob in, 17
    Bungs in, 17
    Chips in, 17
    corresponding descriptions in, 20
    criticism, 1, 13, 18, 25, 51, 54–57, 83, 101, 134, 148, 165
    Doctor Long Ghost in, 17, 27, 55, 89
    Miss Guy in, 17
    Holborn in, 17
    John Jermin in, 17, 27
    language of, 39, 54, 85, 90, 157
    Little Jule in, 17, 27, 88
    narrative, 15, 29, 54–56
    picturesque sketches of, 60
    political tone of, 55–56
    publication, 88
    Queen Pomare in, 18
    Po-po in, 18
    romance of, 43
    Rope Yarn in, 17
    Rover in, 17
    sea-story, 27, 47, 54, 56, 83, 146, 150
    Society and Sandwich Islands in, 35, 55
Ortega y Gasset, José, 141

P

Paradise Lost (Milton), 82
Parker, Hershel, 33, 93
Piazza Tales, The
    criticism, 162–164
    introduction, 163
    publication, 164
    romance in, 163
    stories in, 2, 39, 48, 163–164
Pierce, Franklin, 7
Pierre; or, The Ambiguities, 1, 190
    battling for truth and right in, 144
    criticism, 13–14, 25, 34, 142–163, 173
    Delly in, 153
    failure of, 39–41, 48, 149
    father's memory in, 143–144, 151–152
    Mrs. Glendenning in, 143–145, 147, 151–154
    incestuous relations in, 142–143, 145, 147, 150, 153
    Isabel in, 143–145, 147, 152–155
    language of, 142–143, 146, 152, 156, 159
    Lucy Tartan in, 143–145, 151, 153–155
    metaphors in, 157–158
    Pierre Glendenning in, 142–145, 147, 150–156
    psychology of madness in, 147, 151
    reviews, 34, 142
    self-analysis in, 176–77
    social immorality of, 143, 145, 147, 153–155, 160
    Stanly Glendenning in, 153–154
    suicide in, 150
    writing of, 69, 175
Poe, Edgar Allan
    style of, 29, 122, 139, 147
Poetry, xii, 167–173
Pope, Alexander, 105, 161
Porter, David
    Journal of a Cruise to the Pacific Ocean, 37
Porter, William T.
    on *Moby-Dick*, 85–87

Q

Queen's Quarterly, 93

R

Rabelais, Francois, 24, 98
   humor, 102, 105
Realism, 30, 107
   narrative, 115–117
   nautical, 109, 111–112, 134
   subjective, 112, 114
Redburn: His First Voyage, 1
   allegory, 60
   criticism, 59–60, 62, 148
   Donald in, 21
   Henry Bolton in, 19
   Highlander in, 25
   Jack Blunt in, 21
   Jackson in, 21
   lack of excitement in, 14, 19
   Larry in, 21
   Lavender in, 21
   Liverpool in, 47
   Max in 21
   narrative, 19
   Nathaniel in, 20
   Captain Riga in, 20
   romance in, 47
   sailor's yarn in, 27, 60, 95
   tone and taste of, 19, 27
   Wellington Redburn in, 19–20, 25
Reynolds, J.N., 135
Richardson, Charles, F., 29
Richter, Jean Paul, 155
Rime of the Ancient Mariner (Blake), 26
Ripley, George
   on *Moby-Dick*, 77, 91–93
   on *Redburn*, 59–60
   on *White-Jacket*, 61
Robertson-Lorant, Laurie, 33
Robinson Crusoe (Defoe), 55–56, 89
Rousseau, Jean Jacques, 37
Russell, W. Clark
   on Melville's sea stories, 25–28
   on *Moby-Dick*, 94–96

S

Salt, Henry S.
   "Marquesan Melville," 33–43

Schiller, Friedrich, 64
Secret Sharer, The (Conrad), 101
Shakespeare, William
   Hamlet, 34
   influence of, xii, 26, 63, 68, 82, 90, 105–106, 108, 139–140
   Macbeth, 92
Shelley, Percy Bysshe
   Cenci, 155
Sigurd the Volsung (Morris), xii
Simms, William Gilmore, 45
Skepticism, 69, 71
Smollett, Tobias
   influence of, 39, 96, 101, 105
Socrates, 69–70
"Socrates in Camden, with a Look Round" (Buchanan), 28, 42
Song of Myself (Whitman), xii
Southey, Robert
   The Doctor, 81
Stedman, Edmund Clarence
   on Melville's poetry, 170–173
Stephens, Ann Sophia
   on *The Confidence Man*, 165–166
Stevenson, Robert Louis, 29–30
   Black and White, 44
   influence of, 32, 45, 105
Stewart, George R.
   "The Two Moby-Dicks," 138
Stoddard, Richard Henry, 32–33
   on Melville's poetry, 169–170
Strachey, John St. Loe
   "Herman Melville," 43–45
Studies (Lawrence), 117–118
"Sunday up the River" (Thomson), 41
Swift, Jonathan
   Gulliver's Travels, 55, 89

T

Thackeray, William Makepeace, 105
Thompson, Francis, 106
Thompson, James, 105
   "City of Dreadful Night," 41
   "Sunday up the River," 41
Thoreau, Henry David, 5, 100, 189
   Walden, xi

Timoleon, 2
Transcendentalism, xi–xii, 51
    and Melville, 38–39, 107, 115–117, 119, 134, 142, 145, 161, 174
    in poetry, 5, 24
Trent, William P., 45–46
Twain, Mark, 91
    The Adventures of Huckleberry Finn, xii
"Two Moby-Dicks, The" (Stewart), 138
Two Years before the Mast (Dana), 47, 62, 96
Typee, or, A Peep at Polynesian Life, 62, 67, 96
    cannibal tribe in, 44, 51–53, 88–89, 137
    captivity in, 47, 51
    comedic dismissal of, 29
    criticism, 13, 25, 83, 85, 101, 117, 134, 163
    Faraway in, 16, 36, 40, 52, 89, 150
    George Borrow in, 33–34, 36, 45, 47
    ire of missionary interests in, 51
    Kory-Kory in, 16, 89
    language in, 85
    Marnoo in, 16
    King Mehevi in, 16, 39
    myth of the noble savage in, 33, 35, 51
    narrative, 15, 29, 34, 37, 39, 52, 60, 90, 146–147, 150
    politics of, 51
    preconceptions of the Pacific in, 5, 7
    publication, 38, 43, 45, 47, 53, 88
    rhythmical drifting of, 36
    romance of, 43
    success of, 13, 35, 38–39, 42, 51, 148, 165
    Toby in, 16, 45, 47
    Tinor in, 16
    Tommo in, 16–17
    travel stories in, 1, 27, 30–31, 34, 47, 51–53, 55–56, 89, 146–148

U
Urne Burial (Browne), 44

V
Van Doren, Carl, 46–48
    on *Moby-Dick*, 134–138
Virgil, 58

W
Walden (Thoreau), xi
Watson, E.L. Grant
    on *Billy Budd*, 173–178
    "Melville's Testament of Acceptance," 173
Watson, Henry Cood
    on *Mardi*, 57–59
Weaver, Raymond
    Herman Melville: Mariner and Mystic, 173–174
    on *Moby Dick*, 103–106
Webster, John, 105
Whipple, Edwin P.
    "American Literature," 29
White-Jacket; or, The World in a Man-of-War, 1
    corruption in, 61
    criticism, 22, 61–63, 148
    daguerreotype-like naturalness of, 62
    humor in, 62
    language of, 39, 85
    life on a man-of-war in, 32, 35, 47, 61, 95
    log-book, 61
Whitman, Walt, 93, 98, 141
    "Drum-Taps," 168
    Leaves of Grass, xi–xii, 54, 142
    on *Omoo*, 54
    Song of Myself, xii
Women in Love (Lawrence), 117
Wordsworth, William, 18

Z
Zink, Karl E., 76
    on *Billy Budd*, 178–187